WILLY WAS
OUR LANDLORD
IN AMHERST.

English Papers

English Papers

A Teaching Life

WILLIAM H. PRITCHARD

Graywolf Press
Saint Paul

Publication of this volume is made possible in part by a grant provided by the Minnesota State Arts Board through an appropriation by the Minnesota State Legislature, and by a grant from the National Endowment for the Arts. Significant additional support has been provided by the Andrew W. Mellon Foundation, the Lila Wallace-Reader's Digest Fund, the McKnight Foundation, and other generous contributions from foundations, corporations, and individuals. Graywolf Press is a member agency of United Arts, Saint Paul. To these organizations and individuals who make our work possible, we offer heartfelt thanks.

Published by Graywolf Press
2402 University Avenue, Suite 203
Saint Paul, Minnesota, 55114
All rights reserved.

Printed in the United States of America.

ISBN 1-55597-234-9

2 4 6 8 9 7 5 3
First Graywolf Printing, 1995

Library of Congress Catalog Card Number: 95–077952

To Marietta
Without Whom Not

Contents

⌒∞⌒

ACKNOWLEDGMENTS

Lawrence Douglas provided detailed, chapter-by-chapter criticism of the manuscript; Will Pritchard and the late Julian Symons encouraged me in the writing of it. I am grateful for the editorial assistance of Fiona McCrae, Mary Byers, and Ian Morgan at Graywolf Press, and for unstinting, cheerful clerical help from Susan Raymond-Fic.

Rather more vaguely, I should like to thank Amherst College for its hospitality over the years toward this reader and writer of English papers.

Introduction

⸎

Writing about first-person narrative in his preface to *The Ambassadors,* Henry James warned of "the terrible *fluidity* of self-revelation." Such revelation has of late been rife among American university professors, a number of whom have written memoirs dealing with academic life. An article in *Lingua Franca* about such professor-confessors is titled "The I's Have It," and concludes with an anonymous academic asking, "Have they no shame?" In fact, the current impulse toward autobiographical writing about teaching may stem from something more than the usual authorial vanity and love of self-display. Recent years have also seen a number of books about the current state of academic — especially of English — studies in which the impulse is less confessional than diagnostic. I think, for example, of contributions by Stanley Fish, David Bromwich, Frank Kermode, and Gerald Graff, none of whom hesitates to invoke his own experience of university teaching as an important measure of things. To one degree or another, both the confessors and the diagnosticians have been animated by the sense of confusion and uncertainty prevailing today in literary studies.

I have been animated by the same confusions, the same uncertainty, yet found myself wincing when I realized that, in writing my own narrative version of self-exposure, I was joining what is possibly an already overexposed group. Why should my story — similar, no doubt, to that of thousands of English teachers who went to graduate school, earned a doctoral degree, and proceeded to live the life of a practicing academic — be of interest to anyone but myself? And doesn't the adoption of a first-person perspective dangerously open the writer to the "terrible *fluidity*" — the all-too-easy personal disclosures of which Henry James warned? I went there, I read this and that, I studied with X, whom I admired, and with Y, whom I thought an imbecile. I am the man, I suffered, I was there, even if only in the classroom — so Whitman's famous lines could be trivialized by a cloistered account of the making of a professor.

When he reviewed Robert Frost's second book of poems, *North of Boston*, Ezra Pound said that after reading them he knew more about farm life — which meant that he knew more about "Life." Much of my life has taken place in academic circumstances — in courses, departments, classrooms. What possibilities for knowing more about life do they provide? A question not, of course, for the writer to answer; yet in undertaking this account I was at least certain about what I would not or could not provide. Domestic and familial life, habits of eating, drinking, sleeping (all vital activities) have in the main no place in it; nor was I about to hold forth on the pleasures of watching the Boston Celtics over the years, nor the ongoing seriousness with which I watch *Loving*, my half-hour daily soap opera. Unlike some of the confessors, I had no personal revelation to bring, at last, to light; no scandal to confess or transforming experience to relate. I wasn't planning to retire or begin a new career, starting afresh in nonacademic surroundings. Nor did I have — like some professors — the knowledge or conviction of just where and when and how things had gone wrong in English studies. (I believe that they have.) There is also the question of perspective: most of the diagnosticians have spent their lives teaching in large universities and been actively involved in recruiting graduate students, supervising their dissertations, later helping some of them to find employment. They are members of, sometimes have presided over, large and complicated departments of English, filled with competing concerns. That I had spent my teaching life at Amherst, a small liberal arts college regularly identified by *U.S. News and World Report* polls as at the top of the elite, didn't make my perspective more just or pertinent to the larger questions of higher education in the United States. Quite the contrary, perhaps.

What I knew most about, where my perspective was most pertinent, was surely life in the classroom, a subject that writers, even academic ones, tend to avoid. Put it rather that the treatment given that life has been mainly satiric and reductive, from Wordsworth's disparagement of the vain chatter characterizing his years at Cambridge right down to the farce of Jim Dixon's redbrick university in Kingsley Amis's *Lucky Jim*. The "academic novel," as it used to be practiced in this country, made a point of avoiding classroom happenings; you look for them in vain in Randall Jarrell's *Pictures from an Institution* or Mary McCarthy's *The Groves of Academe*. Exceptions only prove the rule: I think, for example, of an argument about Ibsen in Lionel Trilling's story "Of This Time, Of That Place"; or, in James Guetti's novel, *Action*, a discussion about Keats's Chapman's Homer sonnet between students who couldn't care less and a professor waiting for class to be over so he can head for the racetrack. Indeed, the best place to go for a sense of actuality in the English classroom is not to fiction, but to textbooks about teaching such as Benjamin DeMott's *Close Imagining: An Introduction to Literature* or William E. Coles's books on composition. My treatment of the classroom, while less intensive than theirs, is designed to give a sense of what happened in some of the ones I have been in, on both sides of the desk.

Still, the question of motive remains: why write about a life within academy walls? Perhaps the real spur to attempting such an account of one's past must come from the way the present seems to have fallen away from it — betrayed it, even. And no matter how often we remind ourselves that a person's account of his past will inevitably idealize and transform it into something it never was, nevertheless the activity goes on. Robert Frost once said that the motive or inspiration out of which a poem arose was mainly "Animus." He compared it to seeing someone approach you in the street ("someone you're accustomed to abuse") and having something rise in you, looking for its expression in new and original words. The animus behind this book comes from remembering moments and situations that now seem invaluable, as when thirty-five years ago, at the beginning of my teaching career at Amherst, we taught a novel by D. H. Lawrence in an introductory staff course. During a meeting to devise an assignment on the book, there developed among the seven of us a fierce argument about Lawrence. For two hours we sat around a table and disagreed, with three clearly distinct points of view at odds with each other, irreconcilably so. At the end of it I had a headache but knew I had been through something worth experiencing. The knowledge that, for all sorts of reasons, such an argument could not happen now is what has spurred me to write about what has been lost; to effect a recovery of it in imaginative memory. I attempt, in this book, a larger recovery of my life in "English."

Chaucer's line about his clerk in *The Canterbury Tales* — "And gladly wolde he lerne and gladly teche" — has been solemnly quoted all too often in the festschrifts that entomb Great Teachers. Mordancy rather than mellowness is called for, especially since academic happenings are at least as deserving of a comic perspective as those in other realms. And any working teacher needs to have a sane sense of how much waste there is in the process: how many students one never connects with; how humorlessly too many people treat this burden or privilege of educating the young. "Remember," said my teacher, Theodore Baird, "Education doesn't work." So, as with viewing other kinds of experience, a combination of idealism and irony is the best recipe, and it's only after we laugh or despair at the distance between the promise of teaching and its results, as far as we can see them, that Frost's lines about the right way to conceive a vocation may be quoted:

> Only where love and need are one,
> And the work is play for mortal stakes,
> Is the deed ever really done
> For Heaven and the future's sakes.

English Papers

I
Foreshadowings

❦

In his memoir, "The Dogwood Tree: A Boyhood," John Updike comments on the innocence of his youthful assumptions about art, religion, and politics, yet says that as a man he has found no certain substitute for those assumptions. The reflection accords with my own experience. I spent my first years on First Street in Johnson City, New York, a stone's throw from the Erie–Lackawanna Railroad tracks (New York City to Buffalo) and from Johnson City High School. From the front porch of my grandmother Pritchard's unassuming frame house, you could hear the whistle of the locomotive coming up from the ravine to the left; on the other side of First Street stood the schoolyard, gym, wood and metal "shops," and other appendages of the high school proper. Like the railroad, the school was absolutely *there*, no more to be questioned than where my next meal was coming from. I think of this unquestioned assumption as the foundation of my acceptance—throughout life in various forms and places—of "school." And when I hear serious-minded people talk about how they hated their time spent in elementary, secondary, or college classrooms, I am never quite able to credit their sincerity or their sanity.

Johnson City, a village of 17,000, sits on the Pennsylvania border between Binghamton and Endicott—the two other constituents of what are known as the Triple Cities. They were factory towns, Johnson City especially, with Endicott–Johnson, a then-thriving shoe company, leading a pack that also included IBM, Agfa–Ansco (later General Aniline and Film), and other smaller industrial operations. Education in our town was public education and it was taken seri-

1

ously, even though almost no one continued schooling beyond high school. Various members of my family were active in local education: my mother supervised music in the elementary schools; my father, a lawyer for Endicott–Johnson, served on the board of education, for many years as president; one of my aunts taught first grade. There was even an uncle who, ill and overaged as he was, maintained a janitorial position in the high school through what I suspect was my father's covert influence.

Johnson City was a company town, and its school system felt like a family thing to me. My father's position on the board of education meant that school-related documents were available in his desk drawer for my perusal. The one discovery that I cared most about was an alphabetical list of all the teachers in the school system including — most interestingly — their respective salaries. (I inscribed my aunt's annual salary of $1,776 on my mental tablets, and when I told my parents of my discovery they urged me to keep it a secret.) Being the son of a school board member carried perks such as a free pass to all sporting events, including seats on the fifty-yard line at high school football games. A few words from my father got me excused from the required manual training course (wood shop) in junior high so that I wouldn't endanger my precious pianist's fingers on an electric saw. More than once I visited my aunt at the end of the school day and was allowed to sit in the back of the classroom and observe the first graders. On a couple of occasions the janitorial uncle even contrived to let me and my friends into the high school basketball court for a bit of illicit practice.

But my mother's role in the romance of school was paramount. A few years before I was born, she had joined the music department of the Johnson City school system and was beginning to develop what over the next three decades would become an admirable, varied program in vocal and instrumental music, with choirs, glee clubs, band, and orchestra existing on all levels from grade to high school. As a music supervisor, she took charge of seeing that in the elementary grades one to six, in three different schools, serious standards were observed. Students were taught to read music and to sing in part-harmony; they were also encouraged to learn a musical instrument and to "appreciate" famous pieces of "serious" music. There was even a bit of theory and harmony thrown in. It was truly an attempt at systematic ear training.

My own ear training began very early, perhaps most memorably on the day I learned to sing "Old Folks at Home" ("Way down upon the Swanee River, / Far, far, away"). By the time I was two years old I had sung in a children's talent show on the Binghamton radio station. Not too many months afterward I obliged the crowd at a Shriner's fest at their Kalurah Temple with a rendition of "Sailing, Sailing, Over the Bounding Main," belted out in the presence of various Shriners who, in the pageant, were to be understood as undertaking an ocean voyage. As part of one of my mother's elementary school music events I wielded—rather uncertainly—a lariat, while giving vent to songs such as "Take Me Back to My Boots and Saddle," and "Go to Sleep, My Little Buckaroo." So it's fair to say that at a very young age my head was full of tunes and lyrics, a condition that was only to grow until it reached the present point where, as an occasional insomniac, I lie in bed rehearsing them yet once more:

> I know an angel
> On the East Side of heaven
> Who lives in a third-story room;
> We meet on a rooftop
> And dream in the dark
> When the lights of New York are in bloom.
>
> All through the daytime
> It's the same old Manhattan,
> But evening again sets me free;
> Then I turn off Broadway
> To the East Side of heaven
> Where an angel waits for me.

The tune—not provided here—may now live almost exclusively in my head.

My singing career peaked at age four and went steadily downhill thereafter, even though I sang in glee clubs, in a male octet, and regularly in the junior choir at the Episcopal church I began to attend at age eight. But singing was essentially displaced by piano lessons, begun at the same time I entered kindergarten, two months shy of my fifth birthday. The best lines ever written about a child putting in time at the piano are surely Randall Jarrell's in the first section of "The Lost World":

> A prelude
> By Chopin, hammered note by note, like alphabet
> Blocks, comes from next door. It's played with real feeling,
> The feeling of being indoors practicing.

I knew that feeling of being indoors practicing, but fancy that, on the whole, my practicing felt less oppressive, since the challenge presented to me by the keyboard—the almost unimaginable possibility that I could master it to some degree—fueled my early attempts and has never been extinguished. I was fortunate in my teachers and perhaps even more so in the continuing presence of a mother who, from the kitchen or wherever she was in range, would suggest that I play the passage once more, *hands alone,* and yet once more until it reached passable quality.

From the beginning, my piano playing significantly included memorization, and I committed to heart any piece I liked enough to make part of a repertoire. There were yearly statewide contests ("tournaments," they were familiarly called) in which judges were brought in from outside to hear the student perform a carefully selected program (all selections memorized), as well as the spring piano recitals in which one's teacher presented the array of her pupils. (Eudora Welty's great story, "June Recital," has a superb account of such an event.) For me there were also, and increasingly, appearances at clubs of all sorts—from Kiwanis to Hadassah to University Women's—where I would briefly display my musical talents. I was bad at saying no, and more than once headed off to an uninspiring YWCA dance where they wanted someone to play specialty numbers like DeFalla's "Ritual Fire Dance" or the ubiquitous "Clair de Lune" at intermission. The habit of performance, in solo form or as a pianist in a dance band, was enlarged when I took up the clarinet and joined the school's instrumental groups. Later, the high school orchestra's need being deemed great, I attempted to learn the oboe, but was defeated by the ill wind that nobody blows good and forced to recognize the limits of my talents.

From the beginning, then, my sensibility was musically alert, always wanting to hear more. When many years later I came across Frost's little essay, "The Figure a Poem Makes" (it used to precede his *Complete Poems*), I could not have been less than admiring of a way of talking about poetry that seemed wholly natural and eminently sane:

The possibilities for tune from the dramatic tones of meaning struck across the rigidity of a limited meter are endless. And we are back in poetry as merely one more art of having something to say, sound or unsound. Probably better if sound, because deeper and from wider experience.

This emphasis on "tune" and "sound" provided me with a justification, if I ever needed it, for what had been a concerted training of the ear.

The tunes of meaning that in my adolescence and beyond had the strongest effect on me—for reasons, of course, that had to do with more than purely musical values—were popular tunes, the songs of the 1940s as rendered by Frank Sinatra and Perry Como; Jo Stafford, Doris Day, and Margaret Whiting; June Christie, Billy Eckstine, and Sarah Vaughan. I successfully avoided my piano teacher's attempt to introduce me to the principles of theory and harmony—perhaps an early anticipation of what the theorist Paul de Man would call "resistance to theory"—but I could hear what the right chords should be and could usually negotiate the tune into an agreeable harmonic sequence. I cared a lot about, in Frost's words, the "figures" of individual tunes—from "Skylark" to "Indian Summer" to "Tangerine" and beyond—and I played and replayed them on the piano, occasionally having to be reminded that my first order of business was Beethoven or Chopin.

The coming together of words and music in a memorable figure I also experienced in sacred as well as secular tunes. Attending the Episcopal church had a lot less to do with concerns of doctrine, salvation, and sin than with rehearsing and singing every week in the junior choir my mother had begun to direct, and playing the organ—only partially, since I never learned to use the pedals—for Sunday school services. During the innumerable rehearsals and often at the services themselves, I squirmed with boredom, wishing I were playing basketball or asleep or just somewhere out of this churchly oppressiveness. But what counted, in the sense that they remain with me today, were the hymns. "Hymns in a Man's Life," D. H. Lawrence called them in his prose reminiscence, and though Lawrence's Nonconformist hymns were not mine, he identified something I also know about. Quoting "a rather banal" hymn that contains the lines "O Galilee, sweet Galilee,/ Where Jesus loved so much to be," Lawrence wrote that, to him, the word Galilee has a wonderful sound. The Lake of Galilee! I don't want to know where it is. I never want to go to Palestine. Galilee is one of those lovely, glamorous words not places, that exist in a child's half-formed imagination.

He adds that "in my man's imagination it is just the same."

That "lovely, glamorous" word "Galilee" existed and still exists in my imagination because of the hymn that begins "Jesus calls us, o'er the tumult" and has a second verse that says about this calling: "As of old, Saint An-drew heard it / By the Gal-i-le-an lake." That lake was an exciting place to hear about just as was, more alliteratively and ominously, the "Cross-Crowned Cal-va-ry" of a hymn beginning "In the hour of trial, Jesus plead for me." But Lawrence seems to have been more responsive to the words of the hymns than to their music; for me, the music in its melodies and harmonies was preeminent, and the hymns that remain most strongly in my mind were largely written in the nineteenth century by Englishmen like John B. Dykes ("Holy, Holy, Holy, Lord God Almighty," "Eternal Father Strong to Save," and many others) and Sir Arthur Seymour Sullivan, famous for Easter contributions like "Come Ye Faithful, Raise the Strain" and "Welcome Happy Morning." John Irving once wrote that the nature of hymns was such as to make us want to repeat and repeat them; once you have satisfyingly finished one verse, there is nothing to do but to sing another one to the same tune or start the whole thing again from the beginning.

In the hymns, the popular songs, and the "serious" pieces I played and sang repeatedly in my youth, I experienced a powerful version of the "momentary stay against confusion" Frost said poems enact. In my attention to their forms or figures I found satisfying resting places, seldom attempting to move behind them to whatever content or thought might presumably lie there. Here, in retrospect, was the beginning of a lifelong preference for surface to depth—for the primary sensuous claims made by words and music rather than their secondary significations of meaning. As Wyndham Lewis once said about Joyce's *Ulysses*, "Nobody who has ever looked *at* it will want to look *behind* it." The surface, as it were, contained God's plenty, and we should be grateful for it and preoccupied with it. This aesthetic, if it can be so called, may have worked not only to downplay the centrality of "interpretation" to my later study of literature, but also to disincline me toward psychoanalysis and other attempts to investigate the springs and principles of one's inner life. Along with a very active and retentive memory went the conviction that it was less important to figure out why I said or did something than to repeat or improve upon the saying or doing. Perhaps, like Plato, I was concerned with saving the appearances.

Since I spent my first four years in a household that, in addition to my parents, contained two aunts, a grandmother, and a housekeeper who looked after me, the possibilities for attention were legion—especially since my brother had not yet come into the world. My importunings of these elders were directed toward playing games and being read to, and the repeated cry attributed to me was "Weed-a-book." Years before I learned to read I had committed to memory forgotten epics like The *War of the Wooden Soldiers*, which, at the drop of a hat, I would recite for the surprised visitor. There may be nothing extraordinary about this fact, but, as with the hymns and popular songs to come, the activity of memorization and repetition emanated from a sensibility that appeared to be geared toward vocal performance and that took pleasure in doing it again and again. After I learned to read and began to borrow regularly from the school and village libraries, my strongest inclination showed itself not so much in seeking out new books in new areas as it did in rereading ones that had already gripped me. My favorite subjects were in no way unusual: fiction, mysteries, sports stories about real or imagined teams and athletes, myths and legends like *The Nibelungenlied* or *The Song of Roland*. What may have been novel, or at least slightly more distinctive, was the almost guilty pleasure I took in signing certain books, again and again, out of the library. Many years later a comrade in graduate school chastised me for not being adventurous enough to seek out new titles rather than rereading *The Great Gatsby* or *The Portrait of a Lady*. I took him seriously and tried to modify my ways; but there was a way there to be modified—retentive, preservative, conservative.

As for the public library in Johnson City (called Your Home Library), I loved it—loved the smells of its different rooms, delighted in moving beyond the confines of the children's section into adult alcoves, appreciated the coziness of its warmth in winter and its cool respite from summer heat. Anyone thinking about the library as it has appeared in poems quickly thinks of Jarrell's three library-based ones, of which "Children Selecting Books in a Library" contains the following:

> What some escape to, some escape: if we find Swann's
> Way better than our own, and trudge on at the back
> Of the north wind to — to — somewhere east
> Of the sun, west of the moon, it is because we live
>
> By trading another's sorrow for our own; another's
> Impossibilities, still unbelieved in, for our own.

But Jarrell believed his childhood was a sorrowful one and that reading was a compensation for an unsatisfactory life. Unless I deeply mislead myself I had on the whole a happy childhood of which reading — like playing the piano and playing basketball — was one of the good parts. If anything, I treated reading as an extension of my life, or of myself, rather than a substitute for some inadequate life and self. But mainly, as an obedient boy who usually believed what his grade school teachers told him, I thought that reading was one more of the activities that would surely make me a better and smarter person. I'm not sure when, if ever, I learned that the escape provided by reading (and our teachers told us it was *not* an escape) to somewhere — in Jarrell's words — "east of the sun, west of the moon," was different from moral self-improvement.

As an adolescent, I thought the acme of taste in reading were the detective novels of S. S. Van Dine and his smooth-talking aesthete of a sleuth, Philo Vance. I read and reread *The Bishop Murder Case, The Greene Murder Case,* and the others, convinced that I was getting something out of the ordinary when Vance provided disquisitions on Egyptian art or Turkish cigarettes. Since I had absolutely no luck in recommending these books to my contemporaries, I decided I was quite a sophisticated fellow. Otherwise my favorite writers were ones that most American boys who read would have been reading in the 1940s: the marvelous sports novels of John R. Tunis (*The Kid from Tomkinsville,* reread recently, has lost nothing of its savor); the Horatio Alger novels of an earlier generation, available, though tattered, in a box in our attic. I avoided "classics," whether American, English, or Continental, and somehow no one urged me to read *Moby-Dick* or *The Scarlet Letter* or *The Three Musketeers* or *Oliver Twist.* My parents, after a full day's work, had little time left over for reading, although my mother belonged to a book club. The only book I remember my father bringing home was the celebratedly steamy *Forever Amber*, by Kathleen Winsor; as I recall he did not get far with it, nor did I, when a quick turn of the pages revealed precious little of the requisite hot stuff. Much more fulfilling in the line of sexual information were James T. Farrell's Studs Lonigan novels, recommended to me by a reading pal across the street. The Lonigan trilogy, especially *The Young Manhood of Studs Lonigan*, offered a heavy and welcome concentration on smoking, drinking, and various kinds of sex, just the sorts of things a respectable small-town American boy from a decent family wanted to hear about. I hid them from my parents, having no interest in sharing with them tales of life on the mean streets of Chicago.

Poetry, in which I was to invest so heavily later on, remained a strictly academic subject, something to be identified or memorized in classrooms presided over by mainly dedicated, predominantly spinster teachers. We stayed away entirely from English poetry and from odd-ball Americans like Emily Dickinson and Walt Whitman (except for his conventional "O Captain, My Captain"). I never read a line of Shakespeare until I was in tenth grade, when we were piloted through *The Merchant of Venice*, and that was a "play," not a poem, it seemed. Our examples of verse were almost exclusively American and—with the exception of Frost and Carl Sandburg (especially "Fog")—were chosen from the nineteenth-century "fireside" or "schoolroom" poets: William Cullen Bryant, John Greenleaf Whittier, James Russell Lowell, Henry Wadsworth Longfellow, Oliver Wendell Holmes, with bits of Edwin Markham and Eugene Field thrown in. We read "Thanatopsis," "Barbara Freitchie," the prologue to Lowell's *Vision of Sir Launfal;* "Paul Revere's Ride" and "The Village Blacksmith"; "The Skeleton in Armor" and "The Deacon's Masterpiece." "Build thee more stately mansions Oh my soul," the first line of the concluding stanza of Holmes's "The Chambered Nautilus," sums up perfectly the mainly oppressive and solemn air that gathered around these poems. In the classroom, poetry "study" was usually met with a groan, whereas it would be quite acceptable for a teacher to read aloud a story by Kipling or O. Henry. Compared to current practice, when poetry is likely to get into the secondary school curriculum only in minimal ways (if at all), I don't regret my time spent with these admirable American sages. But for the most part my teachers were pretty uncomfortable themselves with the art of verse and seldom able to suggest any connection

between it and what Wordsworth called "the grand elementary principle of pleasure." That *pleasure* could be involved in reading or writing
poems did not occur to me, or perhaps to them.

Things got worse in English classes as I became older. Ninth grade
featured our first "classic," *Ivanhoe*, which my classmates cordially
hated but I, ready for a classic novel, found wholly welcome. We studied *The Rime of the Ancient Mariner* mainly, it seemed, to learn what
was simile, what metaphor, and what personification. Tenth grade
brought more unpopular classics: *The Merchant of Venice* (from which
we memorized Shylock's "I am a Jew" speech and Portia's "The quality of mercy is not strained"), *Silas Marner*, and *A Tale of Two Cities*,
the last of which people simply failed to complete, even in a short-
ened, excerpted form. And that was pretty much it. What my English
teachers knew how to teach was grammar; complete with diagram-
ming of sentences, workbooks, quizzes, and a rational grading standard, it was much less problematic to deal with than literature. The
modest literary education I managed to acquire happened outside of
school, on my own time and serendipitously, and was conducted
exclusively in prose since it would not have occurred to me to borrow
a book of poems from the library. My standards for poetry were fairly
conventional, especially after encountering some free verse from early
in the century. In an embarrassing, four-square poem written for the
school paper I aired my prejudices in the following stanza:

> And though I may be old-fashioned
> I like a poem that rhymes;
> You can have Carl Sandburg or John Gould Fletcher
> And others of our times.

(I had just finished claiming to admire Holmes and Whittier and
Longfellow for their directness and sincerity.) Yet, fifty years later, I
find myself speaking up for the virtues of rhyme and stanza in contemporary poetry and usually preferring poets who work well in these
established forms. Updike's remark about finding no certain substi-
tutes for one's youthful assumptions confirms itself.

If it is difficult to identify the budding teacher or critic in my procedures as a young reader of literature, it is easier to locate such an
impulse in relation to professional sports, especially baseball. Unlike
literature, which was immense, chaotic, and about whose world I
didn't know where to look for guides, baseball seemed comprehensi-

ble, well catalogued, and with statistics at the ready for anyone who was interested. I began to pay attention to baseball during the 1941 World Series between the Yankees and the Dodgers, indeed in the notorious fourth game when, with two Yankee outs in the ninth and the Dodgers about to win by a run, Mickey Owen dropped a third strike, allowing the batter to reach first base. There followed a demolition by the wrecking crew—Henrich, DiMaggio, Keller, Gordon, and Dickey—and the Dodgers were through for the series. Next spring I prepared for the season by subscribing to *Baseball* magazine, which provided rosters of the different teams, estimated their strengths at various positions, and evaluated their probable finish at season's end. This kind of ranking and filing spoke to me on a level deeper than actually playing the sport. I memorized all the players at all positions on all the teams; I made out file cards with my own evaluations and wrote critiques of each team's outfield and infield, pitching and catching strengths. I made up a scrapbook of pictures of the greats and not-so-greats, complete with pithy one-line captions beneath the pictures ("Barney McCoskey, sharp-hitting rightfielder for the Bengals"). Most weeks I bought the *St. Louis Sporting News*, the extraordinary baseball paper that reported on all the teams and carried all the box scores for the previous week's games, both major and minor leagues.

I also put in my time on the diamond, playing a good-field no-hit game for the South Side Vagabonds, as we called ourselves. But stronger allegiances were to the New York Yankees and Giants—we had a class A Yankee farm club, the Binghamton Triplets, which played its home games in Johnson City—and to keeping track of things through the media and my own records. It wasn't long before I learned how to make a line score, inning by inning, with all the little symbols sketched in neatly. It was impossible to receive Yankees and Giants games on upstate New York radio; however, New York City's WHN carried the Brooklyn Dodgers games, so I was fortunate to be exposed to the voice of Red Barber and followed Brooklyn (even though I favored the Giants) through the wartime seasons of struggle and postwar ones of success. Red Barber's idiom was in itself a civilizing and witty resource. When he described a "rhubarb" (an argument between players and umpire), or opined that the "Brooks" were "tearin' up the pea patch," or presented us with "Old Higlebee" (Brooklyn pitcher, Kirby Higbe) or "Old Gromyko" (second baseman

Eddie Stanky, who drew a lot of walks, thus reminding Barber of the Soviet delegate's walkout at the UN), Barber gave memorable value to the hours I spent listening to what was, after all, just a game. His voice was especially important on the days when the Dodgers were playing in the West while the broadcasters sat in their New York studio, receiving reports of the game every so often over the teletype machine. This meant there were no sounds of bat meeting ball or the roar of the crowd; just lots of dead air, broken by the tick-tick-tick of the teletype, then by Barber re-creating what supposedly happened during the last minute or so. It meant that you were all alone with this single author- ity who kept you listening entirely by the dramatic shifts he could conjure up through his remarkable voice. My relation to baseball was primarily literary, academic even, in its commitment to convention, tradition, inherited rules — to the pedantry of statistics and the plea- sures of notation. Something like it went on, to a lesser degree, in my trackings of professional and collegiate football and of the local high school basketball wars. It was an interest, perhaps surprisingly, not widely shared among my friends; just as you didn't come across many fellow readers with whom to share enthusiasms and tastes, it was hard to locate someone who cared not only about sports but about keeping track of them. The connection, when occasionally made, was a signif- icant one. I finally met such a person in the boy who played left field for the Vagabonds. He was a passionate Dodger fan, extremely critical of players who failed to perform successfully, and he had a particular animus toward a hapless Dodger pitcher during the war period named, memorably, Ed Head. One day it was reported that Head had suffered a back injury while attempting to bend over and tie his shoes. We found this hilarious and would act out poor Head's shoe-tying attempt and ensuing collapse on the clubhouse floor. From then on we shared base- ball lore and statistics, even after Ed Head had departed the scene.

But if I was excessive in my study of baseball, it was probably the only such excess allowed me. In the areas of education, music, and religion, I fully complied with powerful constraints that nothing be carried to an extreme. My parents certainly approved of — or in my father's case at least tolerated — my churchly activities; but if I had decided to become a truly intense young Christian gentleman, they would have been worried, even appalled. Although my work at the piano continued steadily and even, one summer, approached daily practice of two hours, there was a guiding sense on the part of both my parents that, really, the life of a professional concert musician was terribly risky and probably not worth the things I would have to give up for a shot at success. My father's unquestioned piety about the virtues of a college education ("the best years of your life," and so forth) allied with his fear that musicians were on the whole unsound people who not only might not make enough money to live on but also were likely to turn out odd, in one way or another. No one, neither parents nor friends nor music teachers, ever gave a passionate speech on the glories of the artistic vocation, and perhaps it was just as well. As I entered high school, the possibility of opting for such a life receded.

As for the education part of it, what I thought of as a good elementary school training conformed to the conditions of public school in an industrial town with a minimum of "tracked," separatist learning ventures. We were all more or less in the same boat. The only attempt to cater to the needs of the clever student was at an early stage to double-promote him or her, thus "skipping" a half year, as I was twice allowed to do. From time to time my parents would express regret about how much time I must have been wasting in class while the "slower ones" had this and that bit of knowledge or technique drilled into them. I did not mind it at all; indeed, I was fiercely democratic and wanted nothing more than to fit in with, to be accepted by, those slower classmates, some of whom in other ways were enviably fast. The very suggestion of being sent away to private school, never discussed seriously in my family, would have disturbed me greatly. So I endured the wasted time and disciplinary sloppiness of many class hours, learned Latin at a needlessly slow rate, sat through vacuous discussions, in social studies, of "the community" — rather than reading history and politics. Once the New York State Board of Regents examinations were passed at the end of the eleventh grade (we prepared for them endlessly by going over old exams), one's high school work was essentially finished. My final year of English consisted of a semester of "Debate," in which we argued about whether people should go along with the group or assert their individuality, and a review course in the fundamentals of grammar, designed to better equip the few of us who were bound for college.

I had more or less assumed that my academic success (I was a valedictorian) was tantamount to acceptance at just about wherever I decided I would be happiest. For reasons not at all clear to me, Princeton University appeared to unite the virtues of a major institution with some of the charms — bucolic compared to Harvard or Yale — of a small-town college atmosphere. Accordingly, to Princeton I applied, and to Princeton only. My resourceless high school guidance counselor gave me no counseling and no guidance of the slightest use. The notion that, even in the remote days of 1949, it might be prudent to apply to more than one place never crossed his or my parents' or my own mind. When there arrived at the beginning of June a terse letter of rejection from Princeton, the effect was catastrophic, an alternating of rage and tears. After things settled a bit, my father ascertained from a Princeton acquaintance that my age — sixteen — had been against me and that a year of preparatory school was in order. This would not do at all, the three of us agreed, and we began to cast about for alternatives. One of them was Amherst, which I had looked at briefly on a trip through New England the previous summer, the college simmering and shut tight in the mid-August heat. Amherst had an excellent reputation and, in addition, a band in which I could continue playing the clarinet. My father wrote a letter to Amherst's dean of admissions, pleading the case of his talented son. In reply, Eugene S. Wilson, an admissions dean of some repute, invited me to send along my college board scores and said that if they proved acceptable I would be admitted to the Amherst class of 1953. And so it came to pass.

It is fair to say that no one in Johnson City, New York, had even heard of Amherst College. Where was it? Was it a law school? Wasn't I going to law school since my father was a lawyer? I tried to answer these questions with a semblance of a confidence I lacked. Meanwhile there were ceremonies to close out my life and good times as a public schoolboy, capped by a commencement at which the top three graduates gave orations on subjects that couldn't have been further from our hearts. Certainly mine, a disquisition titled "Health," was a thoughtless performance, full of concern at how important health was to us all and how disastrous it would be if the Truman administration succeeded in putting through some form of "socialized medicine." I copied statistics from some pamphlet or other and fed them back to the proud parents; dutiful applause was received and credited. It was not at all a good way of taking leave, and even though the less than stimulating topics (the other two were "Housing" and "Prejudice") were ones suggested to us from higher up, I wish that at least a part of me had rebelled and somehow managed to do something else. Much better was the following night, the informal Class Night, where five of us put together a popular-swing combo that produced acceptable music. Here at least one could be sincere and not embarrassing, controlled but not stuffy.

Thus, at age sixteen I didn't know much about anything except baseball and statistics, the words of popular songs and sacred hymns, and how to play the piano. I liked movies and fantasizing about girls; I "knew" that I would go to college, have stimulating relationships, probably continue on to law school, get married, have children, and live some sort of small-town suburban life. Philip Larkin's musing speaker in "Dockery and Son," with his quite different set of circumstances ("To have no son, no wife, / No house or land still seemed quite natural"), wonders where these "innate assumptions" come from and he concludes

> They're more a style
> Our lives bring with them: habit for a while,
> Suddenly they harden into all we've got
>
> And how we got it: looked back on, they rear
> Like sand-clouds, thick and close . . .

I knew nothing about any of that, but presumed that the "well-rounded man" Amherst College claimed to create or educate served well enough as a vague goal.

II
An Earthly Paradise

In *Begin Here: The Forgotten Conditions of Teaching and Learning,* Jacques Barzun has described what he imagined to be an incoming freshman's response, half a century ago, to the American college:

> In most cases the boy or girl had never been away from home and was now alone responsible for the use of time and resources, no longer pupil but student. He or she was called Mr. or Miss in class, without irony. The whole intellectual landscape was new; here were grave faculty members, friendly but not chummy, devoting a good many hours a week to teaching certain definite matters of agreed importance and also doing that mysterious thing "research." It seemed to give their words the authority they claimed and did not hesitate to exercise. This enchanting new atmosphere found its counterpart in the work to be done — many hours of reading in real books, written by adults for adults, who were deemed capable of understanding all the words and of singling out the important points to remember.

Since Barzun goes on immediately to claim that today's college and the university around it — he seems to make little distinction between college and university — is, by sad contrast, "a motley organization dedicated to the full life," one may ask whether his fifty-year-old vision of the old-fashioned American college is accurate. On the basis of my encounter with Amherst College that fall of 1949, I would have

17

to say yes, that's pretty much the way it was. The college was in the process of scaling down, after heavy postwar enrollments, to its "norm" of eight hundred and fifty students. The catalogue for that year ("Amherst — A Liberal College") announces rather proudly that it "has no wish for a greater enrollment." Amherst was an institution "devoted to the individual student and his development." Its teacher–student ratio was one to ten. It was a college of "the liberal arts," and although science courses were offered they were considered "part of a broad liberal education." Originally most graduates entered the ministry; now fifty percent of them "go directly into business." The catalogue praises Amherst's faculty as both scholars and teachers; even as laboratory research gets done and books get published, the professors "are at the same time an understanding, interested, friendly group of men to whom a student may turn for academic or personal guidance." It is noted with pride that the college is currently second in the number of its graduates appearing in *Who's Who*. The final sentence puts the emphasis on what Amherst offered its students: "a sound, purposeful education for life."

This reassuring little document did not need to go on at great length, since its assumptions were evident to its readers. For example, it contained not a single word about proper behavior on the part of undergraduates. A few years later the following "rule" was added: "Conduct befitting a gentleman is expected at all times of students at Amherst College. It is assumed that undergraduates will understand what constitutes gentlemanly conduct without specific regulations forbidding particular actions." The emphasis fell rather on the curriculum, Amherst's main source of pride — the New Curriculum as it was called, instituted in 1947 and destined for a life of almost twenty years. The New Curriculum involved a required completion of three two-year courses in science, history, and the humanities, to be taken during the undergraduate's first two years. In addition, there was a language requirement as well as modest ones in physical education and public speaking. The required two-year courses in what can be roughly designated as the three "divisions" (science, social science, humanities) could be satisfied in slightly different ways; but all freshmen took a year of physics-mathematics (there were two levels of difficulty), a year of history (Western, from the Greeks through World War I), and a humanities package consisting of a Great Books course and one in English composition. All sophomores took a year of American Studies, in which various historical and political issues were considered; they took a humanities course (music, drama, fine arts) or an introduction to literature (critical reading); and they took either a chemistry-biology sequence or a sequence called Evolution of the Earth and Man. Accordingly there was no necessity for any advisory assistance during one's first two years: the map was fully laid out.

By my calculations I spent roughly twenty hours a week in the classroom my freshman year (not counting science laboratory and phys ed) and slightly fewer hours as a sophomore. Classes met Monday through Saturdays (ceasing at noon Saturday) and attendance was required, although after first term one was allowed as many cuts over the course of a semester as there were course hours in the week. Except for a break at Thanksgiving—classes ended the day before at noon, resuming Monday following—and cancellation of Saturday classes on two football weekends, there was no respite from one's courses. Nor was it possible, as for years it was at Harvard College, to put off doing the work of a course until a preexamination reading period in which a semester's catching up could be attempted. At Amherst the course in composition required handing in a short paper three times a week (thirty-three over the semester); in history there was likely to be a weekly quiz on the assigned reading material; and other short-term quizzes and papers provided a spur to keep up with the assigned humanities reading, math problems, or language translation.

This singleness of academic pursuit was strengthened by a paucity of alternatives in the social realm. Except for the three army veterans in our class, freshmen were not permitted to keep a car (one or two did secretly, I believe), and without such transportation, and assuming one was interested in such activity, access to the female population at Smith and Mt. Holyoke became more difficult. Since freshmen could not join a fraternity until spring, there was an absence of places to entertain a young woman, one's room being off-limits and the cramped social space of a dormitory basement hardly an attractive spot to frequent. You could go in for communal or solitary drinking, but I saw little and did nothing of either that fall of 1949. We were encouraged to attend the football game on Saturday afternoon ("Freshmen sit together as a class . . . ") and to participate in jousts with the sophomores such as the formally organized rope pull or informally unorganized water fight. But there wasn't much to do, really, except study.

This limiting of possibility felt like the opposite of deprivation since—in Barzun's words—I had entered into an "enchanting new atmosphere." I had been once to a summer music camp and had visited New York City more than once, but to be "away from home" and responsible for my own time was something new. I was indeed called Mr. in class, without irony, and I was expected to spend many hours reading real books written by adults for adults. The faculty, all male, all white, were, it is fair to say, friendly but not chummy. I was invited to tea at a music professor's house and for cider and doughnuts with the dean of admissions, and sometimes along with classmates I had lunch or supper in the dining hall with a faculty member, but that was the limit of socializing with what I presumed were my superiors (I did not think or care much about any "research" they might or might not have been doing). Such mild socializing as this actually enhanced, rather than detracted from, the ambience. For me, and I suspect for others, there had been nothing like it before and—truth to tell—there has been nothing quite like it since.

The state of being enchanted does not, of course, necessarily or even possibly go along with anything like intellectual clarity. The history course in Western civilization was straightforward enough, the march of events clearly laid out in well-organized lectures ideal for note-taking: here was the Roman Empire, there the Renaissance; over there World War I. And French was taught much in the manner I had been accustomed to in high school. But I hadn't the foggiest notion of how to proceed or of what was going on in the badly taught (so others assured me) physics introductory (I had avoided science in high school and didn't expect to take to it at Amherst). And the humanities course was mysterious in another sense, since I had little idea of how to enter the conversation about great books into which I was invited. My section was taught by John Moore, a brilliant classicist trained at Harvard, and equally at home, it seemed, with English poetry as with Greek and Latin. In class Moore would ask questions about *The Iliad* or the Bible that were speculative and wide-ranging, often tinged with fancy and playfulness: What if Socrates had said this rather than that? Suppose Pilate had done this rather than that—what then? A classmate, visibly annoyed after fifty class minutes spent, it seemed, in going round the mulberry bush, complained to me as we walked away from class, "He keeps asking these questions and then doesn't answer them"—as if Moore's intellectual limitations and pedagogical trickery had been thus exposed.

All these courses, however, were as nothing compared to the course in composition, another matter entirely and a most puzzling un-note-takeable-on activity that challenged, bewildered, and often defeated the freshman who had been told, all through high school, what a good writer he was. English 1 was by all odds the most radically upsetting course in the New Curriculum, setting things in motion for me that had immeasurable repercussions on my future as a learner, teacher, and human being. Directed, indeed invented, by Theodore Baird, it was conducted by him and most other members of the English department in sections of sixteen to twenty students that met three times a week. My section was taught by Armour Craig, who had been a student of Baird's and come back to Amherst to teach with him in this staff course. Craig, who seemed to have read a prodigious amount and whose remarks contained frequent allusions to writers I had never heard of—Bertrand Russell, William James, Alfred North Whitehead—demonstrated early on that he would be a hard man to satisfy. On opening day of class, after a few preliminary procedural remarks, we were invited to write a paragraph or two in which we said something about our expectations concerning this course titled "Composition." What did we hope to get out of it? Like most of my classmates, it turned out, I couldn't think of much more to say than that I hoped to learn to write, or (if I knew that already) to improve my writing. When at the next meeting Craig briefly addressed these statements of expectation, he appeared puzzled by them: "Most of you say that in this course you want to learn how to write. But surely the question is, write *what*?" What on earth was Craig talking about? I wondered. What was wrong with my modest, sensible hope, elicited under pressure of a question, that I should learn—in freshman English at this admirable college—to write?

The playfully contentious twist Craig gave to our pious answers was a harbinger of things to come, as, over the course of thirty-three short papers, we were subjected to questions to which I never managed to come up with the right answers. Each of the assignments presented us with questions we would deal with in a short paper to be handed in at the next class. Those papers, in turn, provided the materials for discussion in the class to come. There was no textbook, no accompanying assigned literature. It soon became clear — though it didn't feel much like clarity — that the subject of the assignments was language, or rather our individual successes and failures (mostly the latter) as users of language. Many of the assignments began by directing us to recall a situation — from our experience, real or imagined — in which we told someone the "right name of something" or the "wrong name of something"; how did we know the name we told him was right (or wrong)? What about a time when we were puzzled and could not say the right name — what did it mean to be "puzzled"? Recall a situation in which we needed to ask, about something (not a word), "What does *that* mean?" or in which we were able to say with confidence, "*That* means . . . " How would we define "confidence" or "meaning" or "right name"? What happened when we became dissatisfied with a "vocabulary" or when a vocabulary failed us? As we came nearer the end of term, the assignments focused explicitly on the matter of communication, as in the following, number 30 in the sequence:

> Recall a situation in which you shifted your terms in order to communicate successfully.
>
> a) Where were you, to whom were you speaking, and in what terms? Illustrate your situation by quoting some of your statements.
>
> b) When did you shift your terms? Why? Give some examples of new statements you made.
>
> c) Why could you not make these new statements in the terms you were using in a)? Answer with reference to at least two words or phrases.
>
> d) What, then, generalizing from this example, is Successful Communication?

Although I did not know it then — indeed, I never fully realized it until ten years later when I found myself on the other side of the desk teaching English 1 — "situation" was the key word here and we were being asked, time and again, to imagine a situation. It wasn't enough vaguely to "recall" a situation or to invent one if nothing came to mind. Composition — the act of putting words together into sentences and paragraphs — involved paying attention to the act, to the art, of writing in ways I had never been asked to before. As freshmen confronting the same assignment thrice weekly we argued about what "they" (the

English staff) meant or believed about language, about the relation of words to things. Rumors circulated to the effect that mysterious though colorfully named figures such as Alfred Korzybski or S. I. Hayakawa or Ludwig Wittgenstein—perhaps Pragmatism—stood behind the course's assumptions. Meanwhile the real work of engagement was going on elsewhere, in the recurrent struggle to make verbal formulations that were somehow, for the moment, adequate. Very seldom, in my case and in that of most others, was the struggle officially designated by the professor as a successful one—and that kept the course irritatingly alive and kicking.

The papers we handed in were read and commented on (thought not graded) by our instructor. In most classes, selections had been mimeographed to be read aloud and then examined to see what they yielded. Occasionally the mimeographed material consisted of a group of sentences taken from various papers to illustrate different ways of talking about the assignment question. The class discussions focused wholly on our ideas and the sentences in which we formulated them, rather than on the mechanics of writing (it was assumed we knew about those, although mistakes were corrected). For one whose high school valedictory oration ("Health") ensured a high level of flatulence from the orator, the analytic approach of English 1 was invaluable as well as highly disturbing to a young man's self-confidence as a maker of sentences. In the final, longer paper we were invited, after being provokingly ushered into the subject, to write about some difficulties in communication and what advice we would give writers to help overcome them. I tied myself into knots in my awkward attempts to express these difficulties; yet my writing at least revealed some effort, a sense of strain that had been, in my high school prose, totally absent.

English 1 had a heady flavor. Those of us who flattered ourselves that we eventually "caught on," and who were at least rewarded with respectable grades, caught on to something we took to be an all-important crucial difference between words and things, language and reality—between mind and the world-out-there. That world we now understood to be chaos, without pattern or design, awaiting only our human strategies—verbal ones—for running lines of order through it. I had not yet read *The Education of Henry Adams* (that would come in my sophomore year, in two different courses), nor did I know what an important part it had played in shaping Theodore Baird's sensibility, nor that, in an earlier form the composition course had once spent a semester with Adams's book as the single text for reading and writing about. But Adams's formulation, "Chaos was the law of nature; order the dream of man," seemed an authoritative one to sum up what we had learned over the weeks of a term. And we learned also how tenuous and uncertain a relation there was between our operations as users of language, as order makers, and the people and things "out there" with whom we were attempting to communicate, whom we wanted to move around to fit our dreams of order.

As with Adams's chapter from the *Education*, failure was a livelier, more invigorating notion to play with than was success. Armour Craig liked to use a homey illustration, which would pass into course mythology, of how one's order-making dream might receive shocking comeuppance when the external world refused to cooperate. One might, he said, be in the act of backing one's car out of the driveway, intent upon getting first to point B, then subsequently to C, and fail to notice the oncoming presence of Skibiski's truck (Skibiski was a successful entrepreneur who sold farm machinery in nearby Sunderland) with which one disastrously collides. Chaos was the law of nature, and in that encounter with Skibiski's truck the law came to sudden vivid life. The notion that failure rather than success might be a good subject for a writer helped form my developing sense of irony, even as it stayed just below the surface of consciousness. But I'm convinced that an important reason why the deconstructive turn (with its emphasis on aporias, slippages, dangerously floating signifiers) had the effect on me of being very old news indeed, was the skeptical attitude toward language cultivated in the English classroom decades previously.

There was also a touch of playful irreverence about English 1 that, in the pretty uniformly sober academic classroom of 1949, pleased and enlivened, as if "English teachers" liked to fool around as much as the next person. Early on we heard of the infamous final examination that the now-sophomore class had been given the previous year: it consisted of a fairly complicated situation of noncommunication between the student as Earthling, bound to certain vocabularies in which he expressed the "right names" for things, and a visitor from Mars who spoke a very different language. The details of the situation don't matter, but they led, through a series of questions, to the exam's concluding question: "Now, define Mars." (It was rumored that more than one puzzled or disaffected student had chosen to answer, "A candy bar," and handed in his exam.) The point about discourses

WILLIAM H. PRITCHARD

being bound by their terms, and the difficulties that ensued when 1
ther participant was able to shift his terms in accommodation, wa
familiar one; but the instruction to "define Mars" gave it new flavor.
For the concluding, longer paper in our semester it was proposed that,
in three different situations someone asked us, "Who do you think
you are?" to which, in each case, we replied "Einstein." The results
were markedly different: in the first situation a mathematics professor smiled; in the second, small boys requested an autograph; in the
third we were carted off to a padded cell by institutional attendants.
The long paper didn't ask us to define "Einstein," but its line of suggestion is perhaps evident. It was a touch of wit that sometimes made
for wit in others, as when my fairly solemn roommate called up our
professor at home and anonymously asked for some information.
When Armour Craig asked who it was on the other end, my roommate replied, emphatically, "Weinstein," then hung up (indeed, Weinstein was his "right name").

More than one alumnus or faculty member who studied or taught
at Amherst College under the New Curriculum of 1947–66, has
likened the experience to boot camp, the all-male classroom helping
to encourage trials and testings that, while rather mild in comparison
to the training of U.S. Marines, had analogous aspects. Although Craig
was studiedly polite with us, other teachers were not. Paragraphs of
papers that contained irrelevant or pompous writing were boldly
crossed out by the instructor, with marginal notations such as "gob-
bledygook" being especially popular. "I stopped reading here," wrote
one teacher after encountering some inanity and drawing a bold line
across the paper. A frequently encountered teaching stance was that of
the instructor as gadfly or enigmatic critic, perceived as knowing
something we didn't about what "the course" was getting at. In
response to our puzzlement and questioning, sincerity was not the
preferred mode of address; rather, we would be met with another question or a teasing bit of obliqueness. Among those of us who fancied
that we were beginning to get the hang of things, there was a tendency
to impress ourselves and perhaps others with just how much of a special experience we were undergoing. We delighted in using the current
classroom vocabulary extracurricularly, as it were, by subjecting real-
life events to English 1 terms. This sort of thing must have been perceived by outsiders as exclusive, perhaps offensive, although every so
often one of them—perhaps a female taking some more traditional

How would Willy know?

English course someplace else—would remark, with amazement and, we hoped, admiration, "You Amherst men all talk alike."

Although in the humanities course we read the Great Books and spent a few classes savoring famous poems (Shakespeare, Marvell, Keats), my literary education really began the following year. English 1 made it a point of pride *not* to assign any books; the sophomore English course, titled "Introduction to Literature," advertised itself correctly as dealing with "a small number of works of prose and poetry" in such a way as to illustrate principles of critical reading. That course, taught in sections as was the composition course, was largely the creation of Reuben Brower who, himself an Amherst graduate, had returned to teach both English and classics at the college after his graduate work at Harvard and especially at Cambridge, England, where he studied with both I. A. Richards and F. R. Leavis. I was only vaguely conscious of Brower's presence behind the course, although he did take over our section for a couple of classes when our professor, C. L. Barber, was ill. But it was apparent, in comments heard from all the sections, that this course, familiarly known as "close reading," occupied itself in strenuous engagement with the words on the page. We were never *not* looking at a poem, a line, a word—whether the material was a Shakespearean drama, a novel by Henry James, or *The Education of Henry Adams*. My sophomore year the readings for the first semester consisted of a poetry anthology (we concentrated mainly on Wordsworth), a selection of Frost's poems, *King Lear*, and Ben Jonson's *Volpone* and *The Alchemist*. In the second term we located ourselves slightly more within a particular century, reading Jane Austen (*Mansfield Park*), Adams's *Education*, parts of *In Memoriam*, James's *Portrait of a Lady*, with a concluding look at E. M. Forster's *Room with a View*.

Learning to read critically had to do with discovering—to use the term Brower employed in his book *The Fields of Light*—the "imaginative designs" displayed by poems, fictions, poetic dramas. These were of course designs of language, enacted in verbal performances of richness and complexity (I am using words that my eighteen-year-old ears were beginning to register). The place where such designs and displays, such performances could be most concentratedly experienced was in the lyric poem, and that is why Brower invariably began his introducing of literature with various examples of lyric. To help us in our attempts to describe the designs of poems, we were provided with useful terms as inherited from Richards and the New Critics (especially Cleanth Brooks and Robert Penn Warren) but developed and refined by Brower himself: tone, attitude, dramatic situation, metaphor. If the method sounds potentially mechanical, capable of being abused, that was certainly the case. What saved it from abuse, especially in class, was the agreed-upon procedure that one should begin and if possible end by reading the poem aloud. So a short lyric like Wordsworth's "To a Butterfly" ("I've watched you now a full half-hour/ Self-poised upon that yellow flower") became the ideal, because manageable, object on which to concentrate.

We were invited to try the poem out by performing it orally; adjustments and modifications could be made in the speaking voice to provide an invaluable check on interpretive overeagerness, indeed on abstraction of any sort. I now think that this emphasis on sound was a good deal more important than anything we figured out about metaphor or attitude. Tone, tone of voice, was the key to realizing the poem; if we could get that right—whatever "right" meant—the rest would follow in due course. But the practice of reading aloud, whenever possible, before the interpretive argument began—although, of course, it had already begun in the decisions made about how to read aloud—was also a way of promoting the sense of freshness of response essential to the good critic. R. P. Blackmur put it this way in his characterization of that critic's task:

> He knows that the institution of literature, so far as it is alive, is made again at every instant. It is made afresh as part of the process of being known afresh; what is permanent is what is always fresh, and it can be fresh only in performance—that is, in reading and seeing and hearing what is actually in it at this place and this time.

At that point I had never heard of Blackmur, but something like his recommendation of the value of performance was being practiced in the literature classroom as I experienced it.

Blackmur's eloquence is doubtless too much for the more modest reality of any single course to live up to. And note should also be taken of the distance between the excellent principles and careful pedagogy of "English 21: Introduction to Literature" and what an individual student like me was able to make out of it in his work. In our attempts to become close—at least closer—readers, we were on one occasion turned loose on *Lear* (there had been a fair amount of preliminary classroom analysis of scenes) and invited to identify a particular "train" of images or metaphors we saw as contributing to the expressive texture of the play. The exercise was directed more toward seeing than hearing, and it was squarely in the line of modern attempts, by Wilson Knight, Brower, and other critics, to emphasize the way Shakespeare's dramatic poetry worked—the emphasis being directed at language rather than at theme or character. After scrambling about I finally came up with a group of related references I classified under the rubric of imagery involving small animals, the sort of humble fry that Edgar, disguised as Poor Tom, alludes to on the heath, in the third act: "Poor Tom, that eats the swimming frog, the toad, the tadpole, the wall-newt and the water." I tried to convince myself that I was on to something that had perhaps been overlooked or insufficiently attended to. My professor, Cesar Barber, was not convinced, even though his comment on my paper sought to modulate skepticism with kindness as it began: "Your little animals finally don't amount to much, although not, I think, because you've overlooked anything." In my attempt to look at literature under the microscope and not neglect any minutiae, I had nitpicked or newt-picked my way into triviality, not evidently the proper alternative to talking largely about Lear's tragic agony. Even at the time I took some hard satisfaction in Barber's criticism, since I hadn't really convinced myself about the small animals either. Now the anecdote seems to me a nice example of the difference between the admirable aim of a course, as expressed in a single exercise, and a particular individual's attempt to carry out that aim, inadvertently resulting in parody.

Yet for all the comedy of such individual failures, "Introduction to Literature" was a proper follow-up to the course in composition. There we had been confronted time and again with instances in which the language we were using failed to work, in which the gulf between words and experience seemed more impressive than any possible connections to be made between those realms. "Introduction to Literature" relaxed the skeptical bent of "Composition" and acted as if language, intelligently used, could describe a relation between the reader and the words on the page he was engaging with. It was a course that, rather than insisting we come to terms with literature, suggested some possible terms for our experience of it. And if we sometimes acted as though the critical vocabulary of tone-attitude-metaphor-irony was a magical key to unlock poetic structures, that was perhaps forgivable; at least it helped us attend to the details, the particulars of organization informing the work. In discouraging—or certainly, not encouraging—talk about biography or "ideas" or other larger contextual possibilities, the course may have too confidently advised us to think small (of small animals), and my own future reluctance to talk about contexts rather than texts was probably encouraged by this sort of critical training. Yet the materials presented for our attention— Wordsworth and Frost, *Lear* and Ben Jonson—surely demanded a strenuous engagement with words on the page.

Given the impact both these English courses exerted on me, it seems odd that I failed to sign on as an English major but opted instead first for political science, then for philosophy. Partly this must have had to do, shamefully, with the fact of not being immediately rewarded by high grades in English, suggesting to me that perhaps my strongest talents lay elsewhere. It probably had something to do as well with the foolish idea I had of myself as a budding lawyer with "relevant" courses in political science under his belt. How irrelevant to the core of my being those courses were I was not to find out until I had been thoroughly bored by "Elements of Politics" and "Public Administration." Philosophy, by contrast, seemed much more attractive, with a small intelligent group of majors and a remarkable historian of philosophy, Sterling P. Lamprecht, who took us through the great names, from Plato to Kant. By this time, my junior year, I was an agnostic, thanks mainly to a course in ethics in which we read Nietzsche, John Dewey, and Walter Lippmann. Philosophy, I thought, might give me something comparable in the line of faith—if not Christian, at least cosmic and metaphysical. The aspiration was all there, if not memorably so, in a long paper I turned out for a course in the philosophy of religion. As the final effort of the term, members of the class wrote a paper titled "My Religious Philosophy," in which we attempted to come to grips with intimate and ultimate concerns. The papers were returned ungraded, though with comments, by our somewhat bland professor: "An honest and (thus far) a fruitful approach" began his evenhanded remarks at the end of mine.

I had by then decided that law school was not for me, an altogether sensible realization prompted by a sharp-tongued senior who said, in response to my talk of a legal career: nonsense, that clearly I was cut out to be a teacher and not a lawyer. I am still surprised by the inevitability with which his assertion cut through my hitherto not very carefully examined future plans. But since the men I most admired in the world were my Amherst teachers, what better than to emulate them by joining their profession? How many others have decided upon the academic life in similar terms, I can't say. I do know that in the half-joking but really quite serious educational scenario my friends and I scripted in our imaginations, and in the incessant conversations we had about favorite faculty members, their role in the play was not to be underestimated. To alter the sense of Freud's famous phrase, it was a species of family romance in which different professors stood in for real or nonexistent family members I had left behind or never had. Armour Craig was the severe Calvinist father, but (unlike my real father) he read literature and philosophy and proposed enigmatic questions about books. Sterling Lamprecht was a benign, grandfatherly figure, who could speak with beautiful lucidity about the *Ethics* of Spinoza, or Locke's *Essay Concerning Human Understanding*. Theodore Baird was the deeply sardonic uncle who showed up on occasion to jolt us out of some complacent assumption. ("Oh, Mr. Hazlitt, so you *identify* with Romeo, do you? Well, isn't that just lovely!") John Moore, the mischievous gadfly who asked unanswerable questions about *The Republic* or the Bible, was perhaps an extremely gifted older brother or cousin everyone knew was a genius. There were of course no women in this family romance — there were no women at Amherst except on weekends, when they were brought over on leave from Smith or Mt. Holyoke. I still remember my surprise when I found out that my blind date from Holyoke not only majored in philosophy but knew far more about logic and the philosophy of science than I did. But she didn't manage to break into my family romance.

The romance was not exclusively with our teachers. Various discovered novels and poems were endowed with supreme artistic power: *The Portrait of a Lady, A Portrait of the Artist as a Young Man, The Great Gatsby, The Waste Land* — books like these (and others, not all of them from this century) were read and reread, their substance consisting of nothing less than ultimate aesthetic truths about life that needed to be often rehearsed. It was something like Walter Pater's adventuring of the soul among masterpieces, though perhaps without quite so much incense as the Paterian flame demanded. My notion of the best way to win the interest of someone of the opposite sex was to engage in a conversation (with me doing most of the talking) about the incontestable merits of Fitzgerald or Frost or whomever. Although I don't remember conspicuous success in this tactic, it was undeniably invigorating to advertise the powers of art as found in the special virtue of this poem or that novel. For good or ill it was the teacherly impulse asserting itself. Many years later I discovered that a much more intrepid reader than I, Randall Jarrell, who by age eighteen had consumed, among other things, prodigious amounts of imaginative literature, liked nothing better than to get himself in the position — especially with young women — of recommending lists of books with which they absolutely had to become acquainted. Probably the main way in which my advertisings of a self through recounting literary discoveries resembled Jarrell's was in how sexual feeling got diverted or turned into something else, presumably of aspect more sublime.

Meanwhile I continued to try to pass myself off as a respectable student of philosophy, even though my manifest weakness in logic, in the philosophy of science — indeed, in anything requiring concentrated analytic skills — was painfully evident. As a senior honors project, the completion of which was to be an essay of some length on a philosopher or philosophical question, I chose William James, arguably the most "literary" of thinkers and one whose writings could be taken in by a mind derailed by Charles Sanders Peirce or Bertrand Russell. My treatment of James also observed conventional literary lines insofar as I considered the books chronologically, identified their main themes, and described their stylistic and writerly methods. The best parts of the essay had little to do with propounding a "thesis" but rather were moments in which I tried to respond effectively to some vivid and appealing bit of Jamesian prose from the *Psychology* or *Pragmatism* or *A Pluralistic Universe*. Although my own writing, judging from this culminating performance as a graduating senior, left much to be desired, the Amherst philosophy department seemed more than satisfied with the finished product. So, evidently did a committee from the philosophy department at Columbia University, which, on the basis of my record at Amherst and a submitted paper on causality in the philosophy of science, accepted me as a graduate student for the following fall.

In that spring of 1953 the Korean peace treaty was still a few months off, and the draft very much in evidence, so there was additional reason to carry on one's education. Yet my classmates who were going on to graduate work in philosophy or English—mainly to Harvard and Columbia, or to Fulbright Fellowships in England or France —did so out of fairly pure, if professional motives. The passport to a career in college or university teaching lay in a Ph.D., and none of us wanted to interrupt academic life. In that respect, life four decades later has precisely reversed itself, with the rule that anyone graduating from college plans a one- to three-year hiatus between that event and reentry into school—not just graduate school in the humanities, but in law, business, and even medicine. (Of course, there is now no draft to contend with.) My class was filled with people headed for Harvard Business School and Harvard Law School and we happy few—our little group of English and philosophy majors—measured ourselves as morally superior to them. After all, *they*, those hopeful bankers, businessmen, doctors, and lawyers, were all going to make a lot of money; *we*, although not planning to starve, had renounced dreams of financial glory in the service of something higher. We would be paid, as Armour Craig put it, to read books, and that seemed an excellent arrangement. For other than the financial limitation incurred by choosing a career in teaching, no evident drawbacks presented themselves. It never crossed anyone's mind that, upon the near completion of graduate study with the dissertation in process, there would be the slightest difficulty in landing a job. And indeed there was no such difficulty. So although our motives in choosing a teaching career were, as motives go, reasonably respectable, the component of superiority exercised in relation to those benighted souls who were happily ready to lay down the books (no more John Donne, no more Henry James) and make friendly accommodations with the facts of American commercial and professional reality, was strong and satisfying to the point of complacency. We reserved special contempt for advertising, for "Madison Avenue," the shorthand way of referring to the kind of American success (why did we assume all admen succeeded?) that was most despicable. Indeed, some of these successful people knew nothing about metaphor and the difference between words and things. On one memorable occasion a graduate of the college gave a talk to prospective admen in which he expressed his heartfelt admiration for the product he was boosting. A knowing member of the undergraduate audience decided to have a little fun with him by confronting him with the "lies" routinely told by advertising—such as that the flavor of Jell-O was locked in. How could they talk that way, asked the skeptic, only to be astonished when the salesman came back by insisting that, in *his* product, Jell-O, the flavor really *was* locked in! We thought this an obscenely beautiful instance of the chicanery, self-delusion, and general corruptness that characterized a world we were rejecting.

I have been speaking about "we"—the group of would-be teachers who hung around together, talking about books when doubtless we should have spent more time reading them; talking incessantly about our professors; distinguishing ourselves from the philistine element in our classmates ("philistine" was a recently discovered word, although we had not read Matthew Arnold's *Culture and Anarchy*). But what about the curious unstable compound of motives and impulses that was my twenty-year-old self? Amherst's course catalogue praised its curriculum in the liberal arts as promoting "the undergraduate's all-around development," as providing "a sound, purposeful education for life." But my liberal arts curriculum, the courses I had taken and the ones I spurned, had helped produce something other than—as the phrase went, mocked by us even as we sort of believed in it—"the well-rounded man." My non-well-roundedness may be verified by noting some aspects of liberal study that played no part in the self I was becoming. First there were the physical and biological sciences—touched on, admittedly, in the required science courses of the first two years, but leaving only the most superficial traces. It is no misrepresentation to say that my understanding of physics, chemistry, biology, or geology was for the most part nonexistent; and that my knowledge of mathematics ceased after a little calculus in my freshman year, never approaching anything like theoretical sophistication—it was essentially just more high school problem solving without the ghost of a reason why. In the social sciences, I had wholly avoided economics and psychology, and anthropology and sociology were not yet part of the curriculum. My grasp of history barely extended beyond the required freshman survey from the ancients to World War I, and the only history I really knew anything about was the history of philosophy. In the American Studies "problems" course we looked briefly at the Puritans, the revolution, finance capitalism, and other matters. The only aspect of political science that survived from four courses I took in the field was an introductory look at American constitutional development, especially with respect to the Supreme Court.

As for the humanities, a semester of French enabled me to satisfy the language requirement, and I thereafter left languages entirely alone until I took a semester of German with the graduate school language exams in mind. I avoided the fine arts, both in their historical and practical aspects. It was music in which I invested my time and heart: keeping up, to some extent, my status as a pianist, by accompanying various stage productions and Gilbert and Sullivan operas; singing in fraternity chorus competitions; playing piano in a dance orchestra and clarinet in the college band; playing and listening incessantly to American popular music and to jazz as well as to "serious" music. Most of this activity—except for courses in Beethoven and in Palestrina to Schubert—was outside the curriculum. Inside it, and at the center of my education, were fifteen or so courses in philosophy and English.

Those elders—especially the alumni of Amherst and other colleges —who currently lament the lack of a prescribed curriculum and who believe there was a time, a few decades back, when an undergraduate was exposed to something like an "all-around" education, should examine the components of my own, as I have detailed them here. Even, that is, with two years in which one's courses were rigidly prescribed, one could manage to leave a lot out, neglecting to touch on all sorts of presumably worthy subjects that today's undergraduates, choosing their course items like customers in a cafeteria, may just touch on. This is not to say that my studies lacked intensity or purposefulness, although I was never convinced that I worked hard enough or read carefully enough. It is rather to emphasize the peculiar slant, the warp, the bias, that was beginning to shape my aspirations as a learner. I was in the market for spiritual enlightenment—though I would not have said so at the time. There needed to be something to fill the void that a Christian faith had once filled. Couldn't it be filled by the great philosophers who would teach me the wisdom and moral insight that they surely possessed? And perhaps even more dramatically, by the great poets and novelists and dramatists who had given expression to the best that is known and thought in the world?

Or was it the great critics, more specifically the twentieth-century Anglo-American critics who, along with my favorite teachers, held the keys to help me unlock the culture hoard? (Matthew Arnold used the terms "culture" and "criticism" more or less synonymously.) My fascination with critics and criticism can be seen as wholly appropriate to the time. After all, 1953 was the year Randall Jarrell, himself a marvelous critic, published *Poetry and the Age* containing his famous satirical essay, "The Age of Criticism," which I read when it appeared in the *Kenyon Review* in 1952. Yet the Amherst English department gave us no encouragement to read critics, almost never assigning secondary material about literature and usually speaking as if they had arrived at their critical insights independently. My obsession with critics was fueled rather by a precocious classmate, William Youngren, who more or less on his own had been reading Pound's pronouncements about the state of literature, as well as I. A. Richards's *Principles of Literary Criticism* and *Practical Criticism*. The latter book, with its responses from Richards's university pupils to various unsigned, undated poems he gave them to read and comment on, presumably demonstrated that these students had great difficulty in distinguishing a good poem from a bad one. An ability to discriminate was exactly what I wanted to possess, and not just with regard to poems. Criticism would help me possess that ability, especially if I found the right critics to read—such was my thinking.

Youngren referred me to Stanley Edgar Hyman's recent book *The Armed Vision*, which contained chapters on various modern critics and their approaches. Hyman had provocatively arranged the chapters by ascending order of virtue, beginning with critics he assessed negatively (Edmund Wilson, Yvor Winters, and, surprisingly, T. S. Eliot) and concluding with four who won his special seal of approval: Richards, William Empson, R. P. Blackmur, and Kenneth Burke. I barely had time to dip into any of these but promised to remedy that after graduation. Meanwhile it was exciting to read a critic discriminating among the critics who would help me discriminate among works of art. Never mind that I had experienced few of those works; the *idea* of criticism provided a forcible motive for literary endeavor, promising to help me tell the good from the bad (as if all poems were either "good" or "bad"). And then there were those authoritative little magazines, in their heyday, appearing quarterly with the latest bulletins. The big four as I perceived them—*Partisan, Hudson, Sewanee,* and *Kenyon* reviews—seemed magical in their combined publication of original work and (even more attractive to my criticism-struck sensibility) of the back pages with their omnibus review chronicles and other reports on new books.

But if I expected from both philosophy and English something like

Arnold's "culture" or "criticism," I also realized increasingly that there was a sharp incompatibility between the way teachers in those disciplines went about their intellectual business. Sterling Lamprecht's lectures on the great philosophers were models of coherence and development over the course of a fifty-minute class, and although I lacked the sense of mastery when I tried to read Aristotle or Kant or Santayana, my lecture notes on Lamprecht were full, seemingly comprehensible. There was Spinoza, or Locke, set down in lengthy, careful sentences spun out over the course of the three or four lectures he gave on each. Lamprecht was an empiricist, a "naturalist," as he and the group of philosophers associated with Columbia loosely referred to themselves—an admirer of Aristotle and more recently of Frederick J. E. Woodbridge. He was as well a man of reasoned calmness who accepted the universe without God and still found that it was good. His confidence in order, in the coherence of things, in the ability of language truly and usefully to refer to the world's body, was manifest and reassuring. He was approaching retirement with the same graceful acceptance of the inevitable that seemed to characterize him generally. But what was a twenty-year-old like myself attempting to do with this example of studied, some would say stodgy, composure? I didn't question myself too carefully on that point.

By contrast, the dominant presence in the English department, Theodore Baird, the director of freshman composition who also taught an influential course on Shakespeare, was crackling and anarchic, a wicked wit with a loudly intimidating, teacherly manner. Baird was full of mischief and mockery, juxtaposing with Shakespeare various contemporary items he had encountered in the daily newspaper or heard about on the radio. Never was an atmosphere less "academic" than in his classes. The organization of his Shakespeare course was simple, in a sense conservative, consisting of nothing more than a careful examination of the language of four plays—first semester, *Romeo and Juliet* and *Hamlet*; second semester, *Antony and Cleopatra* and *The Winter's Tale*. These were studied not in order to discover their imaginative design (in Brower's words) but through a basically philological approach that kept moving excitingly into the historical, the human. So a reference in *Romeo* to charnel houses would bring on talk about Elizabethan attitudes toward death, then further talk about modern funerary customs. If the ghost of Hamlet's

father were in question, Baird might move from talking about Elizabethan notions of death, spirits who came back for a visit, to contemporary ways of dealing with the departed—Hallmark Cards to send
with the words that we couldn't find to express our sadness. It was a
spirited, sometimes riotous classroom; at other moments Baird was
muted and sober, as he steered us through various difficulties and odd-
ities in Shakespeare's language. But it was always language that was at
issue. Why was the ending of *Romeo and Juliet*, where Friar Laurence
tediously tells us at length what has just happened, so boring? Answer:
"Shakespeare didn't know how to end a play." What an outrageous and
yet wholly salutary thing to say! Why didn't Hamlet kill Claudius
sooner rather than later? Answer: Shakespeare deferred the murder,
since he had various verbal things he wanted Hamlet to do, such as
strike off a number of soliloquies. The move was away from explain-
ing a play through the analysis of character and always toward the
writer as controlling hand. To make students pay attention to that
hand, to the words it disposed in lines of blank verse rather than to the
supposed insides of characters' heads (as if they were real people, just
like you and me), seemed to be Baird's pedagogical aim. But it
expressed itself in a dramatically unsettling manner indistinguishable
from radical playfulness, a playfulness quite alien to the cooler
inquiries of philosophy, as represented by Sterling P. Lamprecht.

So I pursued a degree in philosophy at Amherst while looking long-
ingly over my shoulder at people who were writing about Milton or
Joseph Conrad. Of course the English department itself was less
monolithic than I make it sound. Although Baird and Brower got
along well as colleagues, the assumptions and style of the two staff
courses they directed importantly diverged. Baird's emphasis was pre-
ponderantly on the discontinuities, the gaps, between mind and
world, language and "things"; Brower's emphasis, through the practiced technique of close reading and describing, was on the connections between reader and text that could be made through articulate
discourse. By contrast to them both, Cesar Barber was a myth-and-
symbol critic, deeply interested in psychoanalysis and how it could
help us in reading literature. And Armour Craig had evolved a complicated, sometimes obscure, interpretive vocabulary for talking
about what went on in nineteenth-century English novels, or in the
poetry of Donne and Milton. Unlike Sterling Lamprecht, neither

Brower nor Barber was easy to take notes on; but they were easier to take notes on than Baird or Craig, who seemed programmatically committed to keeping things off-balance and confusing.

As spring of our senior year arrived, the thought of leaving Amherst —"An Earthly Paradise," Reuben Brower called it in his own farewell speech to the class and to the college (he had accepted an offer from Harvard)—and my decision to become a teacher combined in a rush of nostalgia and dedication. I managed to drench the whole business in sentiment, idealizing, with few or no moments of ironic qualification, both my recent past and the future as I dreamed it. Trying to make sense of Santayana's *Scepticism and Animal Faith*, while reading in the philosophy seminar room of the library from which the college chapel could be distinctly and handsomely glimpsed, was an exercise in exhilaratingly divided attention. In a desperate attempt to prolong my residence in paradise, unwilling to face another summer in Johnson City, New York, I approached the dean and suggested that for a reasonable sum I might be permitted to rent a room for the summer in one of the college dorms. This was not done unless very good and necessary reasons presented themselves in justification, such as employment by the college. I had no such employment, and when the dean asked me my reasons for wanting to stay in town I replied that I hoped to make use of the library. He was unimpressed: "Mr. Pritchard, Amherst [pronounced Am-ust] is not a summer resort." Our conversation was concluded almost before it had begun. Amherst was indeed not a summer resort, but a place I had grown intensely, even perilously, attached to. Such, such were the joys, now about to be concluded—the echoing green (its sport no more seen) fast becoming a darkening one.

III
At the Universities

Sometime during the winter or spring of my senior year, when I had decided on graduate study in philosophy, I went to see John Moore, my humanities teacher from three years previous to ask him to tell me what graduate school was like. He provided a surprisingly reassuring account of a place (he had been at Harvard) where students had the time to read more fully, to explore more deeply subjects in which they had begun to be interested. There were others of like minds, of shared interests, and it was possible to lead the intellectual life in its most satisfactory form. As for academic demands, Moore said they were not inordinate, not a turning up of the heat from undergraduate requirements. It was, in short, something I should look forward to — it might even be possible to have a good time in graduate school. I was extremely reassured by what Moore said, even if I couldn't quite believe it. At any rate, I made no effort during the following summer to solidify or extend my abilities as a student of philosophy; indeed, the only philosophy I seem to have read then, on the evidence of my notebook, was A. J. Ayer's *Language, Truth, and Logic,* written in just enough of a popularizing mode for me to be able to follow it and feel I had been introduced to logical positivism.

Other than Ayer's the books I read were literary classics I had not gotten around to in college: Boswell's *Life of Johnson,* Gibbon's *Autobiography,* Coleridge's *Biographia Literaria;* at an easier level, novels and stories by F. Scott Fitzgerald, Evelyn Waugh (*A Handful of Dust*), and Nathanael West (*Miss Lonelyhearts*). I managed to get a job playing piano in a small dance-jazz band at a hotel in Lake Geneva, Wisconsin, forty-five minutes north of Chicago. There were five of us in the combo—two of them good friends of mine—and we holed up in fairly primitive dormitory-like accommodations, made music six nights a week at the hotel, and had the days free to spend as we wished. For me that meant a minimum of beach visiting and a maximum of reading, even in the steamy heat of our garret-like abode. I had brought along my first selection from the Reader's Subscription Book Club, the five-volume Viking Portable Library *Poets of the English Language*, edited by W. H. Auden and Norman Holmes Pearson. My idea was to read through it while memorizing various exhibits that struck me as especially beautiful. I wanted to make myself into a treasure house of lyric at its best, a walking Palgrave (whom I had not heard of), and this I managed to do, at least to the extent of putting a few poems where they have never been dislodged—such as Thomas Carew's "The Spring":

> Now that the winter's gone, the earth hath lost
> Her snow-white robes; and now no more the frost
> Candies the grasse, or casts an ycie creame
> Upon the silver lake or chrystall streame:
> But the warme sunne thawes the benummed earth,
> And makes it tender; gives a second birth
> To the dead swallow; wakes in hollow tree
> The drowsie cuckow and the humble-bee.

Carew goes on to describe the spring in which all nature smiles, the only creature out of harmony with things being his lady ("onely my love doth lowre"), who will not submit to his entreaties. The moment when things move from sweet to sour is also a moment of fine stylistic power, heard especially through the enjambment that reading aloud (and I was reading aloud) could bring out:

> Now all things smile; onely my Love doth lowre;
> Nor hath the scalding noon-day sunne the power
> To melt that marble yce, which still doth hold
> Her heart congeal'd, and makes her pittie cold.

The feeling was common enough, Carew's poem just one more entry in the long list of complaints sung by the poet about his mistress's coldness. But what gripped me in the poem was something that had nothing to do with a "point" being made, but rather with what, appropriating some words from Wordsworth's *Prelude*, might be called a "pure organic pleasure in the lines." The pleasure in listening to, in enacting through reading aloud, in recalling from the memory on different occasions, a sequence like "Nor hath the scalding noon-day sunne the power / To melt that marble yce"—this seemed to be the sort of experience I wanted more of. Just how the study of philosophy would further such satisfactions was an uneasy question I preferred not to face directly. By the end of July, a truce was signed with North Korea; I had my deferment for the academic year and tried to think of studying philosophy as something that couldn't hurt and, in fact, would surely do me some intellectual good. But it felt increasingly like a diversion from what I wanted to do most in life.

I was headed for Columbia University because of affiliations between its philosophy department and Amherst's. Three of Amherst's four philosophy teachers had taken their degrees at Columbia, and a shared emphasis on the history of philosophy, along with reverence for naturalist-humanist luminaries like John Dewey and F. J. E. Woodbridge, made for friendly relations between the departments and a readiness on Columbia's part to accept Amherst applicants. My first semester at the university I signed on for two courses with John Herman Randall (his son, Francis, had graduated from Amherst the year before me), the famous and fearsome historian of philosophy. I also elected, among others, a course in the philosophy of art given by Irwin Edman, whom I had met when he visited Sterling Lamprecht the previous spring. Columbia seemed like something of a family affair.

But what I was signing onto more significantly was New York City and its premier university. I took a room in a decaying building on Broadway and 115th Street. What had once been a large apartment was broken up into spaces not much more than cubicles, with a kitchen used in common by the five or six or us who lived in proximity to one another. My room was so narrow that I could sit in a chair against the wall and stretch out my legs to touch the wall opposite. Large obscene pigeons made a racket outside on the window ledge. Then there was the city itself. To move from the earthly paradise we half-truly believed was Amherst to the distinctly nonparadisal world of Morningside Heights and New York's Upper West Side, and from the intimate classroom to the prevailing lecture-room style of Columbia graduate instruction, was, to my small-town and small-college sensibility, shocking in the extreme. There was also the ethnic difference between the two places. Amherst's philosophy department had recently hired one of the very few Jews on its entire faculty (a man from Columbia), while the English department was WASP to the core; Columbia's philosophy department, with the notable exception of John Herman Randall, was in the main Jewish. In some ways this difference wasn't important — certainly I thought little about it, nor did I encounter situations in which I was made aware of incompatibilities of behavior between Amherst and Columbia professors that had to do with class or religious or ethnic background. But a wider world was impinging on me, often in a way that felt less than benign, as on registration day in Columbia's gym with lines of students the likes of which little Amherst never saw.

Columbia's philosophy department was noticeably laissez-faire in its attitude toward graduate students. A certain number of courses needed to be completed in the regular manner, for academic credit and a grade; but a smaller number could "count" on your record, without work handed in or a final grade. This opened up the possibility, which I had never before entertained, that if a course proved too difficult I might neglect to do the work, yet still have it count for nonacademic credit. This I began to do when things came to a head in November and Randall handed out a midterm examination in the history of ancient philosophy. It was a "take-home" exam, something I had never encountered. At Amherst an examination was written and handed in at a specific place, during a two-hour time period.

Randall's examination consisted of six questions, all of which we were expected to answer: the first was about the pre-Socratics; the other five were divided between Plato and Aristotle. Two examples may suggest what I found myself up against and why it defeated me:

> 1. In what respects does the *Republic* exhibit Plato's "artistic attitude" toward human life and experience? How is this same attitude reflected in the *Protagoras,* the *Phaedrus,* the *Meno,* and in the *Philebus,* the *Gorgias,* and the *Timaeus?*

> 2. What is the "theory of Ideas" often attributed to Plato that is examined and rejected in the *Parmenides?* According to Parmenides what difficulties must be considered, what steps avoided, if an adequate understanding of the function is to be

forthcoming? In what manner does the *Cratylus* go
on to suggest and develop a functional conception
of "Idea"? How is this "functionalism" put forth in
the *Republic* and further developed in Aristotle's
De Anima and *De Partibus Animalium*?

These and the other four questions were equally and utterly terrifying
in their assumption that, after six weeks of what was presumed to be
extensive reading in primary and secondary sources, we could write
with authority and in detail about the works of these greats. Just how
many pages altogether were we expected to produce on the exam?
Rumors flew, some of which mentioned a student who had taken the
course the previous year and written sixty pages of commentary. The
length seemed on the one hand reasonable, since each of the six questions could easily justify ten pages of response; on the other hand, such
length was impossible to manage, what with my other four courses
and Thanksgiving vacation coming up in two weeks. I made a start on
one of the questions, wrote a couple of pages, and then abandoned the
examination, consigning Philosophy 161 to the category of H credit.
Malcolm Brown—an Amherst classmate who was also a graduate student in philosophy—and I headed out for a beer and an assessment of
the situation.

This was a watershed moment in my academic life, since for the
first time I had backed away from a test, and not in some discipline
where I lacked competence, but in a subject and even a *kind* of philosophy—historical rather than logical analysis—I had chosen to pursue
and was being partially subsidized for by a fellowship from Amherst.
Looking back at this midterm exam forty years later, it still seems to
me crushing to the spirit. Of course Randall—or whatever assistant
read these papers—would have entertained less than the highest
expectations about how graduate students were likely to perform.
Probably the point was for us to give it a try by demonstrating some
evidence that we had read around a bit in Aristotle and Plato; to make
a stab at dealing with these questions by giving back, at least in part,
what Randall had doled out to us in his very impressive lectures of the
past weeks. But I was unable to see it that way, nor could I feel anything but its all-or-nothing aspect; and since I didn't have a prayer of
producing all, I chose to produce nothing.

Instead of hunkering down to the typewriter and knocking out paragraphs of commentary on Plato's theory of Ideas, I proceeded to frequent, promiscuously, the classrooms of a number of Columbia's more famous lecturers. Jacques Barzun, a university contemporary of Randall's, has described (in *Teacher in America*) the lecture room as "the place where drama becomes theater":

> This usually means a fluent speaker, no notes, and no shyness about "effects." In some teachers a large class filling a sloped-up amphitheater brings out a wonderful power of emphasis, timing, and organization. The speaker projects himself and the subject. The "effects" are not laid on, they are the meaningful stress which constitutes, most literally, the truth of the matter. This meaning—as against fact—is the one thing to be indelibly stamped on the mind, and it is this that the printed book cannot give.

This is acutely said, and it characterizes Barzun's own lecturing. Impeccably dressed, and with a white pocket handkerchief on display, he spoke in elegant, sometimes supercilious, ironies as he detailed extravagances from the French Revolution, often looking out the window while the class looked at him. By contrast, Marjorie Hope Nicholson ("the best man in the English department," was Irwin Edman's feline joke) spoke with little inflection, no irony, and no notes as she impressively laid out Donne's relationship to the "new philosophy" of Copernicus and Galileo. Then there was Randall himself, a stocky bulldog of a man usually with the remains of a cigar clamped between his teeth and a fierce cough punctuating his delivery. His lecture-room behavior was quite different from and much more idiosyncratic than the midterm exam he gave us; aggressively personal, it was a no-punches-pulled account of his thoughts and feelings about each philosopher and philosophic movement. Plato and Aristotle were both heroes: the first for the poetic and dramatic creations of his dialogues, the second for being *maestro de color che sanno*. My notes on Randall, as he began the unit on Aristotle, are as follows:

> Now if I were to say that Aristotle is the only true philosophy—along with certain Aristotelians like Spinoza and John Dewey—but I won't say that—YET.

> What we seem to want in philosophy is a gospel, and
> all Aristotle tells us is the way the world is. Aristotle
> is the philosophy of the morning after, after the great
> wild spree of modern philosophy. The first of the great
> knowers.

Randall (who sometimes looked as if he had firsthand acquaintance with a few mornings after) loved to digress, as do great lecturers, and in a parenthesis would take off after Reinhold Niebuhr and the neo-Orthodoxists "across the street" (at Union Theological Seminary), or Dwight D. Eisenhower ("the best president since Ulysses S. Grant"), recent head of Columbia whose departure was unlamented by most faculty members.

Testimony to the strongly personal nature of Randall's engagements with the philosophers was the constant reference, in my notes, to "Jack believes," or "Jack won't accept that," or "Jack says, on the contrary." To reduce this scary figure, author of a famous history (*The Making of the Modern Mind*), to "Jack" was a way of dealing with him. Randall's problems came, not on the lecturer's podium, but when he had to meet students in a smaller group. In his account of lecturing, Barzun describes how a good lecture course should break up for its third or fourth hour into smaller section meetings where "the lecturer should himself be available for questioning by his students"; he must "correct without wounding, contradict without discouraging, coax along without coddling." Randall professed to believe in the importance of our biweekly section meeting, in which he pledged himself ready to answer our questions; but in fact these meetings were a fiasco, since he had no notion of how to engage us in conversation. In one such meeting a brash graduate student suggested that Aristotle was confused in his employment of the term *ousia* (substance). "No," replied Randall, "*you* may be confused, but Aristotle is perfectly clear." The student tried to recoup, suggesting in slightly different terms that Aristotle was perhaps inconsistent in respect to this or that aspect of the substance problem. No, was Randall's reiterated answer. "Aristotle is perfectly consistent — *you* may be confused." End of the "conversation."

The only course I managed to complete for regular academic credit that semester was one taught by the popular lecturer and celebrated wit — so he seemed to regard himself — Irwin Edman. Edman was

gentle, roguish, and lisping, full of anecdotes about the Greats—
Santayana, Dewey, Woodbridge—and the author of a number of popularizing reflections on life and letters that brought him mild fame. (He
would have been good on the radio quiz show *Information Please,* and
indeed probably appeared there.) But his credentials as an aesthetician
were slender since they consisted mainly of a short popular account of
the subject, *Arts and the Man* (1939). This book dealt rather superficially with subjects like "Art and Civilization" and "Art and Experience"; its way with particular examples of art did not inspire
confidence, as in the following paragraph from the chapter "World,
Word, and Poet":

> The poet is indeed chiefly engaged in awakening the
> torpid imagination by the liquid loveliness of sounds,
> by the march of his verse, but not least by the evoca-
> tive words he uses. . . . He will fill his verse with the
> concrete and specific sensuous detail; he will enumer-
> ate the colors, smells, tastes, and touches of that
> world which has become to the hurried and practical
> adult a routine.

There follows, by way of illustration, a poem of Rupert Brooke's, "The
Great Lover," "in which the effect is simply that of an exquisite com-
memorative reminder of those tense and tingling moments of sensa-
tion which in health and in youth we enjoy." Rupert Brooke! We never
talked about him at Amherst, and Malcolm Brown and I would read
aloud and chortle at the "liquid loveliness of sounds" Edman found in
Brooke's lines:

> The benison of hot water; furs to touch;
> The good smell of old clothes; and other such—
> The comfortable smell of friendly fingers,
> Hair's fragrance, and the musty reek that lingers
> About dead leaves and last year's ferns.

We especially loved those friendly fingers and their comfortable smell.
    Columbia's proven strength as a college with its prescribed curricu-
lum—different from Amherst's, but rigorous in the amount of reading
required in the humanities and social sciences—may well have made
it less attentive to and inventive about educating its graduate students. There were rumors about various professors who gave highly

successful undergraduate courses but refused to teach in the graduate school, or, as was said of Lionel Trilling, did it perfunctorily. So although I quickly failed as a graduate student in philosophy, perhaps the institution also failed me. At any rate, by the end of first term I pretty much knew it was all over, with my one completed course— and in the softest of philosophical atmospheres—an embarrassment. More positively, two events, their convergence mainly temporal, helped redirect my intellectual desires. The first was an exposure to the writings of Kenneth Burke, especially to Burke's *Grammar of Motives* and its pages devoted to reading the history of philosophy in (Burke's word) "dramatistic" terms; the second was exposure to Lionel Trilling and his brand of moral criticism. Both these men offered powerful alternatives to the Columbia philosophers.

I had previously encountered Kenneth Burke's name in *The Armed Vision*, Stanley Edgar Hyman's survey of modern critics, and from Armour Craig at Amherst I learned that Burke's earlier *Permanence and Change* (then out of print) was full of helpful tips about symbolic uses of language. "All Living Things Are Critics" was a subheading of "Orientation," the first chapter of *Permanence and Change*, and it began in the appealing, somewhat mischievous style that was his trademark:

> We may begin by noting the fact that all living organ-
> isms interpret many of the signs about them. A trout,
> having snatched at a hook but having had the good
> luck to escape with a rip in his jaw, may even show by
> his wiliness thereafter that he can revise his critical
> appraisals. His experience has led him to form a new
> judgment, which we should verbalize as a nicer dis-
> crimination between food and bait.

I found this breezy, confident way of proceeding irresistible, read most of *Permanence and Change* and went on to dip into Burke's other books from the 1930s such as *Counter-Statement* and *Attitudes toward History*. I could see connections—admittedly not carefully traced out—between Burke's intensely language-orientated analysis and the sorts of treatments of situation we had practiced in English 1 as freshmen. And when, in his *Grammar of Motives*, which I never read seriously until my year at Columbia, Burke turned his attention to the philosophers, his analysis of their language felt different, more radical in its bearings, than traditional capsulizations from some history of philosophy of what the philosophers *meant* by that language. For example, in his section on Thomas Hobbes, whom Burke treated as an example of materialism in philosophy, he quotes from the opening chapter of *Leviathan* where Hobbes calls life "but a motion of limbs" and compares man's heart and nerves to the springs and wheels of a watch. Burke comments:

> Ironically, though Hobbes warns heatedly against the deceptions of metaphor, he is here in effect announcing that his book is to be organized about the metaphor of the machine, in taking it as the *Ausgangspunkt* of his vocabulary. Next he expands his figure into a proportion: as man is a machine, so the State is a gigantic man.

Burke continues in this fashion, comparing a passage from *Leviathan* to Menenius's parable of the body in *Coriolanus*. The emerging sense was of Hobbes as a writer, as much a maker of metaphor, even though a philosopher, as the poet Shakespeare.

This seems elementary, yet didn't feel at all so at the time. If we now are willing at least to entertain the notion of philosophy as "a kind of writing"—in Richard Rorty's language about Derrida—it was not a common way to talk in 1953, certainly among the limited number of philosophers with whom I was acquainted. In treating different philosophical systems as competing terminologies, as attempts by the individual writer to move things around linguistically in ways that would "solve" the problems the philosopher had posed himself, Burke had recourse to an analytic playfulness not unlike the sort employed by an inventive reader of poems. And in fact an appendix to *A Grammar of Motives* contained chapters on Keats's Grecian Urn ode and on the poetry of Marianne Moore. So with the enthusiastic simplification that a more practiced observer of the scene might have complicated, I heroicized Burke as someone who could "do" philosophy but in an unacademic and, it seemed, unrecognized way (nobody in the Columbia philosophy department ever mentioned him) I saw as confirming the rightness of things learned from Amherst English. Not the least of his attractions were temperamental and stylistic, seen in the passage about the trout quoted earlier. As Hyman pointed out, one of the most ingratiating features of

Burke's style (Burke spoke of "style as ingratiation") was its constant reliance on jokes, puns, and a wry humor to make his "serious" points. It was a style to which I aspired, even though I was light-years away from achieving it.

As the second term of my Columbia year moved along, I spent more time reading and thinking about Burke than on my courses. Class notes taken on philosophy lectures became increasingly sparse; instead, I spent class time writing out various poems I had memorized: Marvell's "To His Coy Mistress," Donne's "Good Friday, 1613, Riding Westward," Wordsworth's "She Dwelt among the Untrodden Ways," and the opening lines of Tennyson's "Tithonus." On one page, after a brief note of what Marcus Aurelius said about some ethical matter, there is Yeats's "The Second Coming"; in the margins of another page there are lists of novels by James, Faulkner, E. M. Forster—also lists of critics and an attempt to rank the top ten English poets. How large a part Lionel Trilling played in this increasingly souped-up romance with literature, it would be hard to overestimate. In the fall of 1953 the first titles in the Anchor paperback series appeared, and Trilling's *Liberal Imagination* (along with D. H. Lawrence's *Studies in Classic American Literature* and Edmund Wilson's *To the Finland Station*) was among the earliest. People told me I should attend Trilling's undergraduate class and since I was shopping around the English department I eventually showed up, along with Malcolm Brown, at his course in Hamilton Hall. I'm not even sure we were polite enough to ask permission to join the small classroom where he held forth to what must have been a select group of thirty or so undergraduates. (It certainly contained some talented young men, among them the novelist Sam Astrachan, English professors-to-be Alvin Kibel and Harold Skulsky, and others who have, I am sure, made their way in academic and literary circles.)

We were lucky to find a couple of empty chairs that we set up on the side of the classroom, feeling conspicuous, though neither Trilling nor the Columbia undergraduates paid us any heed. For the first semester the subject was fiction: novels by Jane Austen, Dickens, and D. H. Lawrence; second term it was poetry: Wordsworth, Keats, Yeats. Classes usually followed the same format with Trilling pacing about the desk up front, his eyes underlined by enormous pouches, his coloring on the jaundiced side. Sometimes he smoked a cigarette, intensely, using a holder. Most typically he, who was to write that he thought of literature as concerned with "great elaborate fights about moral issues," would direct the class to some scene or moment in the novel under consideration, then pose a question about it. In *Persuasion*, for example, Trilling detected in Austen's tone toward some of her minor characters, an animus more powerful, a sarcasm more savage, than in her previous work. When she mocked the "large fat sighings" of Mrs. Musgrove was this not cruelty? To what extent did they, the class, think that purely aesthetic motives were sufficient to judge human behavior? What did they say in response to Lawrence's onslaughts on, not merely his characters, but his readers as well? Lawrence was the sort of writer who delighted in throwing a stone through our windows; did we say in response, merely, what a pleasant noise the glass made as it shattered? With Keats, whose letters as well as poems were assigned, Trilling spoke about the poet's "geniality" toward himself, adducing the letter in which Keats tells his correspondent how, when he is feeling seedy and depressed, he spruces himself up, knots his shoelaces, then sits down to the task of poetic composition with new vigor. Could the class imagine there being something "moral" about sporting a clean pocket handkerchief?

Trilling's interest in literature was finally not in the words on the page but in what they might tell us about life—about, as he called it, the moral imagination. He used the word "moral" a lot, and I began to see it as an indication of the seriousness of his literary stakes. Certainly his strong response to Wordsworth's poetry was to something other than or beyond its brilliance of metaphor or its tonal varieties. In discussing "Tintern Abbey" Trilling paused over Wordsworth's assurance to his sister ("Knowing that Nature never did betray / The heart that loved her") and remarked to the class challengingly, "It betrayed Dorothy Wordsworth, didn't it?" as he proceeded to describe the pitiable physical condition of her later years. Trilling seemed fascinated by Wordsworth's later attempt at moral realism; by his rejection of earlier, now judged to be illusory, assumptions about nature. In the "Elegiac Stanzas Suggested by a Picture of Peele Castle," the poet imagines how, if he had been a painter in his younger years, he would have given the scene an ideal life, adding "the gleam / The light that never was, on sea or land, / The consecration, and the Poet's dream." Now, his own brother dead at sea, he understands the violent, inhuman power Nature subjects human beings to:

Such, in the fond illusion of my heart
Such Picture would I at that time have made:
And seen the soul of truth in every part,
A steadfast peace that might not be betrayed.

So once it would have been,—'tis so no more;
I have submitted to a new control:
A power is gone, which nothing can restore;
A deep distress hath humanised my Soul.

The acceptance of natural betrayal—as if Nature could betray the heart that loved her—has led to a new affirmation. But might this one be equally illusory? The point was that a Trilling classroom discussion focused on issues and ideas, not at all on the stiff quatrains and uncomplicated syntax in which they were presented. It was as if the value or interest of "Elegiac Stanzas" had nothing to do with the way it was written and everything to do with its moral life.

Columbia undergraduates responded vigorously to Trilling's provocative, often deliberately provoking, questions. Unlike at Amherst, where classroom behavior was cooler, more laid back in its cautious and sometimes complacent style, in the Columbia undergraduate classroom—at least Trilling's—people argued, talked too much, went too far in some of the things they said. It was a lippy place, more urban than urbane, and these undergraduates sometimes treated their professor irreverently. One day, before Trilling had arrived, two class members sarcastically anticipated the line he would take about the day's text; I was surprised that they should treat this august figure with anything but the deepest respect. Yet class discussion and argument were surely the better for their relative lack of self-consciousness and—on the students' part—deference (although Trilling was the essence of politeness). It was wonderful to observe a situation in which both parties to the dialogue seemed to listen to each other. On one occasion a student—whatever the subject was I can't remember—delivered a strong personal statement that attempted to say just what he believed about the issue at question. Trilling listened hard, did not immediately respond, then said in a measured way that he would "think about" what Mr. X had said. That was all, but I had not quite heard its like before. Trilling's writing confirmed the moral seriousness with which he took his classroom. "Of This Time, Of That Place," a story he published a decade previously, is about Frederick Tertan, a psychotic student whose professor (a stand-in for Trilling) must decide what to do with him. Tertan's madness is established in part by setting him in relation to other students in the class, at least one of whom, a very model of conventional business-oriented white-shoe enterprise, the professor later decides is—in his own way—also mad. But the play of voices as Ibsen's *Ghosts* is under discussion in one of the story's scenes constitutes one of the few plausible classrooms in literature, and it could have been written only by someone who had spent years of listening—to himself as well as to his students.

In retrospect, at least, there was a connection between my experience of Trilling, in class and in *The Liberal Imagination*, and my reading of Burke, especially *A Grammar of Motives*. For Burke, literature was, like other uses of words, symbolic action; for Trilling, literature was the most powerful and serious way of presenting moral issues—it made statements about life with which we had to grapple seriously. Both critical approaches distinguished themselves from more purely aesthetic ways of taking poems and novels—neither Burke nor Trilling cared about the literary text as a thing in itself—and both combined to make impossible, if my performance had not already done so, my career as a philosopher. It was also a question of glamour, if it must be confessed, since both Trilling and Burke in their ways were glamorous figures, equipped with swagger, panache, and more vibrant ways of being an intellectual than anyone in the Columbia philosophy department demonstrated. By that spring I had ruled out another year in the study of philosophy, at Columbia or anyplace else. But it never occurred to me to approach Trilling and ask him about possibilities for graduate study in English with him, since he seemed to me unique, nothing like the other teachers of English I had heard at Columbia. Furthermore, I was in correspondence with William Youngren, who was studying English at Harvard. Youngren had provided me with reports on what Brower was doing there and told me about other members of the Amherst group engaged in graduate work in English. Harvard was a possibility I filed away in my imagination as I headed home to Binghamton via the Erie–Lackawanna Railroad on a mild evening in the middle of May, engrossed in my Modern Library edition of Lawrence's *The Rainbow*, feeling like a failure.

I was not the first stalled and uncertain young man who looked—or tried to look—at military service as a temporary solution to his uncertainty. Saul Bellow's protagonist at the end of *Dangling Man* put it this way: "Hurray for regular hours! And for the supervision of the spirit! Long live regimentation!" But as I resumed life, rather embarrassedly, at my parents' house, spending as much time as I could politely manage in an upstairs room (the den) reading literature, the practical step of enlisting—or perhaps getting drafted, now that I had no academic status—began to lose whatever attraction it had briefly held. More than once I must have talked about studying English at Harvard, though never suggesting that I wanted, or deserved, to proceed there immediately. But my father, himself a graduate of Harvard Law School and with a sentimental affection for Cambridge—even though he'd been unhappy there, to the extent of suffering something like a nervous collapse on the occasion of his law school final exams—eventually took a hand in things by suggesting that I might proceed to Harvard and forgo this unpleasant affair with the U.S. Army. If so, he would stake me to another year at least. It was an irresistible offer, and I set to work to see what could be done.

By then it was the middle of June, and applying to graduate school for the coming fall term could only have been undertaken (and successfully) in a simpler age than the present one. The person who was instrumental to my being admitted was Reuben Brower; he had just completed his first year teaching at Harvard and had now been installed as master of Adams House, along with Eliot House the most literary of Harvard's undergraduate residences. Brower's support of my application had less to do with any firsthand experience of my critical performance (I had never taken a course with him) than with his misguided respect for me as a student of philosophy and as accompanist for a production at Amherst of Gilbert and Sullivan's *Trial by Jury* he seemed to have been highly amused by. At any rate, his letter, along with ones from Theodore Baird and Armour Craig (both of them, like Brower, Harvard English Ph.D.s), did the trick. After what seemed like an interminable two months of waiting, while the McCarthy hearings provided daily sustenance and I sweated it out through an upstate New York summer in the den, Harvard admitted me as a first-year candidate with intentions, so I said on my application, to specialize in the nineteenth-century English novel.

It's fair to say that I entered Columbia philosophy mainly unprepared for what I found there; by contrast, Harvard, though certainly not a known quantity, was relatively well scouted-out thanks to

accounts received from the lips and pens of Amherst graduates studying English there. Youngren, who had earlier turned me on to criticism
and was now as vehemently anti-Pound as he had earlier been a disci-
ple, made sure I would have no illusions about encountering lively
classroom teaching from members of Harvard's English department.
Nor should I expect the kind of New Critical sophistication that "we"
felt at least partly in possession of. With the exception of Brower—
who although learned and "scholarly" enough, was essentially a
critic—and Albert Guerard, Harvard's youngest tenured professor in
English and a novelist-critic of "advanced" psychological bent, Harvard English was solidly traditional in its commitment. Although the
philological tradition, vigorously represented by the Anglo-Saxon
scholar F. P. McGoun and the Chaucerian B. J. Whiting, was a much
reduced version of its former self, the overwhelming majority of the
department consisted of highly productive, respected scholars and his-
torians of English literature. There was Hyder Rollins, whose editions
of Tudor miscellanies, Shakespeare's sonnets, and Keats's letters were
highly regarded; his friend George Sherburn, the biographer of Pope,
had recently retired, but Douglas Bush continued to turn out a series
of big books on mythology in the Renaissance and Romantic traditions, and on seventeenth-century English literature (the Oxford history of that period). Herschel Baker's histories of ideas in the
seventeenth century were also well known; he was collaborating with
Rollins in a massive anthology of English Renaissance literature and
was also chairman of the department. Alfred Harbage, a dullish but
sound professor of Jacobean drama, knew everything about theater history. Perhaps the department's brightest light was Harry Levin,
acknowledged by all to be learned and brilliant in French as well as
English literature, and engaged in building up an impressive critical
oeuvre. While still in his twenties he had published a pioneering book
on Joyce, then followed it with a pamphlet on Stendhal (part of a
longer work in progress on French realism) and a study of Christopher
Marlowe. Levin lectured on Shakespeare, or on Proust, Joyce, and
Mann, to throngs of students. Walter Jackson Bate covered the later
eighteenth century, had just finished his book on Samuel Johnson (*The
Achievement of Samuel Johnson*), and had edited an anthology of the
major critics. On the American literature side of things Harvard
offered Perry Miller, with his daunting surveys of the New England
mind and his unmatched knowledge of Puritan religious history;

Howard Mumford Jones, who specialized in nineteenth-century American writing in its social aspect; and the courtly Kenneth B. Murdock, who had published relatively little but was a link to F. O. Matthiessen with whom he edited Henry James's *Notebooks*.

Herschel Baker received me in his chairmanly office for the obligatory conversation each fledgling graduate student had with Authority. I had been told that he spoke in a Texas drawl and was fond of the phrase "dish of tea" (it had always been "cup" to me), but I listened in vain for the phrase, though the drawl was there all right. He expressed some puzzlement, even a shade of annoyance, at the way Amherst English professors — mainly Baird — behaved in their letters of recommendation. Something other than due respect for Harvard had been detected somewhere along the line, and he wanted me to know he was aware of it. I conducted myself, I thought, piously and humbly, very glad to have been admitted and signing on for a traditional four-pronged load of "period" courses: Chaucer, an early-eighteenth-century survey, Romantic writers, and Victorian poets. Baker warned me about the three language exams — one ancient, two moderns — I would have to pass and which could throw a monkey wrench in the works of graduate progress. He did not care how I prepared for these exams: I could take a course or study a handbook or (and this is what stuck in my ears) "meditate the thankless muse." It was the rather dandyish way those lines from Milton's "Lycidas" flicked off his tongue that both fascinated and unnerved me. At any rate I promised to do my best, and retired.

The Harvard department prided itself on its eclecticism, its lack of orthodoxy, of any single point of view or set of assumptions about what literary study should or must consist in. (In this respect it distinguished itself from Yale, where a strongly New Critical atmosphere reigned.) Harvard provided no advocated perspective from which subjects were to be viewed or papers written, and one was allowed to be as textual or as contextual as one pleased. Except for a couple of courses that asked for a bibliography as part of the term paper, I continued to go on writing the sort of thing — except longer — I had learned to write at Amherst: a "reading" of a novel or poem conducted pretty much within its own terms, with minimal glances, if any, at history or biography or scholarly apparatus. In general there was little "professional" emphasis, partly because many English department courses were designed to serve both undergraduate and graduate students. In retrospect the mixture of students was probably a good thing, since it made the classroom atmosphere less restricted—most of the students taking Chaucer or Victorian poetry had no intention of becoming professionals in the field. These courses had relatively little structure and consisted of assigned readings lectured on and sometimes discussed with the class but tested only at the conclusion of the course, with a long paper and a final examination. So there was little teacher–student interaction over the term, unlike at Amherst. Professors surely announced their office hours, but I never showed up at them that first term except for Douglas Bush, who suggested we come to his study in Widener Library in order to clear a subject for the final paper. If you had no subject, Bush would obligingly suggest one—"You might trace the theme of the river in Matthew Arnold's poetry," I heard him tell an unresourceful class member.

Harvard English then could be said to have been open-minded, undogmatic, pluralistic; other words for it would be undirected, pointless, and pedagogically empty—even anticritical, as I began to feel early on. Strong responses to works of art, especially of a negative sort, were discouraged, as if it were bad form to behave so passionately. Instead we were encouraged to consider the poem or the novel "in its own terms," which evidently meant that adverse value judgments had no place. Although I had been warned not to expect anything from Harvard like a training in criticism, I still felt the absence of a critical viewpoint in the courses I elected that first semester and beyond. B. J. Whiting entertained the Harvard and Radcliffe students by working through *Troilus and Criseyde*, making many fine jokes and droll formulations, while reading aloud famous gaffes committed by those previously enrolled in the course. Hyder Rollins turned his note cards and uttered pithy, old-fashioned remarks about the Romantics while chewing on something we thought might have been Sen-Sen, a breath freshener popular at the time. We learned from Rollins that Southey called Coleridge's *Rime of the Ancient Mariner* "a Dutch attempt at German sublimity," but we never considered that or any other poem in detail. The three short papers required by the course came back with grades of A– on each and the (recurrent) one-sentence comment that my attempt at interpretation had been "interesting." Rollins seemed more attentive to and troubled by my footnotes: "Odd arrangement," he noted, in response to my incompetent attempt to follow MLA style and line them up correctly. His course examinations regularly included a section in which we were asked to match items from two lists, something I had not been asked to do since seventh grade.

The only place where I was aware of a critical mind operating in the classroom was in Bush's Victorian poetry course in Tennyson, Browning, and Arnold. A notable scholar and historian, Bush was also an extremely kind and generous man. A low-key presence in class, he spoke in a nasal drone, scarcely raising his voice as he proceeded through a chronological survey of what seemed to him the most important poems by each writer. At the time Bush was jousting in public with the New Critics, Cleanth Brooks especially, by upholding the importance of history and biography with respect to understanding a writer, and warning against the dangers of excessive ingenuity in interpretive exegesis. On another front he was upholding Christian humanism against the secularists and deconstructors of that era. But in class Bush pretty much stayed with the poems themselves, occasionally read them or parts of them aloud, and even looked now and then as if he were genuinely moved by their language. Once when he was talking about *In Memoriam*, something in one of the sections reminded him of Eliot and he began — off the cuff, it certainly seemed — to quote lines from *Four Quartets*, a sequence from "Little Gidding," I believe. From this I concluded that Bush loved poetry, as he surely did, and I found that immensely heartening. (He was also one of the few English department members who regularly attended poetry readings by contemporary poets in Sanders Theater.)

Bush had opinions and couldn't help expressing them from time to time, even as he tried to be resolutely fair-minded and open to different poetic and critical styles. In my term paper on some Matthew Arnold poems I compared "The Buried Life" unfavorably to Eliot's "Portrait of a Lady," which alludes to Arnold's poem. In his minuscule handwritten comment at the end of the paper — all Harvard professors seemed to write their comments in pencil — Bush raised what he called a "particular hazardous question" by asking me if I thought that a century from now Eliot's poem would stand up as well as Arnold's: "It seems to me likely to be a minor period piece," he remarked about "Portrait of a Lady," while emphasizing that he was speaking about that one poem, not Eliot's poetry as a whole. This was refreshing, regardless of whether Bush was right (and I now think he was). I had begun that semester to read the criticism of F. R. Leavis and had come across his delighted quoting of a passage from Robert Graves's autobiography, *Goodbye to All That,* in which an Oxford official says to Graves, rather disapprovingly, "I understand, Mr. Graves, that the essays which you write for your English tutor are, shall I say, a trifle temperamental. It appears, indeed, that you prefer some authors to others." Such preferring, which I was desperately eager to practice and get better at, was alien to the overall spirit of Harvard English; so an exception to the rule—like Bush's preferring "The Buried Life" to "Portrait of a Lady" and saying so—felt all the more welcome.

But in the main, my courses that first semester were notable for an absence of what I had come to understand as teaching: the articulated effort to criticize, correct, refine, and qualify through argument and commentary, a student's responses to writers and writing. My professors—productive scholars and decent human beings—seemed without the ghost of an interest in making something called a *class* come to life. They were too busy "covering" the ground: English literature 1700–1740, with its major and minor figures; Romantic poets and prose writers and all the things they said about one another, from "This will never do" (Jeffrey on Wordsworth's *Excursion*) to "The maudlin prince of mournful sonneteers" (was that said about Samuel Bowles, by Coleridge? or about Coleridge by some fierce critic?—consult your notes). The flavor, or lack of flavor, in these bland presentations of literary material, can be best tasted by a look at the final examinations that were a significant part of determining one's course grade. At Harvard they were three hours long, a barbarous practice in itself since it subjected the hand to painful cramping and reduced the mind to its less noble elements. Exams were divided into three or four sections, but essentially the same question was asked over and over again in each. There were identifications in which we were told to describe the work in question and consider its general significance, or to identify the poem from which an excerpt was taken and to comment on its characteristic qualities. We were invited to write thirty minutes of thought on such topics as "The importance of Wordsworth in the history of the sonnet"; "Lamb's contribution to the criticism of Elizabethan drama"; "The function and problems of the poet in the modern world, as set forth, directly or symbolically, by Tennyson, Browning, and Arnold"; or "Why is the friendship of Wordsworth and Coleridge perhaps the most important friendship in the history of English literature?"

I was skillful enough at shoveling back, in my wretched handwriting, plausible "answers," but it was a curious and pedagogically prim-

itive situation. The question not to be asked, either by student or professor, was who in the world would have any interest in reading the
answers to such questions? If that forbidden question had been asked,
earth's foundations—or at least those of Harvard English—would
have tottered. In fact, the only point was to get one's A or A– (B+ and
below meant that you were in trouble as a graduate student) and go on
in the next semester to take more courses until the required sixteen
had been completed. It is easy enough to say that neither these courses
nor the examinations that concluded them did anyone any real harm;
and one could certainly make an argument for the sensibleness of
being asked to identify passages from the literature read during the
term. Whiting's examinations in the Chaucer courses consisted
almost wholly of identifying forty-some lines or passages from *Troilus*
or *The Canterbury Tales*, the only preparation for which was to read
and reread the works in questions—surely a good use of one's time.
But as a routine standard of question and expectation, the courses and
exams did no one any real good; they simply kept the academic system
running that had been running the same way in Harvard English for
decades. To someone who had experienced a very different sort of
inquiry, first in Amherst English and then in Trilling's classroom at
Columbia, it seemed like high school all over again, even as I sat in the
venerable precincts of Sever and Philosophy halls in the Harvard Yard.
Were these people getting away with something?

The notion was reinforced when an Amherst friend sent me a final
exam Armour Craig had given in his literary history course at Amherst.
It opened with the instruction that "the purpose of this examination is
to supply you with materials for an essay on your reading in this
course." In the first hour students were asked to compare passages from
Spenser and Pope to show what they signified to a student of literary
history. The second hour directed them to Fielding's preface to *Tom
Jones* in which Fielding offered the reader "Human Nature" as his subject and described himself as "the founder of a new province of writing." Craig then comments: "But, clearly, Human Nature had been the
'province,' the 'provision,' the subject of many writers before Fielding.
What then is 'new' in *Tom Jones*? What, particularly, does the reader of
Swift and Pope find new in it?" Who knows what the "right answer" to
this question was? I find it as challenging now as the student probably
did who encountered it on the exam back then. What that student was
really being asked to demonstrate was not that he possessed correct

information about Spenser or Pope or Fielding but rather that (thinking back to the English 1 assignment sequence treated earlier) one of his "right names" was "student of literary history." He had to *do* something to make that case, had to become active as a critic and historian, rather than passively disgorging facts previously swallowed. There was nothing particularly ingenious or fancy about the examination: no tricks, no showing off on the examiner's part, just enough direction to give shape to the inquiry being conducted. But it was significantly more than a topic thrown out ("The importance of Wordsworth in the history of the sonnet") with the word "discuss" at the beginning or end of it. ("The word 'discuss' is an invitation to chaos," Theodore Baird once remarked.)

Nothing radically different happened in the other classes I took in my two years of course work at Harvard. The only exciting lecturer I heard in those classes was Walter Jackson Bate, whose three weeks or so of commentary on Samuel Johnson (much of it read from the galleys of his forthcoming book) were memorable for their originality and passionate advocacy. The three seminars we were required to take were in their different ways instructive: with Albert Guerard we read, reported on, and argued about William Faulkner, a rather daring figure (because contemporary) to be studying at Harvard. Reuben Brower, in the final stages of composing his book on Pope's poetry of allusion, led us through the major texts. And, after failing to be admitted to Levin's seminar in comedy, I settled for John Kelleher and *Finnegans Wake,* which we fussed at, picked over (my twenty-page paper was about a mere two pages of the *Wake*), and somehow finished. Still, my expectations of anything really decisive or mind-changing happening within the Harvard classroom and system of courses were reduced even from the modest ones I had upon entering. This was not in any sense a devastating experience: first of all I was not about to fade out as I had at Columbia; and second, I had the enormous challenge — in fact, the support — of what we now call the literary canon. The large amounts of reading I had to do, even to begin to catch up to where a Harvard undergraduate English major had gotten after four years; the satisfactions there were in "covering" numbers of writers, no matter how dull (the Elizabethan sonnet, say, or Samuel Daniel); the authentic thrill of taking on a major poet like Wordsworth or Tennyson and reading him, for the first time, in bulk as well as, from time to time, closely: these combined with the mystical presence of fair Harvard and old Cambridge to propel me along forcefully. I got good grades, even while disparaging the literary values and procedures of the men who awarded them to me. And the institution smiled on me. In March of 1955 came a letter from Herschel Baker informing me that I was part of a preferential list of candidates for teaching fellowships the following year. Since budgetary negotiations had not been concluded, I was to regard this letter, wrote Baker in his inimitable style, "not as a firm commitment for a teaching fellowship, but simply as a cheerful hint that in the fullness of time you may receive a teaching fellowship." The fullness of time came quickly: in addition to the teaching fellowship I was given money for my second year's tuition, then appointed to a residence in one of the undergraduate houses where I would give tutorials and supervise honors projects, room and board coming with the territory. Harvard was being both paternal and maternal, and that was fine with me.

IV
Against the Grain:
My Education within Harvard

⚜

It was a luxury to be situated firmly enough, though not all *that* firmly, within Harvard English. I had no expectations of an eventual departmental appointment there, and the length of a teaching fellowship was limited to a few years; still, Harvard needed bodies to staff its undergraduate tutorial program and to teach sections and grade papers in large courses, thus relieving the distinguished professors of such tasks. At Amherst, where there were no graduate students, it was absolutely unheard of for any professor or instructor to take on paper-reading assistants, much less to allow them to teach in the classroom on certain days. Harvard by contrast was based on the existence of a large cadre of Ph.D. candidates looking for employment and hoping to make an advantageous connection with a senior faculty member; or simply eager — as most were, I think — to get a taste of life on the other side of the desk, to read and grade an exam rather than write one; to make, rather than spend, money. Although particular components of the tutorial system changed from time to time, the Harvard system in 1955, when I took on my first students, was straightforward and not much questioned. Undergraduates, when they became juniors, designated themselves as honors or nonhonors majors, depending on their overall grade point average and whether they planned to write a senior thesis. If a candidate for honors, the student met with his tutor weekly or biweekly in his junior year, for an hour or so, to discuss the course of semester reading they had decided on (Romantic poets, the nineteenth-century novel). A certain amount of written work was required, in addition to regular courses, and grades were given. The nonhonors junior majors met, more irregularly, in groups of four to six, presumably to discuss the assigned text and receive the benefit of their tutor's wisdom. Little or no written work was assigned, nor was a grade given; in other words, the tutor had no way of enforcing whatever authority he possessed, and students were likely to show up at these group sessions quite unprepared. I had vivid confirmation of this when, naively, I assigned Dickens's *Little Dorrit* to the group. Early in the discussion hour it became evident that there would be no discussion, since no one had a clue about even such elementary matters as story and character. I went around the room asking, in a casual attempt at tutorial sangfroid, how far in the novel each tutee had progressed. The answers ranged from roughly one hundred and fifty pages to exactly eighteen (*Little Dorrit* runs to eight hundred pages). What then were we going to do about this problem? One young man had a suggestion: "Sir, couldn't we discuss Dickens in general?"

The junior honors tutorials were a shade more successful, though in the ones I conducted in my rooms at Winthrop House I never had the good fortune to encounter a really "literary" male or female (Radcliffe students, though technically under separate governance, participated in the same tutorial system). My senior thesis writers, whom I supervised in addition to the junior tutees, were in the main routine: they produced commentaries on Keats's odes and Lawrence's novels that were capable enough, but whose main aim seemed to be to qualify for an honors degree in English. Exceptions to the rule were not necessarily an improvement. A young man who wrote about "pain" in the Hemingway hero, looked himself — in his pinched, pale unease — to be in constant pain. An army veteran was determined to study novels about World War II because, he confided, he could still hear the guns booming in his ears; accordingly, he focused on Mailer, James Jones, and Irwin Shaw, but the results were undistinguished. An especially pointless tutorial procedure, it seemed to me, consisted of preparing a candidate for the general exam he or she took in the spring of senior year. This was one more Harvard English exam, but writ large, and preparation for it involved going over, with the student, a list of excerpts from standard works of English literature — so many lines from *Paradise Lost*, a stanza from Shelley's *Adonais*, some sentences from Carlyle. We were to provide "practice" exams by inviting them to identify the excerpts, after which we would set them right, if need be. The procedure would have made sense if the students had been trained in such analysis of passages. They had not been, however, and so this final gesture at "placing" bits from hither and yon seemed an exercise in futility. But it didn't matter: if one failed the comprehensive, another opportunity to pass it was provided before graduation. I don't remember anyone who failed more than once.

This superficial way of making sure undergraduates picked up enough information to pass the "comps" was mirrored in my own situation of preparing for Ph.D. oral exams. A usual way of beginning study for this two-hour exam was to procure a copy of something called the *Tutorial Bibliography*, a document that listed by periods the major books and writers with whom one would be expected to be acquainted. The corpus of English and American literature was divided into five periods; one could write off two of these periods through course work and then be examined orally on the remaining three. I wrote off the early English period (pre-1600) and American literature, and thus needed to know all about Eng Lit from 1600 to the modern period. It was necessary to pass the orals before being certified as a viable candidate for the doctorate and signed on to a dissertation subject, though for a student who failed it was not the end; he could come back a year later and make another try (some came back more than once). Unfortunately—or perhaps, in another sense, fortunately—Amherst graduates had a spotty record in passing these exams on the first try (three of my immediate Amherst contemporaries failed them), probably because the nature of our undergraduate education had made us weak on "coverage," though strong on analyzing individual works. Rightly or wrongly, we felt the exams were perfectly suited to the kind of mindless absorption of facts or dates or "ideas" ("Discuss the nature of humanism as found in Spenser, Shakespeare, and Milton") in which students from other places such as Harvard excelled.

There was a horror story making the rounds about an egregious example of orals bullying on the part of a professor toward a hapless (though non-Amherst) candidate. The professor, Howard Mumford Jones, had been a terror in my eyes ever since, in the one class of his I had attended (never to return), he spent an hour haranguing students about the proper size of the file cards they were to purchase to keep their notes on. The story, perhaps true, had Jones asking the candidate the name of Byron's last poem. He did not know, confessed the candidate. What was its date? Jones went on to ask. (Of course the candidate didn't know.) What was its metrical form? And so on, till the torture ended. At the time, I didn't know what Byron's last poem was (I now know that it is "On This Day I Complete My Thirty-Sixth Year" and also know its date and metrical form), and I hated to think of all the other subjects on which I could draw comparable blanks. On the other hand, perhaps we Amherst people were just making excuses for our laziness. The venerable and witty medievalist, B. J. Whiting, was rumored to have remarked that there was no reason why candidates from Amherst should fail their orals; after all, they were no stupider than other English grad students. This seemed to be the right note to take.

In sum, my friends and I were cynical about Harvard English even while performing our requisite duties within it. We could afford to be cynical about it because we had each other—had an informal and self-delighting existence in what someone at the time should have been clever enough to call the Amherst Mafia, even though we did little enforcing. Some of us might fail to pass the Ph.D. oral; but even this failure could perhaps be awarded a momentary badge of honor, suggesting that such behavior was preferable to competent success. In Dryden's words:

> The midwife laid her hand on his thick skull,
> With this prophetic blessing: *Be thou dull*.

To be dull we reckoned the ultimate crime, and dullness was a quality that went with a refusal to make judgments or stick one's neck out about the virtues of a poem or novel. It also went along with an exclusively historicist perspective in which work was to be considered "objectively" in the terms of its own period and set of values. Dull graduate students of English didn't take seriously the attempt to keep up on current work; cared nothing, say, about the poems of Robert Lowell or Philip Larkin—two poets we were hearing much of in 1955—because they were immersed in older times and names. These people tended more often than not to be putative scholars; they gravitated toward Hyder Rollins or Alfred Harbage or Herschel Baker, and their dissertation subjects were frequently an edited text of some old English poetic drama, from the sixteenth or seventeenth century. Rumor had it that if you found a play that had not been edited within recent memory—for example, James Shirley's *The Cardinal* (1641)—

you could proceed to make an edition of it. No need for Shirley's play to have any literary merit; the point was to demonstrate that you knew how to conduct yourself in scholarly relation to a text.

Perhaps unjustly, we conceived these young scholars to be already on the way to becoming old fogies, destined for some Midwestern university where they would take respectable jobs and turn out "safe" work. (Why we picked the Midwest I'm not exactly sure, but the University of Illinois or Indiana University seemed appropriate spots.) We Amherst people, on the other hand, were critics, determined at all costs to be lively, controversial, contemporary, and very much concerned with teaching—much more so than with scholarship or the thought of publication. This preoccupation with teaching played itself out almost daily, certainly on the weekends, in our active attempts to instruct one another in matters of literary and musical reputation and distinction.

From the standpoint of forty years later, a fairly confident claim can be made for the achievement of this Amherst group within the academy and in American letters generally. Senior man, at age thirty when I entered Harvard, was David Ferry, who would become known for his work on Wordsworth and for several volumes of poetry, including a highly praised rendering of the epic *Gilgamesh*. Ferry taught English at Wellesley, along with his friend Robert Garis, who, although not an Amherst graduate (indeed, he was an alumnus of Muhlenberg) I thought of as part of the group. He would publish a classic work on Dickens and become a widely respected critic of dance, especially (in *Following Balanchine*) of George Balanchine and the New York City Ballet. Garis had come to Harvard just after the war, knew the territory, and through him and Ferry I met figures from an older Wellesley–Harvard scene, such as the poet Richard Wilbur (teaching at Wellesley at the time), the critic Patrick Quinn, and other academics from the Boston area. More important, through the agency of Garis there was the music critic B. H. Haggin, whose character and impress will emerge presently.

Then there were Richard Poirier and Thomas R. Edwards, both instrumental in the planning and execution of Humanities 6, Brower's long-lived course in literary interpretation. Poirier, a teaching fellow and resident tutor at Kirkland House, had been around: first in the army; then, after Amherst, a year at Yale; then a degree at Cambridge, where he studied with F. R. Leavis; then some teaching at

Williams College. Poirier seemed to know, as the phrase goes, where the bodies were buried. Edwards, who shared an apartment with David Ferry, was a highly respected tutor and section man in Harvard courses; he had graduated from Amherst with one of the highest averages ever recorded there, had been excused from the freshman composition course because of his high performance in secondary school, and now seemed on his way to knowing everything about English literature. Edwards would eventually publish books about Pope and about politics in English poetry, would join Poirier as a colleague at Rutgers University, and would assist him in editing *Raritan*, a quarterly review notable for its originality. Finally there were my Amherst classmates William Youngren and Neil Hertz, and the poet Thomas Whitbread from the class just ahead of mine. Youngren, who had, as mentioned, directed me to Pound and I. A. Richards, was a close friend and companion as well as my musical conscience, through endless sessions of listening to and talking about both classical and jazz music. Hertz, another close friend, came to Harvard halfway through my term there, began in philosophy but grew even more disenchanted than I had at Columbia, so switched to English. He would later become associated with Paul de Man and write a number of densely original theoretical essays on literary theory and psychoanalysis. Whitbread, an aspiring, talented poet who never achieved much of a following (unjustly, it seemed to me), was refreshingly unacademic; he seemed to live wholly for singing opera and Gilbert and Sullivan, or quoting aloud — and at length — his favorite poems, of which there were many.

It should be emphasized that this "group" wasn't rock solid, that not all of its members liked one another equally or went overboard in pious gestures toward old Amherst; indeed, some of them would have resisted the claim that they belonged to any group. Still, we saw a lot of one another: on week nights between eleven and midnight at Cronin's bar in Harvard Square, or on weekends when we would gather at the Ferry–Edwards apartment to listen to music, read poems and plays aloud, and drink a lot of beer or ale. More than anything else we talked and argued about literary quality, not always in a very polite or rational way, but animatedly (lots of loud insisting went on) and with the sense that this was a self-delighting activity, far removed from Harvard classrooms. No younger member of the group ever convinced an older one of anything. I remember working as hard as I could to make a case to Garis for the consummate interest of Henry James's late, not-much-read novel *The Sacred Fount*. Garis, who appeared to know not only James's fiction but his plays as well (a surprising feat), was having none of it and persisted in shaking his head, serious and unsmiling, as he countered my enthusiasm. On another occasion he and Ferry combined forces to shake my assumption of Frost's greatness by calling his "The Road Not Taken" "loud and thin." How could this be—*could* it be? I had to struggle musically as well, pressing Edwards to play the first act of Gilbert and Sullivan's *Patience* on his hi-fi, then finding that Gilbert and Sullivan was not well received by the assembled. A Radcliffe student I had begun to date (we would later marry) fared no better when I introduced her to some of the Boys and, during a listening session, she offered up her LP of *My Fair Lady*, which had just opened on Broadway. The group's response to Lerner and Lowe was, as to *Patience*, decidedly chilly. The most infamous instance of musically incorrect taste occurred at a notorious party where Tom Whitbread persisted in singing Puccini arias, incurring the wrath of B. H. Haggin, in whose honor the party was being given. Henceforth Whitbread was kept away from Haggin.

If this sounds brutal or childish, it seldom felt so at the time. The line between bullying and persuasion—how could you like Gilbert and Sullivan when there was Offenbach? how could you rate *The Sacred Fount* so highly when there was *The Awkward Age*?—was a thinly drawn one. A thought of Frost's I discovered years later in one of his notebooks speaks to the activity we were engaged in during those Cambridge evenings: "Pushing things around—things and people. It may be affectionately or hatefully. It may be affectionately and still roughly and the more roughly the better. But whether affectionately or hatefully it is always playfully." The interesting thing about these words is that Frost used them as one of his many definitions of what poetry was or did. In our evenings spent reading poems aloud, we vied with one another to get the floor (not always waiting our turn) in hopes of introducing some piece of work the others didn't know or properly appreciate. The play sometimes became rough, though never, I think, hateful; more often, one thing led to another in invigorating ways—improvisation was the key. After hearing David Ferry read "War Poet" by Roy Fuller, a poet I had never heard of, I went home and memorized it. I still can't say it aloud or type it out without something like a thrill:

Swift had pains in his head.
Johnson dying in bed
Tapped the dropsy himself.
Blake saw a flea and an elf.
Emily Dickenson stayed
Indoors for a decade.
Tennyson could hear the shriek
Of a bat. Pope was a freak.
Water inflated the belly
Of Hart Crane and of Shelley.
Coleridge was a dope.
Southwell died on a rope.
Byron had a round white foot.
Smart and Cowper were put
Away. Lawrence was a fidget
Keats was almost a midget.
Donne alive in his shroud
Shakespeare in the coil of a cloud
Saw death very well, as he
Came crabwise, dark and massy.
I envy not only their talents,
And fertile lack of balance,
But the appearance of choice
In their sad and fatal voice.

*WILLY
REVEALS
ALL*

I didn't want these things to happen to me; indeed, I had no aspirations to be a poet. It seemed sufficient to be a second-order mind, contemplating the heroic spectacles and follies of a Hart Crane or a Shelley and memorizing their poems—saying them to myself or chanting them aloud:

I saw a staring virgin stand
Where holy Dionysus died,
And tear the heart out of his side,
And lay the heart upon her hand
And bear that beating heart away;
And then did all the Muses sing
Of Magnus Annus in the spring,
As though God's death were but a play.

I was no longer a mere graduate student, who after a few beers at Cronin's headed back to his solitary digs off upper Massachusetts Avenue, but the rapt speaker of Yeats's "Two Songs from a Play."

Unlike the aspiring scholars with their editions of minor Jacobean plays, my immediate elders in the Amherst group were engaged in writing dissertations on major writers, dissertations that were seriously revisionary and ambitious in their aim. Ferry had just completed his on Wordsworth's poetry; Garis was close to finishing his long-in-progress work about theatricality in Dickens's novels, especially *Bleak House*; Edwards was unfolding a complex argument about Pope's major poems; Poirier was writing about comedy in the early novels of Henry James. Each of these projects would later become a book, and all of them were immensely important in helping to establish my sense of a critical self. Each had at its center an active reader, unafraid to speak, in the first person, of his responses to the writer in question. There was no desire to specialize in some aspect of the poet or novelist that had not been sufficiently "noticed" before — nothing less than Wordsworth the poet or Dickens the novelist was the subject of concern. Nor was there, as far as I can see, anything debilitatingly "New Critical" about these studies. It is important to insist on this since a bad fashion has lately grown up of referring to the 1950s as a time when literary study turned into arid word-pattern tracing, neglecting presumably all matters of biography, history, and anything external to the text under consideration. On the contrary, Ferry on Wordsworth was full of psychology; Garis on Dickens brought to bear theatrical materials and, even more important, invoked novelists like Tolstoy and Austen as standards of comparison; Edwards and Poirier used whatever came their way in order to illuminate the practices of Pope and James. You could not imitate their critical procedures, and therefore they challenged you to find a writer on whom might be exercised a comparable largeness of focus and originality of concern. There was a lot of talk about "humanism" in the rhetoric of Harvard English, but I encountered it most strongly in the humanistic enterprises these newly made friends were conducting. I resolved to do likewise.

Not everyone outside our little group of humanist light was, as it were, benighted. In the course of his oral report in Reuben Brower's Pope seminar, a young man read aloud Ben Jonson's "To Lucy, Countess of Bedford" ("Lucy, you brightness of our sphere, who are / Life of

the muses' day, their morning-star") and immediately became someone I wanted to know. This was Paul Alpers, who would produce
notable works on Spenser and on the Pastoral, and who, in his learning
and industry, showed that an undergraduate education in Harvard English need not be crippling. Concurrently, in something like a return of
the repressed, Columbia surfaced in the shape of three extremely
intelligent recent graduates, now at Harvard. There was the prodigious
John Hollander, assembling his first book of poems and writing a study
of music in seventeenth-century English verse; George Kateb, a subtle
political theorist who read Wordsworth and Yeats, Auden and Wallace
Stevens; and Stephen Orgel, already recognized as the incipient expert
on the masque in Jacobean literature. Hollander and Kateb were members of the Society of Fellows, which meant they took no courses but
had three paid-for years of good food and sparkling conversation to be
experienced (so it was rumored) at the Society's functions in Eliot
House. Orgel was a graduate student like me, but seemed to have a
much clearer notion of his future scholarly career. The Columbia
crowd, as we eventually dubbed them in contrast to the Amherst
group, played a lively role in our imaginative lives by representing the
City and the University, by being conversant with French literature
(they were less purely Anglo-oriented than most of us were), and by
exhibiting, on occasion, camp sensibilities.

I responded to these Columbia people with mixed feelings, admiring their conversational wit and quickness, their panache (another
word I soon learned), their easy allusions to Continental thinkers.
After all, *they* had taken the required Columbia courses in humanities
and in contemporary civilization; they had all studied with Trilling,
though they seemed less severely "moral" in their attitudes toward
books and toward life than I thought either he or the Amherst group
was. If "our" modern poet was Frost, "theirs" was Auden; indeed, I
remember a late-hour party in Richard Poirier's rooms in Kirkland
House that turned into a debate between him and John Hollander on
the merits of Frost versus Auden. The rest of us sat on the sideline and
cheered our poet, our college, as Poirier and Hollander, both hugely
enjoying their own performances, used every resource to best one
another and entertain us. Somebody should have brought in an
applause meter so we could have found out who won.

George Kateb, and on another occasion his friend the philosopher
Marshall Cohen, invited me to the weekly Fellows dinner in their

well-appointed Eliot House dining room. Things began with sherry, along with very fast, very witty conversation, followed by an excellent dinner and further talk afterward. On one of these occasions, Robert Lowell was there, holding forth in his seductively rambling and uncertain way; on the other, Edwin Muir (probably brought by the poet Donald Hall, also a Fellow), behaving altogether mildly and modestly. Two moments stand out, however, signifying for me—then and now—my sense of the young man from the provinces up against something formidable. The first of these moments occurred at dinner, when the appetizer appeared, something I had not theretofore glimpsed or imagined: a dark green, rounded object with scalloped leaves. Knife and fork? Fingers? Some other means of ingestion? Furtively I peeked at my companion on the right, a man named Henry Shattuck, who had been, I believe, Harvard's treasurer and who knew exactly what to do with his artichoke (for that was its name) as he proceeded to mediate between fingers and cutlery. I got through it all right, though later artichoke experiences have never been entirely free of that first panic. The other occasion was less personally fraught, but equally vivid, and occurred during the sherry talk before supper. Harry Levin, intimidating under the best circumstances, was holding forth about some rather impressive critic—English or American—and vouchsafed the information that he was "an autodidact, you know." Somehow, like the artichoke, I had never before encountered "autodidact," and the way Levin said the word could make an ignorant listener think the worst of the person who labored under such a stigma or handicap. Only recently I discovered that at least one other person, Edmund Wilson no less, had a similar experience with Levin, though Wilson knew very well what the word meant. In *The Sixties*, Wilson recounts, "I had heard Harry say a few years ago, 'You know he's an autodidact,' as if he were saying, 'He used to be a Nazi,' something even worse than 'He's a Homosexual, you know.'"

Looked at from the outside, the Junior Fellow situation lay equally remote both from official Harvard and from the reaction to it seen in our Amherst group behavior. It was, of course, delightful to be a Fellow, yet it must also have been difficult, with no structured courses to take or designated tasks to perform like passing oral exams and writing a dissertation. Each member of the society was presumably working on a book, though not all of them got completed, or not until much later. Perhaps it was a reverse version of Pastoral in which the

shepherd-Fellows were more articulate, more gifted, more sophisticated—but also giddier, more adrift, more purely living by their
wits—than ordinary students like me from whom they had been ab-
stracted for three years. These brilliant shepherd-talkers were thus
better and worse than the rest of us, but they surely represented a holiday from everyday concerns.

The two major critics I encountered while at Harvard, who would pre-
side over my evaluating conscience for years to come, were F. R. Leavis
and B. H. Haggin. For some reason, I failed to take in Leavis—as I had
begun to take in Eliot and the New Critics—at Amherst or at Columbia. But soon after entering Harvard I began to hear about and then
read this English writer who for twenty years edited a magazine,
Scrutiny, that had just ceased publication a year previously. Poirier
had studied with him at Cambridge, and Youngren presented me with
a copy of *The Great Tradition*, Leavis's study of the English novel, as a
twenty-second birthday present. I read and reread it, especially its
opening chapter ("The Great Tradition") in which the critic cut a wide
and fierce swath though nineteenth-century English writers of fiction.
There followed, in my perusal, *Revaluation*, his book about the line of
"wit" in English poetry; his miscellaneous essays, some collected in
The Common Pursuit; his early account of major modern poets, *New
Bearings in English Poetry*; and his *Education and the University*,
about the teaching of English and related matters.

There was nothing ambiguous in Leavis's attitude toward books and
writers. What he called the Great Tradition in English fiction was inaugurated by Jane Austen. Before her there had been, granted, the eighteenth century, especially as represented in Samuel Richardson and
Henry Fielding: but Richardson, whose *Clarissa* was a "really impressive work," nevertheless offered us work that was "extremely limited
in range and variety" and whose demands on our time were dispropor-
tionate to the results. Having said as much, Leavis tossed off the following parenthesis: ("though I don't know that I wouldn't sooner read
through again *Clarissa* than *A La Recherche du Temps Perdu*"). On the
other hand, Fielding's famous much-praised range and variety were
mainly external, matters of novelistic "action," whereas his attitudes
toward human nature were simple "and not such as to produce an
effect of anything but monotony (on a mind, that is, demanding more
than external action) when exhibited at the length of an 'epic in

prose.' " If Fielding and Richardson failed to qualify as part of the Great Tradition, so too did Walter Scott, who, though a very intelligent man, did not have "the creative writer's interest in literature" that would have enabled him to break away from "the bad tradition of the eighteenth-century romance." (Out of Scott, we were also told, came a further "bad tradition" that "spoiled" James Fenimore Cooper and Robert Louis Stevenson.) As for the author of *Tristram Shandy*, Laurence Sterne, Leavis dismissed his "irresponsible and nasty trifling" in a footnote. An even more vigorous clearing of the ground went on in respect to nineteenth-century novelists so as to make way for the preeminence of Jane Austen, George Eliot, Henry James, Joseph Conrad, and D. H. Lawrence. This meant, of course, that something had to be done with Dickens, and, infamously, Leavis did it by asserting that Dickens, though a great "entertainer," was not, except in a single novel (*Hard Times*), a great novelist. As for Thackeray, he was a "greater Trollope" who apart from some "social history" "had nothing to offer a reader whose demand went beyond 'creation of character' and so on." By contrast, Austen and Eliot were great novelists "above the ruck of Gaskells and Trollopes and Merediths."

The introductory chapter to *The Great Tradition* is filled with many more judgments, most of them dismissing or severely "placing" the writer (Leavis liked the verb *place*) in a hierarchy. Many of these writers I had read only partially, if at all. Yet this did not deter me; in fact, it may even have contributed toward my taking on Leavis's opinions as if they had been my own. It had everything to do with the power of his voice as it emerged out of the sometimes tangled syntax, out of the idiomatic bite of a style that had contempt for "elegance" and smoothness, that delighted in being rough, abrasive, provocative. (Later I learned from Donald Davie the interesting fact that Leavis's schoolmaster at the Perse School in Cambridge insisted his pupils "voice" their essays rather than simply write them.) Leavis knew his mind and seemed to live in order to perform the acts of valuing and discriminating that he (and I) saw as central to the critical task. Even when the emphasis was on the greatness of one writer, rather than the shortcomings of another, Leavis had to get the greater and the lesser writer into relationship. For example, I shall never forget coming across, early in my acquaintance with him, his remarks about Donne in the chapter from *Revaluation* (probably his best book) titled "The Line of Wit." Leavis begins by mentioning that *The Oxford Book of*

Seventeenth Century Verse has appeared and that this will provide an occasion for resurveying the poets of that age:

> Few who handle the new *Oxford Book* will think of reading it straight through, and fewer will actually read through it, but to persist only moderately in the undertaking is to assure oneself that one valuation at least, and that a key one, among current acceptances needs no downward revision. After ninety pages of (with some minor representation) Fulke Greville, Chapman and Drayton, respectable figures who, if one works through their allotments, serve at any rate to set up a critically useful background, we come to this:
>
>> I wonder by my troth, what thou, and I
>> Did, till we lov'd? were we not wean'd till then?
>> But suck'd on country pleasure, childishly?
>> Or snorted we in the seven sleepers den?
>> Twas so; But this, all pleasures fancies bee.
>> If any beauty I did see,
>> Which I desir'd, and got, 'twas but a dreame of thee.
>
> At this we cease reading as students, or as connoisseurs of anthology-pieces, and read on as we read the living.

The paragraph goes on, but the sentence about reading as we read the living made a particular impact on me. I hadn't at that point read any Fulke Greville, and knew precious little of George Chapman (I knew he had translated Homer) and Michael Drayton. But I easily acceded that they were "respectable figures" to set off, by contrast, the genius of Donne. It was Donne's originality of voice and music that Leavis emphasized: the "utterance, movement and intonation are those of the talking voice." And he pointed by way of illustration to the stress that must be given "Did" in the second line of the poem: "I wonder by my troth, what thou, and I / Did, till we lov'd?" Leavis had no interest in doing an interpretation, a "reading" of "The Good Morrow" or of any other Donne poem. Like his master, Eliot, he circled the poem, landed on a spot, and drew from it a particular instance that could stand for a general quality in the poet. It was hard—for me, impossible —to resist, especially since the sharply drawn aggressive posture had so little in common with the genial relativism existing in Harvard classrooms, where minor seventeenth-century poets like Drayton were to be appreciated "in their own terms" rather than used as foils to set off Donne's greatness.

The files of Leavis's magazine, *Scrutiny*, were available only in the stacks of Widener Library, and I borrowed and read them avidly, especially his own contributions, but also those of his wife, Q. D. Leavis, and prominent disciples. I decided—not consciously, really—to use my reading of Leavis and *Scrutiny* as a way of preparing myself for my Ph.D. orals. My pages of notes on major and minor figures contained plenty of dates, character identifications, names of literary "schools" and movements, plus outlines of the plots of *Paradise Lost* and Spenser's *Faerie Queen*, a poem I had read only in part. But they also contained my judgments of particular poems, plays, and novels in which I attempted to distinguish the important works from the less important. Here Leavis played a significant, not to say possibly troubling role, since I used him as a map for the major currents and traditions in English literature from the seventeenth century on. He told me which writers it was essential to read, and who could be skipped— not that he advocated skipping (he had presumably put in his time with Sterne or Thackeray). But someone pressed for time, preparing himself for an exam, might be tempted here and there to pass over the inessential. There was nothing wrong with this emphasis, or at least not until the temporary taking over of a strong critic's valuation became more than temporary. In some ways Harvard English turned out to be right: for a young scholar-critic it was as important—perhaps *more* important—to be catholic in one's taste, to try to enter into as many different sorts of literary experience as one could manage, rather than become too exclusive and prematurely severe. A large dose of Leavis, in other words, needed to be tempered with an equally large dose of a literary sensibility like that of George Saintsbury, who read everything and had something to say, usually appreciative, about everything he read. But nobody directed me to Saintsbury, and I wouldn't have appreciated him then anyway.

For the present, Leavis served me effectively and, as was the case with Trilling at Columbia, helped to widen my sense of what it was important for the literature specialist to know. He reinforced the truth that there was more to literary study than close involvement with the intricacies of lyric poems. Particularly in the introduction to his edition of John Stuart Mill's essays on Bentham and Coleridge, Leavis emphasized the importance of what he called "extra-literary" studies, since, he wrote, "a serious study of literature inevitably leads outward into other studies and disciplines, into fields not primarily literary," and liberal education should exploit that "outward-leading" to best advantage. He even went so far as to claim that "the profit of a real literary training will show itself very largely in other-than-literary fields." Some of those fields, such as economics, religion, sociology, and political theory, would be of natural concern to the literary student coming to terms with Mill — something that would hardly seem to need saying, yet in my case needed to be said. So Leavis, while encouraging me toward a too-ready wielding of judgments based on insufficient reading experience (Sterne's novels really were not worth one's time), also warned against a too purely literary standard of interest: "I don't believe in any 'literary values,'" he wrote later on, "and you won't find me talking about them; the judgments the literary critic is concerned with are judgments about life."

On balance, however, the most important idea I took from Leavis was that being a literary critic didn't necessitate the elaboration of a theoretical statement in which one disclosed one's principles. Challenged to do so by René Wellek, a historian of criticism, Leavis declined to be any more explicit than he already had been, arguing that the resulting general propositions would be clumsy and even misleading in comparison with the actual work of criticism itself: "My whole effort," he wrote, "was to work in terms of concrete judgments and particular analyses: 'This — doesn't it? — bears such a relation to that; this kind of thing — don't you find it so? — wears better than that.'" Of course there is an answer to this insistence, heard much recently; namely, that a refusal to theorize one's position is itself a theoretical statement. But I didn't worry about that possibility; rather I took Leavis's colloquial indication of how criticism should operate ("this kind of thing — don't you find it so? — wears better than that") as a warrant for my own activity in tutorial duties and literary conversations generally. That it could, on occasion, also be confused with bullying, especially when the older teacher was persuading the younger student ("don't you find it so?"), did not occur to me.

Much of the foregoing remarks about Leavis's influence on me could as well apply to that of B. H. Haggin. Some of the influence was filtered through Garis and Youngren, the most musically gifted listeners of his Harvard following; but Haggin was himself on the scene, during summers spent in Cambridge and on the occasional visit from New York City. He was then in a favorable position to command a forum from which to be heard. His long stint as music critic of the *Nation* was ending in the mid-fifties; but immediately he assumed the same post for the *New Republic* and soon after began his quarterly chronicles of music and ballet for the *Hudson Review*. (Later he would also review records for the *Yale Review*.) I became acquainted with him first through a collection of his columns, *Music in the Nation*, a pile of copies being remaindered in a Harvard Square bookstore for fifty cents each. In one of these *Nation* items he defended himself against a reader who had sent in a recent Haggin column with its title, *Records*, crossed out and *Likes and Dislikes* substituted, and where the reader had underlined each statement in which Haggin said he liked or disliked something. Haggin replied:

> As though criticism properly is something more than personal likes and dislikes, and as though such likes and dislikes are mere whims. Actually criticism is as personal as the art it deals with; it begins with the critic's experience of, and response to, the work of art . . . and it ends with his formulation of his judgment — a reasoned statement of like or dislike. My reader underlines my dislike of Brahms's Violin Concerto and again of Szigeti's performance; but he paid no attention to the subsequent statement that "music as pretentious as the first movement, as saccharine as the second, should not be played with fussy, tremulous inflection that exaggerates its faults," which makes it clear that the dislike was not mere whim but reasoned judgment of my experience of the work and the performance.

As far as I know, Haggin and Leavis never read each other. But a few years previously, in *Education and the University*, Leavis had thrown out the following, in his account of what literary studies should consist of:

> Literary history, as a matter of "facts" about and accepted critical (or quasi-critical) description and

commentary, is a worthless acquisition; worthless for
the student who cannot as a critic—that is, as an
intelligent and discerning reader—make a personal
approach to the essential data of the literary historian,
the works of literature (an approach is personal or it is
nothing: you cannot take over the appreciation of a
poem, and unappreciated, the poem isn't "there").

Clearly these critics inhabited the same world of assumptions and procedures; they even shared, so it seemed to me, a vigorously assertive
tone of voice, as personal as they insisted any true response to a work
of art, musical or literary, had to be.

Sometime that first summer in Cambridge I was invited to a small
gathering at Youngren's where the great man—Haggin, not Leavis—
would be present. This was not an undertaking to be attempted
lightly, for I wanted both to be approved of by him but also to demonstrate some independence of spirit and musical taste. To these purposes I decided I would ask a slightly provocative question about one
of my favorite compositions that Haggin to my knowledge had not
dealt with in print: Bach's violin and oboe concerto, which I knew and
loved in the Casals recording from the Prades Festival. The complica-
tion here was that Haggin's attitude toward Bach was somewhat
grudging; while acknowledging Bach's genius, Haggin was at pains to
point out that the enormous amount of music Bach produced made it
certain that some of this music, perhaps a good deal of it, would be
merely ground out, mechanical rather than inspired. In *Music on
Records*, his 1941 guidebook to the best classical (and jazz) recordings,
Haggin divided Bach's works into three categories: The Great Works,
Other Fine Works, and Uninteresting or Unimportant Works. My
question then was, since the violin and oboe concerto was omitted,
into just what category it fell. Could the omission have been deliberate—the piece insufficiently good for positive inclusion, but not egre-
giously bad either—or was it just an oversight?

The conversation at the afternoon gathering was pretty guarded, as I
remember. Nobody sang Puccini and nobody drank very much, mainly
because Haggin was not an admirer of a tongue loosened by drink (he
himself usually nursed a weak bourbon and water, and refused a refill).
At some point I got up the courage to ask him what he thought of the
concerto and he appeared to be untroubled by my enthusiasm for it,

though he didn't share it himself. The whole thing went off relatively painlessly, as if the Leavis bit about "this kind of thing—don't you find it so?—wears better than that" could be a realistic model for critical discussion. It was not until an updated version of *Music on Records* appeared a year or two later, now titled *The Listener's Musical Companion*, that I noticed (in the section devoted to recorded performances of Bach) that a strong recommendation of the Casals-Stern-Schneider performance of the Concerto in D Minor for two violins was followed by this parenthesis ("with the uninteresting Concerto in C Minor for violin and oboe"). So there it was, out at last in print.

More than anyone I had ever met before or since, Haggin was unable to separate his opinion of someone's moral and human character from that person's taste in music. Years later I invited him to give a lecture at Amherst College, soon after I had gone back to teach there. At a small party afterward I introduced him to a colleague of mine, who in the course of conversing with Haggin expressed his admiration for some Furtwängler performances of Tchaikovsky's symphonies. Haggin said little at the time, but later on, as I drove him to the inn, he remarked to me that my colleague seemed like a pleasant young man and wasn't it odd that he would admire those Furtwängler performances? I couldn't imagine what the right answer to that one might be. The lecture he had given earlier titled "The Approach to Music" (not "An Approach" or "My Approach") was designed to illustrate that the only approach to music was through the listener's good use of his or her ear. Examples from Schubert, Berlioz, Mozart, and from Johnny Dodds's "Wild Man Blues" provided the staple of his fifty-minute demonstration. After the lecture a student came up to him and politely wondered whether, on certain occasions, there wasn't a use for musicological analysis of the piece under question. Absolutely not, returned Haggin, refusing to grant the student any ground at all, even as the boy persisted, still politely, in trying to get his qualification approved.

Yet it was exactly that quality of inflexibility that made Haggin exciting and attractive. Randall Jarrell once said about him that Haggin couldn't lie to you if he tried—and as far as I could see, he never tried. Listening to music in his presence was, frankly, exhausting because I never knew whether to venture some sort of appreciating or depreciating comment or whether it was preferable to keep my mouth shut and play it safe. Yet Haggin wanted to hear what other listeners had to say—as long as it made sense to his ears. He had no humorous tolerance for

the misguided efforts of those whose ears betrayed them. When occasionally he tried to be humorous the result was delightfully elephan-
tine, as in this untypical moment from his journalism when he
reviewed, in 1943, a performance of a Bach piece he found distasteful:

> If at 6.29 in the afternoon of February 28 you noticed
> your dog stirring restlessly and whining in his sleep
> and you felt uneasy yourself, that was because at the
> moment *The Nation's* music critic was near death
> from the most lethally dull of Bach's Sonatas for unac-
> companied cello, No. 5 in C Minor, which was being
> played at the final concert of the New Friends of
> Music by Luigi Silva. . . . Two minutes more and it
> would have been all over with me; but at 6.30—that
> was when Rover leaped up with a joyous yelp—Bach
> and Mr. Silva stopped, and Haydn and the Budapest
> Quartet resumed; and so I am alive to write the excit-
> ing story.

Usually he avoided such trips into the whimsical, preferring instead to
report the pains of enduring what was unendurable.

More than once Haggin quoted Bernard Shaw, whose music criticism he greatly admired, along with Donald Tovey's and W. J. Turner's.
For Haggin, Shaw was the finest of music critics because of the
"integrity" with which he employed all his "resources of knowledge,
taste, literary skill, and wit to deal rigorously with his subject as it
required to be dealt with." Shaw also provided him with a motto by
saying that the critic should know no man, that "his hand should be
against every man, and every man's hand against his." In other words,
no cozy club for critics. But consider the heroic severity of the assertion, which brings to mind the Old Testament. It was Shaw as well
who helped Haggin believe in the personal nature of music criticism,
since, in Shaw's words, "People have pointed out evidences of personal
feeling in my notices as if they were accusing me of a misdemeanor,
not knowing that a criticism written without personal feeling is not
worth reading. It is the capacity for making good or bad art a personal
matter that makes a man a critic."

"Who prop, thou ask'st, in these bad days, my mind?" If Matthew
Arnold's notorious question had been asked of me, I would have iden-

tified the main intellectual props, during those first two years at Harvard, as my Amherst friend and mentors, and the critical examples of Leavis and Haggin. To these should be added the literary artist whom I had adopted, not just as an admired novelist but as a guide to life—a moral sage with profound insights into human nature, the relations between men and women, matters of life and death. This was none other than D. H. Lawrence, whose work I had been introduced to in Trilling's class at Columbia, and whom I chose for my major author on the Ph.D. oral exam. The exam consisted of three half-hour rounds of questions on the "periods" one had studied (for me, English literature from 1600 to the early 1900s) and a final half hour centered on the particular text. Leavis's book on Lawrence, in which he made the highest claims for Lawrence as a novelist and as a moralist, had just appeared in England and was about to be published in this country. Leavis placed *The Rainbow* and *Women in Love* at the height of Lawrence's achievement, and I chose the latter novel as my special text. But I also saturated myself in the other novels and short fiction as well his polemical and provocative essays and reviews. (*Lady Chatterley's Lover* still had to be explored surreptitiously, since the famous trial that removed the ban on it was a couple of years away.) Partly this was an attempt to present myself to Harvard English as a modern spirit who supported the achievement of a "difficult" writer about whose greatness there was as yet no consensus. Leavis presented himself as an embattled discoverer of Lawrence's work, heroicizing the novelist and in the process, I'm afraid, himself the critic as well. In choosing, as it were, both Lawrence and Leavis—and choosing mainly to admire them—I was, it may be, following a pattern, or establishing one, that would eventually become clear to me: I was drawn to figures of imaginative excess, writers who were always going too far. One of the gambits in our group's conversational argument was to draw the other person up short at some point by inserting the cautionary "You go too far" into the battle. Soon we couldn't say it without a mock manner of delivery. But in the intensity of their unqualified enthusiasms and detestations, Lawrence and Leavis and Haggin always went too far. On the contrary, I thought of myself, with some justification, as sane (or sane enough to pass as such), and that whatever "sanity" was, it was something to be aspired to in human dealings. For all Leavis's praise of Lawrence's sanity, neither the praiser nor the praised seemed to me notable for that quality, their power emanating from sources that had to be named otherwise. Rapidly casting my eyes over some of the figures I would eventually write books and essays about — Wyndham Lewis, Norman Mailer, Robert Frost, Randall Jarrell, Evelyn Waugh, Kingsley Amis — there emerges a prevailing identification with the "excessive," usually strongly satiric, presence. Of course it could be argued with some justice that in relation to oneself as an "ordinary" mortal, any figure of significance in the worlds of art and criticism is by comparison extraordinary — excessive, since excess is the prerogative or the expression of genius. Still, if all artists must be judged as performing against the grain, my chosen ones performed in notably extravagant, to me deeply satisfying, ways.

As for Lawrence's and my fate when doctoral orals came round: my examining board, presided over by Monroe Engel, a young lecturer and novelist who actually taught Lawrence in class, was a fortunate mixture of the sympathetic and the mildly unconvinced. By the time we reached Lawrence in the final half hour, I had done well enough on the period questions so that failure seemed unlikely. Alfred Harbage did engage me in mild dispute about whether Lawrence was in fact a good writer, citing a number of passages from *Women in Love* (Harbage had done his homework) where Lawrence invoked the color yellow in connection with the look in a character's eyes, as in "a strange flash of yellow light coming from her eyes" and "The wonderful yellow light in her eyes." Harbage asked me, I thought teasingly, whether I could think of any other supposedly "great writer" who in fact wrote so badly, so sloppily. When I named Faulkner, Harbage laughed and laughed (was Faulkner a great writer?) and changed the subject. And that was that. "Harvard" wasn't really convinced, but lived up to its reputation of letting its students go in the way they had chosen, just so long as they knew enough of the facts. I emerged from the English department's bailiwick, Warren House, a step closer to the doctorate.

V
Hum. 6 and Reuben Brower

Two main areas of discovery sustained me in the less than inspiring climate of Harvard Graduate English. There were the older Amherst graduates who helped shape my tastes and aspirations, and there were the examples of Leavis and Haggin as fierce embodiments of critical integrity. But the enterprise that fueled my sense of what teaching literature could be like, and provided a format for first ventures into life on the other side of the desk, was Reuben Brower's course in the interpretation of literature, Humanities 6, known by all as "Hum. 6." Beginning in the fall of 1951, Harvard and Radcliffe students had to complete a general education requirement consisting of the election of one course from a number offered in each of the divisions (humanities, social science, natural science). These were described as "elementary" two-term courses to be taken in the freshman or sophomore years, and the 1954–55 course catalogue lists six such courses one could take to satisfy the humanities requirement. The first five of these courses were sweeping "Great Books" considerations of Western culture: Humanism in the West, Epic and Novel, Crisis and the Individual, Ideas of Good and Evil in Western Literature, and Ideas of Man and the World in Western Thought. They concentrated on classical authors, great poems and novels, and philosophical and moral treatises; they were alike in assigning many pages of reading each week, as well as in their emphasis on Greatness—nothing read was to be less than "major" in impact, so it seemed. For example, Good and Evil, as it was called for short, featured in its spring term a reading list that included *The Pilgrim's Progress*, Hume's *Dialogues on Natural Religion*,

Candide, Moby-Dick, Dostoyevsky, essays by T. H. Huxley, plays by
Bernard Shaw, and Camus's *The Plague*—a good deal to absorb in thirteen weeks. Harry Levin's list of novels for the second term of Epic and
Novel included *Don Quixote, Bleak House, Moby-Dick* (Melville's
whale was everywhere), and *War and Peace.* Probably the most important experience a student might have in one of these courses was a personal confrontation with his or her beliefs about life and the world. So
after reading Dostoyevsky or Melville or Freud, one might have second
thoughts about one's religion, and roommates would argue mightily,
late at night, about whether God was dead or Freud was right.

Thus the sixth humanities course, Brower's creation, cut a rather
distinct—and a distinctively modest—figure, in its statement of
procedure:

> *Humanities 6. Interpretation of Literature*
>
> A course designed to encourage students to become
> more responsive readers of literature. Close study of a
> small number of works, mainly English and Ameri-
> can, with occasional written exercises. The emphasis
> in the first half-year is on learning how to read differ-
> ent types of imaginative literature, especially poetry,
> drama and fiction. In the second half-year more atten-
> tion is given to interpreting works in relation to his-
> tory and literary tradition, in particular to the
> literature of Greece and Rome.

Worth noting is the emphasis on smallness and the eschewal—in its
predominantly Anglo-American emphasis—of world literature per-
spectives, although those were addressed to a certain extent in the
course's second term. Even more important, the mention of "close
study" promised that coverage was not the point; for students to
become "more responsive readers of literature" required time as well
as pedagogical ingenuity. There were all sorts of courses designed to
make you a faster reader, Brower liked to say; here was a course that
made you slow down and look at the details. Critical responsiveness
was in fact a response to detail, since, as Blake would have it, Art
exists only in minutely organized particulars.

Hum. 6 was essentially the course Brower and his colleagues Baird
and Craig had developed at Amherst called "Introduction to Literature." The main difference was that Hum. 6 had a weekly lecture,

usually given by Brower but also by other staff members, that laid out the lines of interpretation to be explored more fully in the section meetings. Otherwise, as at Amherst, the weekly staff meeting was the place where writing assignments were hammered out, where suggestions about what might be done in discussion sections were debated, and where the course's pulse was taken again and again. Although not a member of the Hum. 6 staff in its first two years, I attended most of the lectures and kept in close touch with proceedings. That staff in its first years was heavily weighted with Amherst graduates, Richard Poirier and T. R. Edwards being especially central to the planning and execution of things. At the beginning of the fall term in 1954, Brower handed out to his colleagues a short document titled "Notes for a Preliminary Discussion," in which he attempted to specify the course's major aims. Its "first and last object," he wrote, was "to get the student to respond to the work of literature before him. He must show us that he has responded by making relevant statements about the work." A relevant statement was one that referred, at least by implication, "to particular words and the way the writer uses them."

Although compared to the other general education courses, with their large dealings with good and evil or man and the world, Hum. 6 might seem limited and modest in range, in another sense it was extremely ambitious: for its aim was nothing less than "to introduce the student to the nature of literature," as Brower put it. What could be odder, less equivocal, than such an aim expressed in such terms? Beyond that, the attempt was to avoid pedantry, and in a sentence that inadvertently amuses by its insistence on the importance of *how* the process should be conducted, Brower wrote, "The student must feel that what he is doing is 'fun.' Rigor of method often equals rigor mortis." That combination of "must" with the emphatic "fun" suggests somewhat awkwardly the pedagogical force behind the enterprise. As a classicist, Brower was in no sense "against" translation, but he had learned—probably in part from studying with Leavis—that "a literature exists only in the language in which it was originally written." Therefore the Hum. 6 inquiry was specifically directed at language rather than at ideas. Brower wasn't much for making theoretical statements, at least complicated, well-qualified ones, but he did go so far as to say in his preliminary notes that the course would be dealing with an area of language "between grammar and poetry," what in an older terminology was called "rhetoric" — "*how* language is used to express *so-and-so.*"

Many years later, one of the most distinguished teachers in that course, Paul de Man, wrote in an essay titled "The Return of Philology" that Hum. 6 was where he became aware of the subversive power of literary instruction. He pointed out how remote Brower's interests were from literary theory; that, indeed, he was far more interested in Greek and Latin literature. Nevertheless, the insistence that students make "relevant" statements about the work of literature by referring to the particular ways a writer uses words, had the effect of subverting the notion that literature was equivalent to the human and historical meanings inevitably ascribed to it. De Man wrote that by being allowed only those responses that were supported by instances of specific uses of words in the text

> [students] were asked to begin by reading texts closely as texts and not to move at once into the general context of human experience or of history. Much more humbly or modestly, they were to start out from the bafflement that such a singular turn of tone, phrase, and figure were bound to produce in readers attentive enough to notice them and honest enough not to hide their non-understanding behind the screen of received ideas that often passes, in literary instruction, for humanistic knowledge.

De Man argued that this procedure had far-reaching didactic consequences that showed up in the way certain students were transformed, were never the same again as writers — indeed, would find writing a more difficult activity since they could no longer just say anything that popped into their heads. He concluded that "mere reading, it turns out, prior to any theory, is able to transform critical discourse in a manner that would appear deeply subversive to those who think of the teaching of literature as a substitute for the teaching of theology, ethics, psychology, or intellectual history." In the context, then, of the other Harvard humanities courses, Hum. 6 was indeed subversive of their "use" of literature for such aims.

Yet subversion was far from anything like a motive for the course's existence. Brower was interested in enabling students to become better readers, and he believed that works of literature — good ones, anyway—were designed by an imagination in ways that can be traced and appreciated. His first book, *The Fields of Light* (1951), which had developed out of his teaching in Amherst College classrooms, was subtitled "An Experiment in Critical Reading." Here the experiment consisted in seeing what could be said, after careful looking and listening, about how words cohered to make a work of art. The book's first half concerned itself solely with lyric poems, with examples from Donne, Herbert, Marvell, Hopkins, Yeats, and others who most compellingly demonstrated the intricacies of verbal patterning. From there he moved on to inspect some longer works in prose and verse that could be shown to reveal subtle design: *The Tempest, Pride and Prejudice, Mrs. Dalloway,* and *A Passage to India.* Patent in the book, as it would also be in Brower's lecturing and teaching in Hum. 6, was the faith, almost a certainty, that great literature's greatness had to do with the way it opened itself to the probing intelligence of a clever reader. Designs were there to be discovered and appreciated for the way they promoted satisfyingly unified artistic experiences. In that sense there is something odd in de Man's enlistment of Brower, since de Man's own interpretive procedure, at least in his later career, was programmatically committed to *not* uncovering unifying designs amenable to confident expression in the critic's signifying language. On the contrary, Brower never treated interpretation as terribly "problematic." One simply had to work hard and carefully at having the relevant perceptions and finding the relevant language in which to express them.

I first heard the word "urbane" in an Amherst class of his, used about some eighteenth-century minor poet (Matthew Prior, perhaps), and the word seemed to describe Reuben Brower's own manner, the tone of his address to literature and to life. He was not a particularly humorous man (he seldom told a joke and was sometimes slow at getting the point of one), and he was much taken up with himself, his plans and ideas. The urbane manner, by turns cool, skeptical, insinuating, lightly contemptuous, sometimes turning warm, even passionate when in the presence of something he really cared about—this manner was not bequeathed him but was achieved rather through strenuous self-education. A young man from the provinces, he grew up in Lanesboro, Pennsylvania, not many miles from my own upstate New York town. In fact, Brower, whose father worked for the railroad, rode the daily train to Binghamton where there was a good high school from which he graduated with high honors. At Amherst College he continued these winning ways, and early on won an accolade from Frost, who in the course of visiting a classroom on one of his sojourns in Amherst (circa 1930) heard the undergraduate Brower read aloud an obscure poem by an obscure sixteenth-century English poet. Frost told the story more than once: "My goodness, the way his voice laid down those lines ... I said to him, 'I give you A for life.'" One had the sense of Brower, then, as a prize student whose hand always went up first in the classroom and whose interests — Greek and Latin, architecture and painting, landscape gardening, both as practiced in his beloved eighteenth century and at his home in Belmont, just outside Cambridge, Massachusetts — were very cultivated ones indeed, the interests of a gentleman.

Often it was difficult to penetrate the manner and get Brower to listen to what you were saying, since he tended to decide quickly what you wanted, with the result that misunderstanding was likely. Once I mistakenly approached him directly after he had finished a Hum. 6 lecture and tried to ask him something about William Cowper, whose poetry I had been reading. As soon as I uttered the name "Cowper" he took me to be referring to James Fenimore, about whom, he hastened to assure me, speaking very fast and as if disturbed by what I had asked, he knew nothing ("No, haven't read him for years ... *Last of the Mohicans*, yes, but ... Oh dear, no, can't help you at all ... "). Finally I drew him up short by insisting it was William Cowper, the poet, of whom I was speaking. "Ohh ... *Cowper*. Yes, of course ... I thought you were talking about ..." This habit of beginning to answer you before he had really listened to what you were saying made Brower vulnerable to some amused comments on the part of those of us who worked with him — but only behind his back. He was not a playful man or a good person to tease, even if you were bold enough to forget the difference in age. Our single serious misunderstanding came many years later when I was putting together a selection of essays about Yeats and tried to explain to him why I failed to include something he had written on the poet. Somehow he decided that I was dismissing his work as out-of-date or insignificant; it took some effort on my part to convince him that I had by no means meant to disparage it. He was a man who jumped to conclusions.

After *The Fields of Light* was published in 1951 (Brower was then forty), he was no longer content, as were his colleagues Baird and Craig, to be "just" a teacher of English in a small college, inventing interesting courses and reading piles of undergraduate papers. When

Harvard made him an offer, it was irresistible, especially with the prospect held out of a mastership at one of the residential houses. Adams House, during his tenure there, was widely accepted as a place whose special interests were artistic and cultural, and Brower brought in a number of distinguished visitors to perform for and talk to the students. But he never became a power in the Harvard English department and had absolutely no success in getting tenure for members of his staff (Poirier, Anne Ferry, and de Man were three impressive teachers associated with him who were not given tenure at Harvard). There were always jokes going around about Hum. 6's emphasis on trying to make students better readers: "Remedial reading," Perry Miller is rumored to have called it. When *In Defense of Reading: A Reader's Approach to Literary Criticism*, a group of essays by members of the Hum. 6 staff, appeared in 1962, someone joked that its real subtitle should be "How to Write about Literature without Actually Knowing Anything." But there must also have been some feelings of envy in Brower's critics as they contemplated what was obviously a very successful and influential course: this was, after all, the academy.

That first year (1954–55) when I was an observer of Hum. 6, the fall term reading consisted of a poetry anthology (A. J. M. Smith's *Seven Centuries of Verse*), a few Hawthorne tales and sketches, Shakespeare's *Othello*, and Henry James's short novel, *The Europeans*. A final "reading period" project (Harvard courses always concluded with ten days or so in which classes didn't meet and one worked on one's own) involved another play of Shakespeare's, *Richard II*, and Fitzgerald's *The Great Gatsby*. By any count, the pages to be read in the course of a term amounted to no more than a few hundred, since one of the cardinal principles of Hum. 6 was that "reading" really meant rereading—that you couldn't estimate the interpretive task (put vulgarly, "work load") in terms of the number of pages a course assigned. Still, it was an especially restricted list of texts.

The ratio of lectures to section meetings was two to one. Brower delivered most of the lectures, including all the ones on interpreting poetry and poetic drama; Poirier relieved him when the subject was fiction, lecturing on Hawthorne and James. In the small horseshoe amphitheater of Room 11, Sever Hall, the staff sat together at one end, while the students fanned out in fairly attentive postures. Brower's lecture style took a bit of getting used to, since his voice was unimpressive, tending toward the monotonous and high-pitched. Often he had not finished delivering his lecture when the fifty-minute bell rang and he would ask for just a little more time. Students meanwhile were snapping the rings of their notebooks, preparing to head to another class or to lunch. Brower would then hasten to cram, into the extra minutes, all the summary judgments and further speculations that he hadn't quite gotten into the first fifty. One was advised to listen closely to this extra inning, as it were, since it contained some of Brower's very best commentary. Yet many minds were doubtless elsewhere.

Hum. 6 always began with poems, and in an anthology of poems he and other staff members later compiled (*Beginning with Poems*, 1966), Brower provided a rationale for so doing:

> We begin with short poems because they offer literary experience in its purest form. By beginning with poems we can be reasonably sure that the student learns early to distinguish between life and literature without being unduly distracted by questions of biography and history or by social and psychological problems of the type raised so often by the novel.

Considered from the standpoint of arguments that have beset literary study during recent decades, these assumptions are anything but unproblematic, and the sense that "to distinguish between life and literature" is something that can be "learned" at an early age of critical sophistication is surely a curious one. Such a distinction would have been understood in fairly simplistic terms: "life" as everything that was large, inchoate, messy, impure—the "great blooming buzzing confusion" evoked by William James in his *Psychology*; by contrast (and especially when history, biography, and novels were shoved to the side), literature as small, delicately ordered, and, most important, a *whole*, so that within a class hour or the confines of a short paper a lyric poem could be dealt with. "Poems may come to stand in a student's mind as platonic forms of true and complete literary experience": it is perhaps no accident that one of Brower's favorite examples in the early stages of the course was Marvell's "On a Drop of Dew," in which the dewdrop is celebrated for its purity and entirety, then likened to the soul. Like a poem, evidently, the drop of dew is born in a "clear region" and is enclosed and complete: "And in its little globe's extent / Frames as it can its native element."

The introductory weeks spent on poetry revealed Brower's familiar concentration on certain key terms—speaker, dramatic situation, tone, image, metaphor—employed about a number of short poems, especially by Wordsworth and Keats. From working with one or another term as the particular poem seemed to call for it, the students moved to interpreting the whole by using all the resources they had been given. After a number of short exercises on uses of tone and metaphor in short poems by Wordsworth they were invited to perform a full-dress "Interpretation of a Poem." The guide for such a paper was fairly elaborate, consisting of three parts: first the "Object," which was defined as guiding a reader to "full and relevant experience of a poem"; next the "Preparation," where a number of questions were proposed about what the poem expressed and how it was organized— how the metaphors were connected, how particularities and peculiarities of sound were significant in affecting what was heard; finally after all this note-taking, reading aloud, and trying to improve one's hearing of the poem, they were ready presumably to tackle the third part, "Writing," in which they would make significant points about the poem with telling examples, practicing the kind of analysis they had been doing with their teachers.

The poem in question that fall, for the culminating "interpretation" exercise, was Gerard Manley Hopkins's "Spring," and it is important to see why—along with the other English poems— "Spring" should have been chosen to introduce poetry to the students. It was a sonnet, presenting (in Marvell's words) its "little globe's extent" within possibilities of compass. And, like those other poems, "Spring" was "dramatic" (in Hum. 6's use of the term) in that it exhibited some sort of progression or change of tone in its address, seeming at a certain point to take stock of itself and turn in a new direction. Such a "turn" occurs after the octet's rapturous enumeration of the sensuous richness of the season, when a different voice inspects and generalizes the season's difference:

What is all this juice and all this joy?
    A strain of the earth's sweet being in the beginning
In Eden garden.—Have, get, before it cloy,

    Before it cloud, Christ, lord, and sour with sinning,
Innocent mind and Mayday in girl and boy,
    Most, O maid's child, thy choice and worthy the winning.

Like the other sonnets and short lyrics Brower used to begin the course, Hopkins's "Spring" exhibited in its mode of address a progression that could be called dramatic. And behind the use of that word was Frost's unqualified insistence that "everything written is as good as it is dramatic." That this assertion, if seriously held and acted upon, would render "bad" much or most of Spenser, Milton, Blake, Whitman, Shelley, and Eliot, did not in the least deter Brower from his pedagogical conviction, since he was concerned not with arguing a case but with effectively getting a course into motion. For this purpose some poems "worked" better than others. It would not have done, on his reasoning, to usher in Hum. 6 with Wordsworth's "Resolution and Independence" rather than (as he in fact began the 1954 term) with "To a Butterfly." "Resolution" is surely a better—a more interesting, more various, more complicated—poem. It is also a poem of twenty stanzas and one hundred and forty lines, inconveniently long to work with, and containing moments of dubious poetic value. In other words, it was not as good a "teaching" poem as "To a Butterfly."

The "dramatic" model was what rationalized the choice of texts. That first fall the introductory weeks included, along with the poems, stories by Hawthorne in which matters of tone and narrative control could be inspected in microcosm and where analogies between fiction and poetry were explored. After that, and in some ways at the heart of the course, was a Shakespeare play, usually one of the great tragedies (*Othello* that term, although *Coriolanus* was a special teaching favorite of Brower's). Brower thought of a Shakespearian play as a "poetic drama," and in the introduction to *Beginning with Poems* he wrote: "In reading a play by Shakespeare [the student] can see, for example, that the man speaking the poem corresponds to the character in a play, that Shakespeare has his large metaphors just as Keats has his smaller ones." By thinking of this drama as not, essentially, composed of plots and characters and great thoughts, but rather language, metaphor, trains of imagery, and marvels of rhetorical performance, the notion of "dramatic" could be extended and deepened so as to present Shakespeare as the consummate imaginative designer of them all.

It was no accident that in a course that "privileged" (as some would now say) lyric poetry as the most essential kind of imaginative expression, the novel—a narrative of a certain length which has something wrong with it, as Randall Jarrell wittily defined it—was deferred until late in the semester. Nor was it accidental that the novels chosen (*The Europeans* and *The Great Gatsby*) were not only short (both under two hundred pages) but were ones in which matters of tone and metaphor played a key role. It would not have been appropriate for the course as Brower designed it to have ended with *Vanity Fair* or *Sons and Lovers* or *Sister Carrie*—just to name three good novels that never made the syllabus of Hum. 6. For the more a work threatened to qualify as a loose and baggy monster (Henry James's phrase about Russian novels) the less chance it had of finding a place in the rarefied, controlled atmosphere of Browerian close reading. His handout to the staff at the beginning of the course at one point declares, "A choice of poems is a choice of lives." One might judge, then, that the essential life of Hum. 6 was created at the cost of suppressing, through omission, kinds of lives less neatly organized than the "dramatic" lyrics, plays, and short novels making up the semester's reading.

Whatever criticisms of the course can be made along such lines, Hum. 6 was most carefully contrived *not* to be a purely New Critical exercise in the close reading of one text after another, with attention paid to nothing more than the words on the page. In the face of recent attempts to convince us that literary study in the 1950s was conducted on an arid plane in which all larger considerations—political, historical, biographical, theoretical—were declared illicit, it is important to insist how different was Brower's inquiry. His interest in what he called "historical context," and his bringing it into the course second semester as an explicit subject of concern, probably had a good deal to do with being trained as a classicist whose specialty as an English professor was eighteenth-century literature. His first published articles were about Dryden's use of Virgil and the "allusive irony" that characterized Dryden's mature style in his best satires, "Mac Flecknoe" and *Absalom and Achitophel*. But Brower's interest in historical context was more than a matter of elucidating the relation between the writer and some poetic forbear; he also recognized the importance, for any sort of full reading of a text, of placing it in relation to its larger social surroundings. Here Leavis's insistence that serious study of literature inevitably led outward into nonliterary fields was salutary. In notes to the staff concerning the relationship between interpretation and historical context, Brower attempted with some tentativeness to say what he meant by this context:

"Historical" is used here in the broadest sense, for any relationship made between the work and any item of knowledge assigned to a date. The context enters into interpretation in two ways . . . 1. as immediately relevant meaning, inseparable from the words of the text; 2. as part of the process of placing the seemingly timeless experience of reading. After reading the most timeless of poems, "Ode on a Grecian Urn," we realize on reflection that this kind of aesthetic experience was itself a creation of the nineteenth century.

Although Fielding's *Tom Jones* was the major text for study, the course began in the second term with further interpretation of poems —three weeks of reading and writing about Robert Frost's poetry. There were frequent reminders that Frost was preceded by a number of poets who wrote about birds and streams and "nature," and that to read Frost well it was necessary to experience the way literary tradition was alive and operative in him. Meanwhile the students were reading Fielding's eight-hundred-page novel, and in order to define the sort of reader *Tom Jones* assumed they were assigned selected sections from *The Iliad* as translated in different ages by Chapman, Pope, and Richmond Lattimore. They also read Pope's *Rape of the Lock* and considered the tradition of Pastoral, which Fielding and other eighteenth-century writers both delighted in and mocked (as in Gay's *The Beggar's Opera*). In addition to the heroic-pastoral predecessors one needed to read Fielding with reference to, there were Fielding's contemporaries—Chesterfield, Hume, and Samuel Johnson, to name three—who put forth or criticized moral attitudes in ways similar and dissimilar to how those attitudes appeared in *Tom Jones*. Brower referred to this concern as "the ideological context," and suggested it might be appropriate to include examples from Fielding's successors, such as Rousseau, and Rousseau's archenemy, Professor Irving Babbitt. (The last two never, in fact, showed up.)

I have doubts whether this aspect of the course (i.e., the attempt to view an individual work of art within contexts) "took" on the undergraduates the way the insistence on close reading did. Much of the context had to be laid out by Brower in his lectures or by the individual section leader in the smaller meetings, and tended to be expository material that one could take notes on. In my experience, Brower's best instruction (as was the case generally with Amherst English professors) was the sort on which you couldn't take many useful notes. So the planning of these "context" units may have been more impressive looking (as I have detailed one of them) than they in fact turned out to be during the semester. Indeed, it may be pedagogically impossible for a course to make its impact in more than one predominant way, especially if the ways seem, not exactly at odds with each other, but certainly distinct. After drumming in the lesson about close inspection of the poem and close tailoring of one's critical sentences about it, it was probably too much to say, "But don't forget history and biography and ideas and those mysterious entities called contexts." And since most of the staff lacked Brower's commitment to classical languages and literature (Youngren is the only one who comes to mind as also classically trained), there was simply less firsthand engagement with reading "Lycidas" or *Rape of the Lock* or *Tom Jones* in relation to Greece and Rome.

At any rate Hum. 6 soon prospered at Harvard; students continued to sign up for it, many of them realizing that it was distinctively and challengingly unlike the sort of broad humanities survey the other courses offered. My impression of things, incomplete as it was (I had accepted a job teaching at Amherst in the fall of 1958), was that the course was at its strongest during its first decade, up to roughly the fall of 1964, when Richard Poirier left to head the English department at Rutgers. During those ten years, and subsequent to the initial heavy concentration of Amherst graduates in the ranks of its instructors, the staff became more mixed, with especially significant contributions made by Paul de Man and by Anne Ferry and David Kalstone (this latter duo coedited the poetry anthology with Brower). Poirier's departure from the course, however (along with the usual entropy of such enterprises), was a most serious loss, since his lectures and exercises on fiction provided an experimental flair and original brilliance that were impossible to replace.

As someone who long participated in staff courses until they largely disappeared from Amherst English's departmental offerings, I have heard countless times the wise remark from students, "It all depends on who you have for section." No matter how stimulating or boring the lectures might be, a student's sense of a course is determined mainly by his relation with the "section person" who reads and comments on his papers. With his Amherst past in mind, Brower subordinated the large lecture to the small section and reduced the number of weekly lectures to one. Granting the justice of the student's remark then, that "it all depends," I want to supplement my account of what Hum. 6 looked like from the outside, with something of what happened in a particular section taught by an eager and imperfect young teacher—myself.

In the fall of 1956, when I joined the staff, Brower was on leave, replaced by his former colleague and friend and my Amherst teacher, Armour Craig. Things began in their usual way, with three weeks of short poems assigned mostly in paired units to demonstrate differences in the ways poets treated a subject. As the day approached on which I was to conduct my first section meeting, I experienced the to-be-expected mixture of dismay and panic and presumed that the only way to combat such feelings was to prepare myself to the teeth. The period of fifty minutes was to be divided between my returning the students' first short papers and making appropriate remarks about good and bad things they had done in them; then I would take them through one of the poems assigned for that first week, my purpose being to show them what a graceful "reading" looked like and to give them some confidence that they could in time perform similarly.

Instead of allowing them to choose the poem from the list of assigned ones, I did the choosing, figuring that the advantage in preparation would be more powerful than whatever might be gained through spontaneity. But the choice I made, of a venerable, even famous, short poem—Sir Philip Sidney's sonnet of recantation (as it has been called), "Leave me, O love"—proved unfortunate:

> Leave me, O love, which reachest but to dust;
> And thou, my mind, aspire to higher things;
> Grow rich in that which never taketh rust;
> Whatever fades, but fading pleasure brings.
> Draw in thy beams, and humble all thy might
> To that sweet yoke where lasting freedoms be;
> Which breaks the clouds, and opens forth the light,
> That doth both shine and give us sight to see.
> O, take fast hold! let that light be thy guide
> In this small course which birth draws out to death,

And think how evil becometh him to slide,
Who seeketh heaven, and comes of heavenly breath.
Then farewell, world; thy uttermost I see:
Eternal Love, maintain thy life in me.

It was a poem about as remote from the interests of a group of eighteen-year-old Harvard and Radcliffe freshmen as anything I could have selected. In the measured, even gravity with which it unfolds there are relatively few tonal changes to identify; the images are unsurprising, the manner hortatory and didactic. Once you get the point that there is an enormous difference between the love which reachest but to dust and the Eternal Love of the final line, you have the poem more or less blocked out.

At any rate I proceeded, in proper Brower fashion, to read it aloud, and then to move through it line by line, making observations ("Note that 'aspire' in the second line means literally to breathe in, thus we're prepared for the 'heavenly breath' of line twelve," etc.) and inviting students to break in with their own comments or questions. They did not break in, but sat there with perhaps respectful, certainly passive, and expressionless faces. If I hazarded a joke, I can't remember it and it wouldn't have done much for the situation Sidney's poem had helped shape. Looking today at my full class notes for the poem, I see, next to line eight ("That doth both shine and give us sight to see"), an awkward notation: "The new sight refers to both the object and the seer. The beams of the mind are replaced by heavenly beams which create a standard and allow man the possibility of following it." Did I *say* that? Perhaps not in those exact words, but close enough to preclude anything interesting happening in the class.

Probably no section meeting from my first year of teaching in Hum. 6 was as dead as that introductory session, and I would learn in later years not to worry about the stiffness endemic to any first meeting of a course. I do remember the inordinate length of time it took me to get through a set of short papers, what with commenting in the margins, commenting more fully at the end, and giving the product a grade. And I remember that, for someone who thought of himself as a humorous person and spent lots of time with people who had similarly humorous interests, my Hum. 6 classroom that first year was a pretty solemn place, even when the writing under consideration— *Walden,* say, or Frost's poems—was playful and extravagant. Our main texts, Shakespeare's *Coriolanus* and *Wuthering Heights* (along with the Frost and Thoreau), were splendid challenges to the young teacher, and I worked hard, but felt less satisfaction in the classroom results. Oddly enough, my most interesting teaching situation occurred with Jane Austen's *Emma*, a favorite text of Armour Craig's (he lectured splendidly on it) but not easily assimilated by the freshmen. A few of them were bold enough in section meeting to pronounce the book "irrelevant" to their lives, and I found myself bristling with annoyance, yet uncertain how to respond. How to meet such a charge, especially since it could not be done through the techniques of close reading? At least I could see no way to prove the book's relevance by tracing its subtle patterns of literary organization. The moment gave perhaps a foretaste of the late 1960s when the cry for relevance would be more loudly heard. In my attempt to combat the charge of irrelevance I tried to get them to make a relation between their society and Austen's. Didn't many of them come from small towns, provincial American outposts? What did they know of gossip or misunderstandings, assumptions that proved erroneous, conduct that was inappropriate to the "real" situation? The point was not that I convinced anybody to change his or her mind, but that I had been forced to enter an area of discussion and argument slightly murkier but less arid than the clean, well-lighted traversal of Sidney's sonnet had generated.

I continued to struggle in the second term, more or less keeping my head above water, though it must have seemed at times to the class that I was in danger of going under. Preparations to take my orals that spring were at odds with Hum. 6, since on one hand I was stocking my head with the right answers to give the august professors about Spenser and Christian humanism, while on the other trying to devise lively strategies for expediting and complicating students' responses to writers like Gibbon, Henry James, and Henry Adams. It probably shouldn't have been a shock when early in the next fall, the *Harvard Crimson*'s "Confidential Guide" to courses appeared and I found myself written about without enthusiasm as someone who in addition to failing to achieve high marks as a teacher was noted to be an "erratic" grader. The unkindest cut of all!

Probably any teacher has had the experience of moving from a first uncertain year in the classroom to a following one that is decidedly an improvement—where, more than occasionally, teaching becomes fun and not just for the one behind the desk. Such was my experience in a second and final year teaching Hum. 6, especially its spring term. I had gained some confidence in my classroom routines, and the attractiveness of both the books taken up and the students to whom I presented them assured me that I hadn't mistaken my vocation. That semester the reading list showed a new focus on modern, not to say modernist books: Joyce's *Portrait of the Artist* and sections from *Ulysses;* Lawrence's *St. Mawr;* Faulkner's "The Bear" and an extended unit on Yeats's poetry. These four major figures dwarfed the usual second-term focus on how Greece/Rome made itself felt in later English versions of Heroic and Pastoral. To be sure, students were asked to read *The Odyssey* in translation, along with *Ulysses,* and there was a final paper titled "Metamorphosis of a Myth," which asked them to look at a Yeats myth with reference to earlier uses of the same in Virgil and Milton. But what really counted that term were the encounters with major figures—Joyce, Faulkner, Lawrence, Yeats. Not accidentally this was also a term in which, through his own choice, Brower played less of a part than he usually did. He was finishing his big book on Alexander Pope and may not have minded stepping back a little and putting the course's reins in the capable hands of Poirier and de Man, the latter of whom had joined the staff that year. Poirier took charge of the lectures and exercises on Joyce's *Portrait* and *Ulysses* (*Dubliners* had been read during the first term, so students had some familiarity with Joyce); he was also responsible for selecting the works by Lawrence and Faulkner, both of which prominently display protagonists in search of "a world elsewhere" (to use the Coriolanus-inspired title of Poirier's book on American writers). What held that semester's texts together was their penchant for what Poirier called "stylistic imitation"—particularly with Joyce and with Joyce's hero, Stephen Dedalus, but with the others as well: Lawrence's mimicking of English society-talk in *St. Mawr* by adopting a narrative tone that both used and parodied it; Faulkner's providing Ike McCaslin, in "The Bear," with romantic-heroic poetry that is rhetorically vulnerable even as it moves him and moves us.

The semester concluded with a month-long study of Yeats: four lectures and eight section meetings. Putting de Man in charge of this block of classes resulted in an originality—not to say idiosyncracy— of approach absent from more recognizably Hum. 6-ish semesters. His artfully delivered lectures were organized so that each began with one of the four stanzas of Yeats's difficult late poem, "The Statues," and he used them as springboards into various aspects of Yeats's poetry. At the conclusion of the final lecture, de Man read aloud one of the last poems that ends

> "I am of Ireland,
>   And the Holy Land of Ireland,
>   And time runs on," cried she.
> "Come out of charity,
>   And dance with me in Ireland."

When he finished, the entire student population of the course burst into spontaneous applause, not something that was wont to occur in Hum. 6. De Man gave his modestly winning, slightly embarrassed smile, acknowledging the tribute. Meanwhile Poirier, whose lectures on Joyce (good as they were) had met with no such applause, leaned toward me, pretended to glower, and declared balefully, "Next time *I'm* going to lecture on poetry."

There was little or no talking down to students and no jollying them up. Poirier and de Man (especially the latter) were as difficult to follow in their lectures as they would prove to be in their professional writings, which is to say they pulled no punches for the students' sake and devoted all their intellectual energies to making complicated arguments about Joyce and Yeats. In their aggressive ways with books, they were more excessive than Brower, but by that same token more exciting. A lot was asked from these students and in return they gave a lot back, writing over the course of the term fifteen or so short papers or exercises with a longer one at the end and an interestingly difficult final exam involving Lawrence, Faulkner, Joyce, Yeats, and even Dickens (whose *Great Expectations* had been read in the first term). They did this without complaint, handed their papers in on time for the most part, and didn't whine when the grade received was below their expectations. When I hear, in the popular mythology, how "apathetic" students were supposed to have been in the 1950s, I think of the energetic way those Harvard and Radcliffe undergraduates grappled with difficult writers and texts. It was a good time to be studying literature, I'm convinced.

The fact that my experience with the eighteen students in my section was so much improved over the previous year's, had something to do with the presence of two attractive young women who seemed more or less pleased and engaged by my classroom efforts and whose approval helped make me feel I was doing something right. (Coming from all-male Amherst classrooms made the experience that much more vivid.) Both of them were recent graduates of the Putney School in Vermont and had been well instructed there, at least to the extent that when, early in the term, we gave the class an exercise on Wallace Stevens's "The Sense of the Sleight-Of-Hand Man," they professed acquaintance with other poems by Stevens. One of them, who quickly revealed herself to be the best writer in my section, asked me whether she could knit during class (this was a common practice during Harvard–Radcliffe lectures) and I felt rather authoritarian in saying that I wished she wouldn't. She ceased to knit but continued to turn in superb papers. At this point I hadn't thought much about the erotic potential of the teacher–student relationship — not the possibility that you might sleep with one of your students but more complicatedly, if that's possible, the difference it makes when your attitude toward a student is not sexually disinterested. Just married myself, I was trying to figure out how to behave as a husband rather than looking around for diversion. But I'm convinced that the charge these two Radcliffe students provided, impossible to measure, helped enliven my performance in class; and anyway, no one could talk about Joyce or Yeats or Lawrence without engaging, to some extent, in questions about sex and love. It was, at any rate, different from that first-class somber run-through of "Leave me, O love, which reachest but to dust," for all the similarity, in the abstract at least, of Sidney's concerns. In his poem about Freud, Auden called Eros a builder of cities; it may be a builder of teachers as well.

Looking back on Hum. 6, in the final chapter of *Poetry and Pragmatism*, Richard Poirier is at pains to emphasize the difference between Brower's version of close reading and more orthodox New Critical practices, as they went on at Yale and were codified in Brooks and Warren's *Understanding Poetry*. Poirier believes that in choosing selections for his introductory lectures and exercises, Brower consciously sought out pieces of writing that lacked the kind of "coherence" most teachers looked for and thus couldn't be magnified into large stable meanings to be written down irrevocably, fixed for all time. He tells the following anecdote about a Hum. 6 meeting at which I was present:

> One year [Brower] began the course with an exercise
> on a short poem by Edwin Muir which, as an exasper-
> ated newcomer to the staff complained, simply
> "doesn't come together." This only confirmed the
> wisdom of the choice for Brower, who said simply,
> "Well, let's see what they can do with it." "Do with
> it," not "get out of it." The question he liked to ask
> on this and other occasions was, again, simply "What
> is it like to read this poem?"—the very hardest of
> questions, and not one likely to encourage a search
> for coherent patterns.

This is certainly accurate in regard to Edwin Muir's "Then," an exas-
peratingly inchoate poem. But it's also the case that in the majority of
instances Brower chose examples that could be shown to have the
"coherent patterns" Poirier mentions here; he was miles away from
any deconstructionist ambition to discover the self-canceling contra-
dictions in any text and speak admiringly about how its language
undoes itself. Certainly Hum. 6, in asking students "What is it like to
read this poem?" invited them to make a metaphorical answer—if
metaphor, as Frost has it, is saying one thing in terms of another. And
to put the emphasis on what it is like to read a poem, rather than on
what coherent patterns can be identified in it, is to tilt "the interpretation of literature" (as Hum. 6 was called) just slightly away from a certain kind of interpretation—of "New Critical" readings—toward a
less authorized, freer response to the work. That tilt had the effect of
making less than a matter of solemn conviction the proposing of any
particular "reading" of a poem as definitive. Instead, it encouraged a
critical modesty by suggesting that a poem's strength had something
to do with the way it would abide, yet not yield to, our interpretive
schemes.

   This encouragement helped me become the kind of critic of poetry
I became, even to some degree in the dissertation I was about to begin.
Having passed my orals in the spring of 1957, I spent some weeks
deciding on a topic and with not too much agonizing came up with
Robert Frost, a choice that represented an assertion of Amherst values
and a desire to follow in the footsteps of Craig and Brower, who had
introduced me to the poet. There were also good objective reasons to

undertake such a project since, in 1957 and with Frost still alive, there had been few attempts to make an argument at length for the nature and value of his poetry. And I would be writing about poems I cared as much about as I did any I had read. At the time I didn't know that Brower was preparing to write a book on Frost. In agreeing to act as first reader (and adviser) for my dissertation, he said I was to go my own way and write the sort of criticism I felt happy writing. Most of his efforts in the direction of my pages, as I produced sections of the essay for his inspection, were aimed at lightening my touch, deflating sentences that had a touch of the pompous, or discouraging brow-furrowed commentary that made it sound as if I were unraveling the writings of Kant or Hegel. "Don't keep telling us what you're about to do," he advised me; "just go ahead and do it. And try to relax." He was a good critic of hyper-self-reflexivity, and he always held D. H. Lawrence's maxim in mind (used on more than one Hum. 6 assignment) to the effect that if it isn't any fun, don't do it. (From my second reader, the venerable Kenneth Murdock, I received nothing at all beyond politely mild approval.) Brower insisted that I have my own thoughts about Frost (to the extent that he hadn't already implanted them in me) and paid his attention to the sentence sounds I made in my writing.

In the fall of 1957, back at the stand to begin my fourth year as a graduate student, newly married, and with teaching and tutorial responsibilities I was beginning to feel more skillful in meeting, there were reports from time to time that such and such a university English department representative was coming to town to interview prospective candidates for teaching positions. It was made known to me through Douglas Bush's kindness that such a person from the University of Toronto was about to appear — would I be interested in being interviewed? The thought struck terror in me; partly because the University of Toronto seemed a giant step away from the Harvard scene I was accustomed to; mainly because I didn't want to think seriously about the future when I found living in the present so satisfactory. Since I could hold on to my teaching fellowship for another year, I said no thanks to the interview. But I couldn't be similarly cavalier in response to the phone call from Amherst College that came one night in late fall from Benjamin DeMott, then chairman of the English department. Would I come down to Amherst for an interview, with the likelihood that if it went satisfactorily I would be offered a teaching position there beginning the next fall? To say that this offer initiated a train of wholly consequential events is at best an understatement, but the offer clearly could not be refused. With only one way to go I made a date to drive back to the Fairest College and put myself on display.

VI
Home Again

Whether hiring practices in academia are more rational and equitable today than they were thirty-five years ago, or whether both are equally strange, beyond the pale of reason, is hard to say. Today when the English department at Amherst College agrees that it needs to hire a person whose field of concentration is, say, the English Renaissance, with special interest in Shakespeare and Spenser, the requested appointment has first to compete with those from other college departments. Should ours be approved, an official announcement is placed in the fall issue of *PMLA* (*Publications of the Modern Language Association of America,* the official organ of the profession) and in other visible places. Applications arrive over the course of a month and a half or so, perhaps amounting to as many as three hundred. These are inspected by a hiring committee, and a number of the more promising applicants are asked to send along samples of their writing. By the time the MLA convenes for three days just after Christmas, twenty to twenty-five candidates have been scheduled for half-hour interviews with the hiring committee. The four or five top prospects are then invited to the campus during January for a day or two in which they present a talk to the department, meet with individual members, and are interviewed by the dean or the president of the college. Late in January the department sits down to work out a preferential list, hoping that its favorites have not been snapped up by a competitor. Once we agree on a candidate, things conclude themselves, successfully or not.

All in all, it is an expensive, time-consuming operation, conducted in the interest of fairness, equal opportunity, and other admirable values. Of course the competition for jobs is absolutely fierce; an example from the current market, involving a former student of mine, may suggest just how fierce. The young man, who was not only a first-rate student of literature but a fine mathematician (he spent a year in graduate school mathematics before changing to English) and an excellent pianist, did his graduate work in English at Columbia, receiving his Ph.D. eight years after graduation from Amherst (it took me seven years, back in the 1950s). He then applied to some forty colleges and universities who had advertised openings in his field. These applications produced MLA interviews from just two of the schools; the two interviews yielded an invitation to visit Loyola University and a subsequent job offer, made (the candidate later found out) partly because his two competitors had given poor presentation-talks at their interviews. His situation was in no way exceptional; indeed, he was one of the fortunate winners in a game, which, these days, one is likely to lose.

No thought of losing entered my mind when I considered my prospective teaching career after Harvard, so it seemed no extraordinary stroke of good fortune but part of the order of things that I should receive the phone call from Chairman DeMott at Amherst. Although I had made but modest progress on my Frost dissertation, that was of no significant concern to the Amherst English department, any more than was my vagueness about what "field" I belonged in, or whether indeed I *had* a field. I wasn't being hired to offer a specialty, but as an Instructor (a rank that no longer exists, so lowly it was) who would teach three sections of two staff courses; it was all to their liking that I not make a fuss about teaching a course of my own. The Amherst interview promised to be anything but grueling; rather it was presented, by DeMott, as essentially a matter of my convincing the president of the college that I was a respectable, promising young man who would give his all to the communal enterprise. When tenure consideration came round, Amherst evaluated its candidates on three fronts: teaching, scholarship, and service to the community. In fact, it was really only the first of these that counted; many members of the Amherst faculty published little, but all were assumed to be active teachers, available and responsive to their students. Scholarship was distinctly secondary (there was, unlike the university ethos, no publish-or-perish syndrome), and service to the college community (committee work, etc.) was just icing on the cake. Once granted tenure, the only grounds on which one could be dismissed were flagrant (that is, sexual) misconduct. I had no aspirations in that direction. As for the dissertation, I was expected to complete it within a reasonable time, but unlike current practice it was unnecessary to have it "in hand" or even to be close to completing it at the time of hiring.

I drove over to Amherst one wintry morning in December 1957 — there would be a heavy snowstorm before the day was out and I was safely back in Cambridge — to be agreeably welcomed, in turn, by my old teachers, Baird, Craig, and Barber, while DeMott, whom by this time I had gotten to know, accompanied me to the interview with President Charles W. Cole. Cole was an economist who, since 1947, had presided over the New Curriculum, still going strong, it seemed, after ten years. DeMott told me that the president liked to display his across-the-board competence by challenging candidates in the terms of their own professed subject. President Cole was in fact very much like the president of Benton College in Randall Jarrell's *Pictures from an Institution:*

> At first President Robbins talked a little stiffly and warily, but then he warmed to himself. He liked to say, "The secret of good conversation is to talk to a man about what *he's* interested in." This was his Field Theory of Conversation. He always found out what your field was (if you hadn't had one I don't know what he would have done; but this had never happened) and then talked to you about it. After a while he had told you what he thought about it, and he would have liked to hear what you thought about it, if there had been time.

During a recent interview with a candidate for English who professed an interest in philosophy, Cole had asked him whether he preferred the earlier or the later Wittgenstein. The candidate was unable to come up with a satisfactory answer — at any rate he wasn't hired. But Cole spared me such questions, asking instead whether I had read any good academic novels in the past year or two. He had one by an American in mind and my mention of Kingsley Amis's *Lucky Jim* drew a blank. Otherwise he talked amiably about Amherst College — asked me, after glancing over my Harvard transcript, why I had received only a B+ in colonial American literature and accepted my admission that I had conceived a distaste for the subject. Nothing about Wittgenstein.

DeMott, who oddly enough attended the interview, sat silently with his head slightly downcast, and later allowed that I had acquitted myself adequately.

And that was basically that. In due course I received an official letter of appointment, at a salary of $4,800, later upped to $5,000 so as to make me feel there was presidential beneficence. No one asked to look at the dissertation pages I had written thus far, nor did the English department or the president request to see anything I had written during my years at Harvard. No one had any particularly significant advice to give me or in fact had any advice at all, aside from Baird's terse instruction before I headed off to talk to the president: *Speak up!* But perhaps the untroubled ease of the process is hardly surprising, for was it not a classic instance of the old-boy network at work? Baird, Craig, and DeMott were all Harvard Ph.D.'s, and Barber had been a Junior Fellow there; Brower, now a Harvard professor, had tendered a favorable report on my progress in graduate school. There was also the fact that I had established something like friendships with these mentors: Craig had attended my wedding the previous summer; I had played poker one evening at DeMott's, and paid a call on Baird at a visit to the college. Such actions, conducted without, I'm convinced, active intent to propose myself as a fit companion in the English department, must have carried a certain weight. This isn't to say that in order to be appointed one had to be a former student and in the Amherst–Harvard axis; indeed, that same fall, a non-Amherst Yale grad student, John Cameron, went through similar interview procedures and was also appointed. But neither of us competed against a slate of candidates; there was no need to say may the best man win, since there was no competition. Nor was there a question of what was "equitable": hiring transactions were swift, cheap, efficient, and polite.

AND Exclusionary. Willy

Nine years after the September I entered it as a freshman, the college had not significantly changed. There was a signal addition to the faculty in the shape of a psychologist who also acted as student counselor, providing an ear for troubled undergraduates and teaching a "gut" course titled "Marriage and the Family." Otherwise things remained as they had been. Amherst's enrollment had designedly shrunk from 1,189 to 1,025, while tuition had risen from a yearly $1,090 (this included room and board) to $1,732, a figure about which no one complained. The English department consisted of twelve full-time teaching members (DeMott was on leave for the year), and its offerings in total took up less than four pages in the college catalogue. With the required curriculum still very much in place, the staff courses in Composition and in Introduction to Literature, (for freshmen and sophomores, respectively) were of primary significance, with a small selection of upper-level courses: Renaissance literature, American literature, modern poetry, twentieth-century fiction, one two-semester history of English literature and one of American, as well as a semester's Introduction to Literary Scholarship required of all honors candidates. There was, as always, a heavy emphasis on student writing in all courses, especially the staff ones. Creative writing (more chastely spoken of in the catalogue as Advanced Composition) was available, in a very limited format, to undergraduates who revealed some aptitude for producing poems and stories. To students who felt the English department was insufficiently encouraging of original composition, it was pointed out that a number of graduates of the college — among the most prominent of whom were the poets Richard Wilbur and James Merrill — had become admired and published without the benefit of courses in creative writing. Rolfe Humphries, a distinguished translator and poet, taught advanced composition as well as a course in Lucretius. President Cole's recent attempt to bring into the department a little more of what he thought was important contemporary critical thought had resulted in the two-year experiment of hiring Alfred Kazin to teach American literature. This worked out badly, with the department feeling they had been pressured and Kazin feeling like the unwanted outsider from the big city. (In his autobiographical *New York Jew*, his comments about Amherst, college and town, are uniformly negative.) Kazin had now departed and in his place stood Leo Marx, on the verge of making a name for himself in the field of American Studies with his important work *The Machine in the Garden*.

These older, tenured professors comprised the top half of the English department. The other half, the one I joined, consisted of six untenured instructors and one assistant professor in his final year. In a year or so, when another instructor arrived, we would become labeled by a clever colleague as the seven dwarfs. We lived in each other's laps, more or less, sharing offices and carrying on conversations with students at adjacent desks. Most of us rented small compact apartments in a residential "compound" the college had recently built for young faculty (rent was sixty-five dollars a month, and a free garbage can and snow shovel were provided). Before and after classes we would assemble in something called the departmental office, really a sort of locker room, and give each other words of encouragement ("Knock 'em dead!") before a class or pronounce upon its successes and failures afterward. The dwarfs taught staff courses almost exclusively, as many as three a term, and there were two weekly staff meetings in which we joined together to make assignments, suggest possible ways of teaching the book in question, and generally push things around in discussion, sometimes in heated argument. This atmosphere encouraged the already competitive spirit the untenured maintained toward one another. On the surface, and in the better parts of ourselves, we were friends; but that didn't exclude the instinct for survival, and since we couldn't all survive at Amherst the competition was keen. Not surprisingly, postmeeting headaches and digestive problems, doubtless helped along by strong drink and cigarettes, were routine. Nobody ran or walked much or exercised in any way except for the occasional game of tennis, another field in which to display the instinct for survival.

It was a male world, Amherst College in the late 1950s, as much for the faculty as the undergraduates. The main social vehicle for celebrating or at least encouraging communal solidarity was the faculty club, a modest building next to the gym with facilities for bridge and snacks, three pool tables, and a downstairs area where on selected Saturday evenings during the semester a dinner was held (the club did not regularly serve meals). These dinners were an object of mixed regard — of derision and even hatred on the part of some. But it would have been unthinkable for a young instructor not to have attended at least some of the dinners, with their lavish portions of prime rib, filet mignon, and lobster salad at the last meeting in the spring. For reason of frugality or caution or both, no wine was served; in fact, liquor was not consumed inside the club. The answer to this absence was an hour or so of hastily consumed manhattans or martinis (staples of all 1950s cocktail parties) at someone's house before heading to the food. There was an after-dinner speaker, usually from the faculty, who delivered a brief talk. But the atmosphere was unintellectual, boisterous, and carnivallike, as these mild-mannered, slightly tanked-up academics — having successfully navigated the previous six days in the classroom — let themselves go, more or less, for an evening. The occasional guest taken to these dinners by a faculty member was invariably less than impressed by the communal behavior; later, in postmortems, we reflected on the boorishness of our colleagues and the inanity of the whole operation.

During these faculty club Saturday nights one's spouse, if one had a spouse, was expected to take care of the small children or perhaps have supper with another similarly placed woman, her spousal function being that of—and the term was used heavily—a Faculty Wife. Faculty wives were regularly asked, at cocktail parties or other gatherings, what department they belonged to, as if they along with their husbands taught English, French, physics. They were automatically enrolled in their own organization called the Ladies of Amherst, which met from time to time for luncheon, tea, a lecture or musical event. These meetings were always held during the day, the idea presumably being that in the evening the wives would be making supper for their husbands and children. Occasionally a young woman rebelled and declared that she had no interest in joining the Ladies of Amherst. Such rebelliousness was a sign, perhaps combined with others, of not "fitting in." For a faculty wife not to fit in wouldn't necessarily seal the fate of her nontenured spouse, but it couldn't have enhanced that spouse's reputation as a loyal member of the community.

Not long after I arrived at Amherst, the novelist Alison Lurie published her first book, *Love and Friendship*, which was read even by people who did not think of themselves as especially literary, since it was an "Amherst novel." Lurie was at the time married to Jonathan Bishop, who had recently served in Amherst's English department before taking a job at Cornell. As a Faculty Wife, Lurie kept her eyes and ears open for material that she then worked into the novel. In *Love and Friendship* the heroine's spouse is a member of the Language and Literature department at Converse College (Amherst's library was called Converse) who teaches in a freshman English course that is a parody version of Amherst's English 1: absurd questions are put to the students by eccentric, rather silly professors who haven't a clue themselves about how to answer them. Against such a background of folly, the wife's liberation into adultery is to be regarded with a good deal of sympathy, especially since her inadequate husband has a very bad, fully described head cold, for a stretch of the novel. In fact, Lurie's sense of the quixotic course taught at Converse was but a slightly heightened version of what many members of the faculty thought went on in Baird's English 1. The fact that, just as when I took it in

1949–50, no books were read and student papers were the sole materials for classroom discussion seemed in itself rather odd; and the off-
beat nature of the assignments could easily be mocked or denigrated
by those outside the course, and sometimes by those inside it as well.

My first teaching semester at Amherst the English 1 assignments
were ostensibly about the activity of paying attention, and the opening
sequence of exercises kept drilling at the students to tell us what it
meant to say "I paid attention" or "I failed to attend" or "I shifted my
attention" or "My mind wandered." The usual response to the question of what it meant to pay attention was to substitute a synonym
such as "I concentrated" or "I focused on the object"; at which point
there were more questions: what did you *do* when you "concentrated," when you "focused"? After a few variations on this theme, we
switched the vocabulary by introducing the statement "I see what you
mean, but I don't agree with you." What did *that* mean, and what was
the difference between saying it and saying "I see what you see" or "I
see what you mean" when you really didn't see it and didn't mean
what you said? As things proceeded relentlessly (three times a week,
that is) it became evident at least to some students that we were
engaged with matters such as the adequacy of words to express our
inner experience; or the difference between "out there" and "in here";
or the shifting, ever-changing contexts of situation, perspective and
motive; or the notion of a system (like the library's Dewey Decimal)
and how one used it; or the area of "inexpressible" experience (a re-
curring word in the course) in relation to what could be expressed.

The final long paper featured a quotation from Shelley:

> How vain it is to think that words can penetrate the
> mystery of our being! Rightly used they may make
> evident our ignorance of ourselves, and this is much.

What did they think about this statement? How, after thirty-three
assignments, did they now conceive of the relation between words and
being? And how much did they know of themselves and of how much
they were ignorant? How much was "much," anyway? The final exam
explored similar matters more playfully, as students were asked to distinguish between areas of their life in which they normally made mistakes and ones in which they normally did not. How, upon reflection,
did they hope to go about reducing the area in which mistakes were
normal? If they did not expect to reduce that area (in a final question),
"How do you propose to go on living?" The exam was to be completed

in two hours and students were directed: "Make your paper come out somewhere."

But no description of the vocabulary and sequences of assignments can suggest how it felt to teach English 1 day by day, week by week. It was totally consuming, something one could never forget about even on Thanksgiving or the brief holiday afterward. As an untenured dwarf I taught two sections of the course, which meant forty students in all plus a slightly smaller section in the literature course. The freshmen wrote thirty-three times over the course of the term; this amounted to 1,320 short papers, plus forty longer final papers and forty final exams. The two composition sections alternated in Monday-Wednesday-Friday and Tuesday-Thursday-Saturday sequences; at each class the papers students had turned in two days previously were returned, with marginal comments and a final longer comment, and without a grade (though I kept track in a notebook of how each individual was doing). If by some (unthinkable) chance an instructor had not finished reading the current batch of papers by class time, he then had no class to give, since they provided the whole substance of the discussion. Naturally, then, one finished the set of papers. But it was a burden, and the single respite on Saturday night made reading a set on Sunday that much more difficult. In looking at my notebook for that first year, I'm impressed, even appalled, by my diligence in keeping a continuous record of how X or Y had "done" on assignment two or assignment twenty-two. And in these days when, for example, forty-three percent of Harvard undergraduates receive a grade of A– or above in their courses, I'm nothing less than amazed to note the final grade list for one of my sections:

English 1 — Sec. 8

Date	Jan. 23, 1959				
Instructor	Mr. Pritchard				
Arbuthnot D H	69		Lehr J L	87
Bellows P H	71		Mosshammer A A	78
Braemer R J	75		Pasmantier M	75
Clark B	90		Perlmutter J F	72
Cronnell B A	74		Pochoda D J	88
Ditzian M D	80		Siegler R	84
Gesing R W	74		Vanags I	85
Hahn E C	67		Van De Graaff M	86
Hanford T T	69		Younger D W	72
Jones P R	80			

One student, just barely, broke into the nineties; three of them didn't even break into the seventies — and all had handed in all their work, so it was not a question of uncompleted papers. How on earth did I feel able to evaluate Mr. Hahn's (the low man on the totem pole) worth at precisely 67? Yet no one complained about his grade, nor were these grades out of line with what colleagues were handing out in English and in other departments.

I have said that the competitiveness among the untenured English department members was keen, though as gentlemen we more or less tried not to acknowledge it. The most outspoken of the lot, certainly the most provocative, was Roger Sale, who after being denied tenure at Amherst went on to a distinguished career as a literary and cultural critic. Sale had come to Amherst the year before I did and took me under his wing, though that was not a particularly comfortable place to be. One morning, about two weeks after the opening of first semester when he was giving me a ride in his car, he suddenly turned and asked, "Had a good class yet with the freshmen?" I tried to roll with this one and allowed as how, yes, I thought I'd had a pretty good class on assignment five or whatever it was. "I haven't," Sale responded, immediately making me feel like the sort of insufficiently critical horse's ass who thought he had had a "good class." He then described how, the other morning in his class, he had talked about Ted Williams in order to make some point about the matter of paying attention. Ted Williams! Why hadn't I thought of that, instead of dragging into class the quotation from William James's *Psychology*? My only response to Sale's coup was eventually to make use, not of Ted Williams but — in another context — of Rita Hayworth as an example of an absolute (the absolutely beautiful woman). In today's classroom this example would no doubt bring swift retribution, and not on philosophical grounds.

By November I was in trouble with both sections of English 1. My inexperience in teaching such a course with no comforting book or books at the center of things led on occasion to empty spaces that I tried to fill by being provocative, overdoing the teacher's privilege of proclaiming from on high. As I felt less certain of my bearings, the temptation was to become more shrill — to try to get by on improvisational moves that failed to fly. Members of both classes decided there was a doctrine or dogma behind the assignments and that I was — as one brave fellow named Mosshammer wrote on his paper — the "impeccable expounder" of it. This was not a good position for a

[handwritten margin notes:]
AND NOTHING BUT GENTLEMEN, THUS REDUCING THE COMPETITION BY ONE WHOLE GENDER.

WILLY TRIES SOME (MALE) DONNISH WIT.

teacher to find himself in, even though in neither class was the feeling of alienation total. Indeed, one stout fellow, working along uncomplainingly toward a C, encountered me as I headed into the barber shop downtown and let me know that "not all the members of the class" felt I was a tyrant! I was touched, grateful for a solicitude I very much stood in need of.

The "boot camp" atmosphere of English 1 was only one of the complaints made about it. There was more than a sprinkling of hostility toward it among disaffected freshman — sometimes bright, dissident ones — and among faculty members who thought it was the joke Alison Lurie had made it out to be in her novel. Members of the philosophy department claimed we were talking irresponsibly about matters that should have been their concern, such as the notion of the "inexpressible." Psychologists, if they had cared, might have found our engagement with the matter of paying attention to be thoroughly unscientific. Some students were convinced we were a crew of nihilists, out to deny all purpose and meaning to the world outside their heads, or at least insisting that purpose and meaning were wholly a matter of how words formulated them and carried them into action. At any rate, in and out of the classroom the course produced argument, sometimes heated. These flames were fanned by my tendency, and that of others on the staff, to adopt a tone of combative teasing, frequently inflected with sarcasm. One of our staffmates who arrived soon after me was notorious for writing "Mayonnaise" in the margin next to student sentences he thought silly or pompous. The liberal crossing out of words, of whole sentences and whole paragraphs, must have had an abrasive effect on boys who had been praised in high school for their prowess in "English."

Had there been women in the classroom at that time (Amherst would not become coeducational until the 1970s) would it have made a difference? Could we have been as playfully aggressive if girls had been sitting there along with the boys? It is hard to say, though I suspect — for worthy or unworthy reasons — that I would have modulated my tone and scaled down the verbal abuse of the papers. Much of our time in class was spent analyzing examples from papers that I judged bad: slack, slovenly, simpering, slick, and so forth. Anonymity was always preserved, but the anonymous one sitting there knew that his effort was being torn to pieces, and he could hardly have been untouched. Yet I received no bomb threats and no one ever took a swing at me. I never even had to deal with an irate parent calling up to find out why Phil was doing so poorly in English. In fact, it wasn't until many years later, when grade inflation became the order of the day, that I encountered a graduating senior who wanted to know why I had given him an A– instead of the A he was certain he deserved and had received in his three other courses. Amherst College in the fifties, and much of the sixties, was a place where you expected relatively low grades: a place, for example, where a freshman who did poorly on the physics exam (as many did) could be awarded a 42 or 53 to be averaged in with his other marks for the term. It was all part of becoming a man.

Someone once said that the world of a Jane Austen novel is so small, so provincial and limited, so uniform in the assumptions its occupants made about one another, that it was possible for interesting mistakes to be made. Something analogous obtained in the Amherst English department when I joined it in 1958. True, we were divided into the tenured and untenured, but we were all white, male, WASP (with the exception of Leo Marx, the first tenured Jewish professor in the department), East Coast educated—at Yale and Harvard, Amherst and Swarthmore—and married, often with children. Someone in the 1990s might look at this wash of similarity and judge that, naturally, unanimity of opinion would follow from it. Nothing could be more mistaken. Who with a reasonably strong mind, a functioning ego, and a love of literature and teaching would be content merely to agree with his colleagues? Disagreement among us came out more strongly in the introductory literature course than in the composition one, since the literature course was about reading books, and we all had firm opinions about *Macbeth* or Keats's odes or James's *The Bostonians*.

The logistics of English 21 (Introduction to Literature) were similar to English 1 in that someone was appointed chairman who took charge of the general shape of the term. But unlike English 1 the chairman of English 21 was not responsible for making up all the assignments; rather he solicited book titles from staff members and then tried to present a package that would make sense as a whole and more or less please—at least not offend—everyone. In the summer of 1959 Benjamin DeMott, as course chairman, invited us to name some books we might like to teach that coming fall. A number of us suggested Lawrence's *St. Mawr*, to which DeMott responded with strong reservations. He didn't agree with Leavis's wholly admiring account of the "dramatic" integrity of *St. Mawr* but instead saw in it "carelessness, statement without presentation, an arrogance or contempt that seems to direct itself purposefully, consciously at the sensitive reader, impatience with the finicky-heroical labor of thickening the social air, discomforting ignorance about how to represent convincingly the accents and attitudes that the audience is to be taught to detest—in fine laziness about 'essential work.'" Nevertheless he called it a powerfully affecting piece of writing and agreed that we should teach it, along with other late-Lawrence material—*Etruscan Places* and some polemical essays. Then he proposed that we move to Lawrence from someone who was by contrast "all art and a yard deep"—John Keats, in his letters and odes.

Since we had taught *St. Mawr* in Hum. 6 during my final term in the course, it was probably my instigation that brought it into the Amherst orbit. Here the procedure was for a member of the staff to produce, at the appropriate staff meeting, what was designated as the "poop" on the upcoming book or writer—Keats or Lawrence or whomever. DeMott provided us with three single-spaced, strongly argued pages on Lawrence, which sparked a debate (referred to earlier) about *St. Mawr* among the staff as lively and instructive as any I remember in or out of the classroom. It was as if there were no higher stakes in the world than deciding how to present Lawrence to our students. Never mind that some of us were untenured, others tenured and eventually to be sitting in judgment on us; the argument was an example of what members of a department could be at their best, when the usual social chat, academic witticisms and backbiting, were dropped and in their place people stood up and spoke their minds about the moral and artistic values of a piece of writing. It was upsetting at the time—such active, potentially violent disagreement among colleagues. It now seems all the more valuable to me when the much prized diversity of my English department means that most of the time we are as ships that pass in the night, politely keeping our distance while pursuing our various specialties and projects with little common turf for argument. Whatever argument there remains is directed increasingly at how the turf should be staked out and divided, so we wrangle about administrative matters rather than literature, scheduling rather than D. H. Lawrence. The current state of things is reminiscent, ironically, of Harvard English in the 1950s, where department members kept hands off one another's territories—in a phrase of Gerald Graff's, "taking cover in coverage."

The argument about *St. Mawr* in the staff literature course and the arguments about how best to run the composition course could be seen as a vindication of one man's vision of what an English department should look like. The man was Theodore Baird, who had come to Amherst in 1927 and was entering his final decade of teaching at the college. Baird has recalled that when he came to Amherst, members of the department (then three full professors and three instructors) simply did not communicate with one another. At least the full professors didn't, contenting themselves rather with civility. Baird said he respected these men in their individual ways but disdained their avoidance of serious argument. As he put it, he had no interest in simply going to the opening-of-the-year departmental cocktail party (wives invited) at which the social level of things was the only one. He thought instead that professors should ask each other, "What do you think you're doing as a teacher?" It was this sort of conversation — mainly in the context of staff courses, but on a daily basis within the small world of the English department of thirty years later — that Baird encouraged and promoted. Indeed, he insisted on it, and if a man came up for tenure with a record of never having stuck his neck out (skating along politely on the social level), he would be unlikely to have Baird's support.

Throughout his career, as I observed it, he kept saying things to people's faces rather than behind their backs; this made him an unsettling presence, but also an exciting one. On occasions in my early years at the college he said things to my face that, to put it mildly, derailed me; each had to do with one of the staff courses that, in a particular semester, I had been asked to direct and provide assignments for. His distaste for Joyce's *Dubliners*, in particular for the ending of its final story, "The Dead" (which I admired and had assigned an important place in the literature course), led to a correspondence between us that went on all through the summer before we were to teach the book. Baird's main focus was always "What do you think you are doing as a teacher of English?" which could be translated into "How are you going to spend those four class hours we've allotted to X or Y?" To answer this question you had to speak up, act as if you knew what you were doing. The reason he was particularly committed to the composition course — beyond the fact that it was his brainchild — was that it forced instructors to be especially resourceful and inventive, day after day, about what they did in class. As he liked to put it, when teaching a course in one's "field," minutes could be filled by talking to students about the idea of kingship in Shakespeare's *Henry IV*, or drawing on the blackboard to illustrate how Yeats conceived of the gyres. (Actually I couldn't do either of these at all well.) But in English 1 there was nothing to fall back on except the sentences students had produced in response to the previous assignment.

Something like an Emersonian self-reliance was encouraged or demanded; one of its antitheses, so it seemed, was institutional cooperation, whether with other departments in the college, other colleges in the so-called four-college area (soon to be five, with the coming of Hampshire College), or academic professionalism as represented by the Modern Language Association and by university conferences and symposia. Baird's vision of the uniqueness of this small college, Amherst, was informed by an ironic distrust of the visionary, as it expressed itself in large-minded schemes for reform, for "improvements." Even the Amherst curriculum held little interest for him outside of the chance it provided, in the year-long composition course, to make his mark as an educational force. If it were put in "educational" terms, he would have been likely to scoff, to declare that education didn't work and that all he really cared about was the fun of being inventive, of making assignments that asked questions that had not been asked before. He had no love for Ezra Pound and no interest in Confucius, but he was surely a believer in the Poundian–Confucian slogan, Make It New. For Baird, that was the only way to make anything.

In my first few years at Amherst I had very little to do with colleagues in English at Smith or Mount Holyoke or the University of Massachusetts. Whatever *they* did by way of English teaching could scarcely have been, I was certain, as radical as what went on in Amherst classrooms. And, indeed, there was nothing comparable, in our neighboring institutions, to the communal argument that went on in our staff courses. In a similar way, I never thought of looking toward the MLA as a scene for potential self-broadening or advancement. That sort of thing was for others less favored in their local arrangements than I figured myself to be. For it seemed that everything was here, on the Amherst scene, to be discovered and worked at. There were no greener pastures elsewhere — after all, was this not the paradise of my undergraduate experience? I felt myself favored, smiled upon, one who had been invited to come back to the place of his growing up, and I was made to feel welcome by my teachers in the English department and by others in the college. When a person on the outside would ask if it weren't complicated to return home and assume a place among the elders who had instructed me, I agreed that, yes, it certainly was complicated. But in my heart it seemed in the order of things.

Beginning in September 1958, I taught five academic years, three courses each term, until I was granted a sabbatical for the year 1963–64. During that time I was also, in DeMott's word, declared a "keeper," that is, someone judged worthy of being accorded tenure. One did not actually get tenure until one became an associate professor; what I was granted used to be known as presumptive tenure, or, as we dubbed it, presumptuous tenure. Some of my fellow dwarfs failed to make the cut and were, in the gentle phrase, "let go" (being let go is to getting fired as passing on is to dying). Roger Sale, whose being "let go" was a complicated piece of injustice, insisted on telling people that he had been fired. Sale was too much for the Amherst community and for some of the members of the English department. He yelled, threw erasers at students in his class, and caused one veteran professor of history to move out of his office because of the noise emanating from Roger's classroom across the hall. He offended some people; he offended me, on occasion, when I would wake up in the morning in the apartment building adjacent to his and, while worrying about the freshman section I had to teach, would hear him whistling "Haunted Heart" as he started up his reliable old Chevy. He was all set to go and *surely* would teach a better class than I. But fueled by envy and resentment I arose and did my best.

By Saturday noon when the week's classes ended, you felt you had done a piece of work. On the Saturday that ended my first week of Amherst classes, I simply went to bed after lunch, slept all afternoon, and still felt tired at the end of it. But as a rule I tried to make Saturday afternoons a respite from thinking about the set of papers due to be handed back Monday morning. I made it a policy at least to read a chapter of some new novel or old classic that had nothing at all to do with my current teaching. Turning to Iris Murdoch's latest or an account of some remote phenomenon like the Oxford Movement (as treated in Geoffrey Faber's book) was restorative and reminded me that there was a wider world than our intense one of classes, staff meetings, and papers. But most of the time that little world was enough. My wife and I did not own a television until October 1962 (we had rented one to watch the Kennedy convention of 1960), when my mother, out of pity, bought us one. It arrived at the time of the exciting 1962 World Series between the Yankees and the Giants and I suddenly ran into a conflict between an afternoon game and a departmental staff meeting. There was no way I could skip the meeting since cutting meetings for any reasons but serious ill health was unthinkable. But I remember feeling, really for the first time, that I would prefer to have been watching the ball game rather than my colleagues.

Over time I was allowed in the second semester to teach a course of my own and I managed to inherit modern poetry because Cesar Barber was on leave (he would soon depart Amherst for good) and no one else wanted to teach the course. Yeats, Frost, Eliot, Stevens, and others — it was a challenge I spent most of the summer on, outlining classes, reading the poets and critics, preparing myself to perform in a way different from the question-and-answer procedure of staff courses. The students in modern poetry wrote a lot of papers and were scrupulous about coming to class, and it was unthinkable that one would not appear for the final examination. One student, however — a rather excitable and talented actor — did not. His absence was immediately apparent to me, and as the rest of the class began to write in their blue books I phoned the dean's office, reporting that Mr. Timothy Colvin had failed to show up. The dean — still the same man who had informed me, some years back, that I would not be welcome on the campus over the summer ("Mr. Pritchard, Amherst is not a summer resort") — took matters into his own hands by heading over to the Beta Theta Pi house where Mr. Colvin was presumably still in bed. Indeed he was, and he soon shuffled into the classroom, somewhat the worse for wear. Such were the paternal attentions at one time paid its sons by alma mater. Truly a piece of ancient history, or so it feels in relation to anything that could happen in a college today.

My first solo course was fairly successful; the second was a disaster. I had decided to offer a survey of eighteenth-century English poetry, more specifically a course that began with four weeks of Pope, ended with four weeks of Wordsworth, and (sandwiched in between the masters) included short looks at various minor figures. It never occurred to me that eighteenth-century English poetry might not be a drawing card for a course, especially with my relatively untested name on the sign-up sheet. Nonetheless, five students elected it (one of them dropping out along the way), and we met in a dreary, airless basement room at noon, three times a week, to contemplate such figures as Anne

Finch, Countess of Winchilsea, James Thomson, and William Cowper
— minor poets not much less palatable to students than the "major"
ones, Pope and Wordsworth. In October of 1962, just as we were in the
midst of Pope, the Cuban missile crisis began to unfold. For me it was
the first major impingement on the tiny classroom world of a wider
public momentousness, and some faculty members decided to take
time out from their classes to discuss the matter with students,
answer questions, perhaps assuage anxieties. My anxieties, which
were extreme on that Monday noon, would not be assuaged by anything I could possibly contribute about the missile crisis (I had nothing
to contribute), so we spent the hour on Pope's "Epistle: To a Lady":

> See how the world its veterans rewards
> A youth of frolic, an old age of cards.
> Fair to no purpose, artful to no end,
> Young without lovers, old without a friend.
> A fop their passion, but their prize a sot;
> Alive, ridiculous, and dead, forgot.

I have no idea whether the four students in attendance that day were
as grateful for Pope as I was, but I am certain he was a better presence
in the classroom than either President Kennedy or Premier Khrush-
chev would have been.

Except for my very first semester, when some students in the composition course rebelled at what they thought to be my overzealous
expounding of "dogma," I had no trouble dealing with undergraduate
classroom manners. The rather awful fashion of "Sir"-ing the professor was still in evidence (some students managing to make that "Sir"
sound like an insult, or at least a taunt), but politeness was the order of
things. Only once did I rise up and dismiss a student from the room: he
was a scrawny ex-Marine veteran known to everyone as Eric the Rat,
famous, it was said, for living in a room so filthy that the maids (in
their last days of college service) refused to clean it. The Rat had once
been discovered, by a professor about to teach his 10 A.M. English 1
section, asleep on the podium, decked out with the autumn leaves he
had accrued in a night ramble through the woods. A sophomore when
I taught him in the literature course, he surprised me in his first paper
on a poem of Ben Jonson's by referring time and again to "Ben": "In
line three Ben uses . . ." or "Ben pulls off a masterstroke of wit." I
remembered there had been a convention at Harvard among certain

older professors of English of referring to Jonson by his first name, and I thought that perhaps the Rat had somehow gotten onto this convention, young though he was. But when in the next paper he consistently referred to Shakespeare as "Bill," I decided there was something else at work. First-name use was scarcely insubordination, however; that came in a class on *The Rape of the Lock* in response to my asking him what he would "call" the poem. "I'd call it garbage," the Rat jauntily replied, provoking me to declare, "Then you'd better leave the class." He did so without a murmur and nobody seemed particularly to mind.

In April 1960 I handed in my Harvard dissertation—on paper that was required to possess at least fifty percent "rag content"—and received the doctoral degree at Harvard's June commencement. Champagne was provided for the successful candidates. Now the father of a small son and prey to a mysterious, itching rash on my face, I set about during the ensuing hot summer revising the dissertation in hopes of publication. This endeavor had nothing to do with my career as a teacher at Amherst, but increasingly I found myself less immune to the lure of publishing than I had presumed. Part of that lure was provided by seeing myself in print for the first time. The college alumni magazine, which had a review section of books by alumni, invited me to assess Richard Poirier's book on comedy in Henry James's early novels. At the same time a new periodical subsidized by the four colleges (the *Massachusetts Review*, still in existence) suggested that I turn part of my Frost dissertation into an article for their pages. Soon afterward there followed a couple of other pieces: an essay for the Brower–Poirier collection *In Defense of Reading*; and a review of a new book on Joyce.

This modest output—two essays gleaned from a dissertation, and a couple of reviews—was surely not an example of someone getting off to a fast start in the professional world of English studies. It might have just been laziness or the lack of much to say, always reasonable excuses for not getting a lot of writing done. But being a part of the Amherst English department had a lot to do with feeling no need to publish; indeed, it may even have cultivated an actual disinclination to do so. Baird and Craig, my major mentors, had published sparingly, seemingly satisfied with teaching and extensive reading. There was a sense in the air that Amherst English was not bound by the same rules that prevailed in most academic establishments; one would not be judged on whether the University of Arizona Press had accepted one's book on kingship in Shakespeare's plays. I tried to follow my teachers by reading—if not widely at least determinedly—in English and American fiction and poetry, much of it contemporary work. I also read music criticism (jazz and classical), some philosophy, autobiography, history, and political, Hollywoodish, or professional sports gossip of all sorts. One could, having been granted tenure, make an agreeable life out of activities in the classroom and the study, in addition to whatever else was needed to spice up the recipe.

Those few published essays and reviews, however, had their effect, not on an audience out there eager for more, but upon the inner man who, given a taste of print, had found it too heady to resist. There was the assumption when I came to Amherst that one was supposed to have a "field." But I was uncertain what my field was or even whether I wanted to become a specialist in anything particular. So I spent a lot of time reading modern poets, novelists, critics—could one make a "field" out of that? I wasn't sure. It was Benjamin DeMott who provided me with an example of diligent application, outside the classroom, to writing sentences other than those he put on student papers or in staff directives. DeMott owned a small Renault that was seen parked outside the building where he had his office, not just during the day but at times when most everybody else had gone home—Friday night, Saturday afternoon, Sunday morning. He was beginning, successfully, to flood the quarterlies and monthlies with lively reviews of new books and with reports on the contemporary cultural scene. To make a literary career it seemed one had somehow to move beyond Amherst. When asked at a meeting for new faculty what there was to do outside the classroom and on the weekend, DeMott advised newcomers to head, by car or train, for New York or Boston. This evidently was his antidote to provinciality, if not exactly what those hoping to build a stronger sense of the Amherst College Community (as it was called) had in mind.

My reaching out to the metropolis was less a matter of getting on the train than of inviting metropolitan critics I admired to come to Amherst and lecture. To the best of my knowledge I wasn't consciously "furthering my career," but wanted to show to my colleagues and students examples of what excited me in certain kinds of criticism. To this end I brought onto campus Lionel Trilling; the film critic Stanley Kauffmann; Whitney Balliett, jazz critic for the *New Yorker*; John Simon, beginning his career as an all-purpose reviewer (he spoke about recent poetry when he talked at Amherst); Bernard Haggin; and for an extended visit of a few days, Kenneth Burke. There were others, but these were perhaps the most notable. The train station at nearby Northampton still functioned: I remember meeting Trilling there and picking up Kauffmann on a glittering, cold January afternoon the day after our second son was born. My wife and I gave parties after the lectures, partly because it was a way of ensuring attendance at the talk, but mainly because we enjoyed giving them. Some members of the department must have looked upon my behavior as evidence that I was perhaps getting a bit beyond myself — the young man working too hard to get to know the correct people. I saw it as somehow compensatory for the hard work put into teaching, and I didn't slight that teaching because of diversions from the great world; they were more like a shot in the arm, an extension of critical talk in the several areas I cared about.

But by far the most important "outside" presence in those first years back at Amherst was Robert Frost. Officially titled Simpson Lecturer at the college, he showed up for about two weeks in the fall, then appeared briefly in the spring to read his poetry aloud to a packed audience in the chapel. In 1960 I was in the process of finishing my dissertation on Frost and was asked to fill in as his social secretary, since his real secretary, Kathleen Morrison, did not accompany him on these visits. My duties involved calling on him in the morning at his room in the inn, going over the day's schedule (whom he would see, with whom he would have dinner), and on a couple of occasions ensuring that he got to bed at a reasonable hour and didn't overtax himself — pleasurable excitements generated by responsibility for the good gray poet. I was nervous though not tongue-tied in his presence, and attempted to draw him out (usually with success) about other poets. What did he think of X and which were the poems of Y he cared most about? Frost's mind as I experienced it in connection with poetry was full of touchstones, not exactly Arnoldian ones, just couplets or stanzas or whole poems that meant everything to him. Or it felt to me like "everything" from the way he would say aloud lines from poems like William Collins's "Ode" of 1746:

> How sleep the brave, who sink to rest
> By all their country's wishes blest!
> When Spring, with dewy fingers cold,

Returns to deck their hallowed mould
She there shall dress a sweeter sod
Than Fancy's feet have ever trod.

Or James Shirley's dirge from one of his plays:

The glories of our blood and state
Are shadows, not substantial things,
There is no armour against fate,
Death lays his icy hands on kings,
Sceptre and crown must tumble down
And in the dust be equal made,
With the poor crooked scythe and spade.

Or from "The Sheaves," a sonnet by Frost's old rival, Edwin Arlington Robinson:

Where long the shadows of the wind had rolled,
Green wheat was yielding to the change assigned;

and Robinson's final comparison of the wheat to female beauty:

A thousand golden sheaves were lying there,
Shining and still, but not for long to stay—
As if a thousand girls with golden hair
Might rise from where they slept and go away.

Sometimes it was no more than a brief moment, a saying excerpted from a poem that seemed to mean something to him that I could not possibly understand, as in three lines from William Vaughn Moody's "Gloucester Moors," a poem I'd never even read:

Who has given to me this sweet?
And given my brother dust to eat?
And when will his wage come in?

Or it might be lines from what I later identified as a short introductory poem of Browning's ("Amphibian") to one of his late, unread longer ones, about a swimmer who suddenly encounters a butterfly:

A handbreath over head!
All of the sea my own,
It owned the sky instead;
Both of us were alone.

It was Frost's speaking voice, fetching up these bits of remembered lyric he had carried around with him since sometime in the preceding century, that unfailingly heroicized them, made a listener feel in the presence of something lofty, noble, heart-stirring.

That was the accent I was listening for in Frost, although there were other, less lofty ones to be heard. If you were a pious and patient enough listener—as I was, partly because it was my job—you heard more than enough about the absurdity of the United Nations and the dubious claims of internationalism generally. You had to put up with hearing about how canny Frost had been in dealing with the government so as to procure Ezra Pound's release from St. Elizabeth's Hospital (it turned out that Archibald MacLeish was the significant mover in this case); and about how T. S. Eliot played at eucharist while he, Frost played euchre; and how the later Yeats's highly sexualized poetry revealed him as a dirty old man. One sat through these oft-performed routines and waited for something less prepackaged. Sometimes a question would provoke Frost into a musing passage that led to a place he hadn't quite foreseen; this happened most often when the provocative agent was from an old poem of his or from something of someone else's he cared about, as with the lines from Browning's "Amphibian." One of Frost's letters speaks of the difference between "thinking" and "voting" and how much classroom talk by teachers and students was merely taking sides—Republican or Democrat, Unity or Plurality— with the talkers voting one way or the other. Real thinking, on the other hand, demanded "getting up there high enough" where you could see the opposites in play and didn't have to vote for one instead of the other. Something like this ascent occurred in his talk when he wasn't in competition with a rival poet or wasn't concerned to prove post–New Deal society a moral horror.

When I published my first essay on him I gave Frost a copy, but never learned whether he so much as glanced at it—at any rate, he never commented. When I suggested to him that I hoped to publish my dissertation as a book he was unimpressed, advising me to "keep it around," to "deepen" it. (I ended up keeping it around for twenty-four years.) It might be asked whether my commitment to Frost revealed severe limitations on my part, a capitulation to a myth that, especially in Amherst, was all too pervasive. Unlike figures such as Brower, Leavis, and Haggin, who deeply influenced me but against whom I eventually reacted with principled disagreement or satirical mockery,

Frost survived largely untouched by such ironic distancing. Perhaps there was no need to make a pronounced swerve away from him since there were ready ways of detaching oneself from cultish embracings of the bard. It was evident that all sorts of Americans who wouldn't be caught dead with a volume of Eliot's or Stevens's verse in their hands professed to love Frost's, using him as a yardstick to beat up more "difficult" poets. Relatively inarticulate Amherst students—and there were some of those—would show up dutifully for one of Frost's readings at their fraternity house, ask him about baseball, and profess to have been enlightened. I had, in other words, become expert at holding in disdain those parts of Frost that played up to this audience—the part that wrote in a letter from early in the century that he had no wish to be caviar to the crowd but wanted to be a poet read by all sorts and kinds of people. My disdain was ballasted by Randall Jarrell's marvelous essays on the poet in which he found highly imaginative ways of characterizing the Frost he found depressing: "The conservative editorialist and self-made apothegm-joiner, full of dry wisdom and free, complacent, Yankee enterprise: the Farmer-Poet . . . a sort of Olympian Will Rogers out of *Tanglewood Tales*." Jarrell was talking about the public figure he capitalized as the "Only Genuine Robert Frost in Captivity"; this Frost wrote poems "full of cracker-box philosophizing, almanac joke-cracking—of a snake-oil salesman's mysticism":

> One gets the public figure's relishing consciousness of himself, an astonishing constriction of imagination and sympathy; one gets sentimentality and whimsicality, an arch complacency, a complacent archness; and one gets Homely Wisdom till the cows come home.

It was the "other Frost" that Jarrell explored in his essays: the private voice, the dark wit, the lyric cadence. But one's sense of that otherness was invaluably sharpened by Jarrell's deft laying out, in broad comic strokes, of the public Frost, often visible on his Amherst College visits. As a dutiful member of an English department, grading large numbers of papers and taking the task seriously, I was less than amused to hear Uncle Robert telling the undergraduates how, when he taught at the college, he used to give everyone an A, or simply threw away their papers without having read them. And the jokes about interpreters of his poems—as if all interpretation were a misguided activity, performed stupidly and mindlessly—were of only limited interest to someone like me who was concerned to write well about those poems. So it was possible for me to feel committed to "the other Frost" because the "public Frost" was fully on display and easy to disown.

He died in January of 1963, by which time I had ceased to think of publishing my dissertation. I had a new subject, the English painter and man-of-all-letters, Wyndham Lewis, about whom I had contracted to write a book for an English authors series. I had also been awarded a fellowship by the college that would enable me to take a year's leave from academic duties; applications to two societies for small grants had also met with success, and the plan (subsequently carried out) was to spend the academic year in Rome, rounded off by seven weeks in England. The first segment of my teacherly life as a teacher seemed to have completed itself, and probably never again would the activity present itself in so totally absorbing and challenging a form.

VII
Changing Times: 1966–1972

It was well along into the 1960s when I realized that—in the words of Bob Dylan, whose music a student introduced me to (unsuccessfully) in 1967—the times they were a-changing. How could I have assumed that, out there in the world, events like the Cuban missile crisis or an enlarging war in Vietnam inevitably took place; whereas in here, at Amherst College, things went on as they had gone on previously. It wasn't as if I were living in the Ivory Tower and didn't know it; indeed, an English 1 assignment had invited students to investigate and speculate on the differences between the Ivory Tower and the Real World. But maybe I was living in the tower after all in assuming that my Amherst College world of classes and course plans and paper reading was the real thing. What I could not imagine was how fragile and of-the-moment that reality was, and how little it would take for it to break apart.

The first intimation I had of what, in retrospect, was the incipient eroding of a structure came early in 1966, when a group of students from one of the fraternities put together a report on student life. They were thoughtful boys, thoughtful enough to wonder about the nature of their education at Amherst, unwilling simply to swallow what was being fed them on the assumption that it would do them good. The section of the report that especially interested and troubled me was titled "The Displacement of Academic Relevance," and it dealt with relations between students and faculty. The argument went that at Amherst the classroom had become a world unto itself with its own rules and values, a world of "disinterested intellectualism." This "disinterested" approach, they went on, resulted in a failure to learn any broader application of the academic method; the student took his courses and wrote his papers but was put in no position to see "how academic study might be relevant beyond the classroom." Under the Amherst ethos, professors came across merely as disinterested intellectuals; their academic efforts did not bear fruit in important social and personal ways. And how did this disinterested method help the students, most of whom did not plan to become academics? How would they learn to "deal with the social problems they will face" or "perform their responsible roles in society"? Summing up its case about the displacement of academic relevance, the report concluded:

> If the faculty is not fully aware of, or does not appreciate the goal of the students which lies beyond the classroom, it is too much to expect of them to structure their teaching in a manner which will help students to place real significance upon their academic pursuits by relating them to themselves—that is to their own goals and values.

Students and faculty, it seemed, had lost contact with one another, and that was what was wrong with education at Amherst in 1966.

I remember being contemptuous of the report's prose—all that "relating" to, with "structure" used as a verb, with goals and values and "real significance." Had these people not taken English 1 and been affected by it enough to distrust such careless use of language? Evidently not; or rather, it was precisely the detached, ironic stance toward students and their aspirations by that course that the report was complaining about. English 1 said to a student in effect (and I remember saying it in fact): "You are no doubt a fine human being, possessed of a noble inner self with splendid ideals and values. But in this course we're going to deal with the way you have chosen to express that self or selves in language. By your sentences ye shall be known, and by them only." But these students, in their emphasis on what "lies beyond the classroom," were saying something like "we want to be recognized as human beings; we want our lives to be taken into account in a way that you have not been taking them."

More important than the report's prose and its inchoate plea for a different sort of recognition was the historical moment, both global and local, that provoked it. The country was moving ever more deeply into the Vietnam morass; locally, at commencement in May of 1966, a small number of graduates walked out of the ceremonies when Robert McNamara was awarded an honorary degree. This walkout provoked an emotional display on the part of faculty and students as they chose or declined to follow the president, Calvin Plimpton, in standing and giving McNamara a round of supportive applause. Meanwhile, in uneasy tandem with the increasingly large number who dissented from the administration's foreign policy, were the black students, concerned to be recognized as something more than an obedient, token minority. The class of 1965 contained three black students; the class of 1968 contained but eight. Their efforts to gain wider recognition were first felt by Amherst early one morning in 1968 when members of the black community, in an attempt to draw attention to their situation as a tiny minority, occupied a college building—a prelude to such occasions in years to come.

But 1966 also signaled the end of the New Curriculum. That curriculum had suffered attrition, with some weaker staff courses gradually dropping off; but its major enterprises—the required freshman courses in composition and in math and physics—were still in place in the early sixties. Nevertheless, as happens every ten years or so, a curriculum committee was appointed to suggest something new, and by the fall of 1966 the New Curriculum was old history. In its place was adopted a somewhat emasculated version of the committee's recommendations, which reduced the total number of courses required of a student to three: one staff course in each of the three divisions—humanities, social science, and natural science. Called Problems of Inquiry courses, they would last a short time and make small impact. Further educational changes came in the wake of the abandoned New Curriculum and conspired to ensure that its successor would be a good deal less severe in the demands it placed on both students and teachers. For one, the faculty voted into being a new class schedule, with eighty-minute classes on Tuesday and Thursday instead of across-the-board fifty-minute ones. This transition was carried out in the interest of eliminating Saturday classes, many faculty members having testified to their dismay at having to teach students on that morning. One might have thought this a curious educational argument, but it prevailed, and Saturday classes became a thing of the past. Second, and out of administrative benevolence, an already less than onerous teaching load (for tenured faculty, three courses one term, two the other; three and three for nontenured ones) was reduced to an equitable two courses per term regardless of rank. This, of course, meant the loss of a considerable number of teaching hours, making the staffing of team-taught courses more difficult. A third custom that disappeared in the 1966–68 period was the hoary phenomenon of morning "chapel," a brief coming together of the college in which the Doxology was sung and a short secular address delivered —usually by the president, the dean, or a member of the faculty. Students were obliged to attend two of these four weekly meetings. After some outcry and hand wringing, chapel was abolished in somewhat the same manner as were Saturday classes, on the grounds that students did not want to be there on demand. (The faculty supported their wish.) Although the word was not yet in the air, "liberation" was the name of the game, and it's not absurd to suggest a connection between the new contraceptive pill, issuing in the sexual "revolution," and the loss of other social regulations. "Sexual intercourse began in 1963," Philip Larkin's poem begins; at Amherst various beginnings or endings (as with compulsory chapel and Saturday classes) testified that a new spirit was abroad. Faculty salaries had risen steadily since Calvin Plimpton became president in 1960; among the faculty there were more parties, presidential and otherwise, and a further relaxing of the Calvinistic conscience that had informed the college in leaner days.

Meanwhile the new Problems of Inquiry courses, which supplanted the required first-year ones in English, history, and math–physics, cloaked themselves in a dubiously self-important rhetoric as if to say: Other people think or have opinions or study; at Amherst, we *inquire.* The humanities inquiry I designed was a course in the practical criticism of selected works of literature, music, the fine arts, and philosophy. But an immediate overselling of the product, before it had begun to prove itself, was evident in our planning sessions when we tried to say what would be new about it. It was suggested, for example, that we reverse the authoritarian and intimidating teaching posture characteristic of many classrooms under the old New Curriculum. We would instead serve as midwife to the students, delivering them of (in a colleague's words) "the largest, most interesting questions they could ask." Our students had a proclivity to ask questions, and it was our task to encourage this. Moreover—and this was a sentiment heard from more than one faculty member—*we* could learn from the students if we but took the time and energy to listen. They had things to tell us; instruction was in no sense a one-directional process; true interchange could be effected if we would only surrender some of our egotistic desire to be in control and stop asking questions whose answers we already knew.

Although I did not realize it at the time, there had been a rehearsal for this educational scenario early in the century during the years when Alexander Meiklejohn was Amherst's president. In Meiklejohn's inaugural address in 1912, he set forth his notion of the "liberal college" as an "intellectual place" where boys would be introduced to the intellectual life for its own sake and be saved thereby from pettiness and dullness — saved from becoming one of "the others":

> There are those among us who will find so much sat-
> isfaction in the countless trivial and vulgar amuse-
> ments of a crude people that they have no time for the
> joys of the mind. There are those who are so closely
> shut up within a little round of petty pleasures that
> they have never dreamed of the fun of reading and
> conversing and investigation and reflecting.

By contrast, Meiklejohn said, he would like to see all Amherst students "plunged into the problems of philosophy," and thereby rescued from worldly vulgarities and distractions.

It was an extraordinarily high-minded beginning for a presidential enterprise that came to grief some years later when, with a divided and unhappy faculty, the trustees finally asked for and received Meiklejohn's resignation. The story has been told elsewhere; I mention it merely to draw a parallel with the assumption, fifty years later at the same college, that the new Problems of Inquiry courses would plunge students into philosophical problems and liberate them from conventional pedagogy — bring them, in Meiklejohn's words, into the fun of "conversing and investigation and reflecting." Robert Frost, who had been brought to Amherst College by an enthusiastic Meiklejohn, but who for various reasons soon fell away from both the president's goals and his practical decisions, reflected mordantly a few years later on what had happened to the college under the now-deposed president:

> The boys had been made uncommonly interesting to
> themselves by Meiklejohn. They fancied themselves

as thinkers. At Amherst you *thought*, while at other
colleges you merely *learned*. (Wherefore if you love
him, send your only son and child to Amherst.) I
found that by thinking they mean stocking up with
radical ideas, by learning they meant stocking up
with conservative ideas—a harmless distinction,
bless their simple hearts. . . . They had picked up the
idea somewhere that the time was past for the teacher
to teach the pupil. From now on it was the thing for
the pupil to teach himself using, as he saw fit, the
teacher as an instrument. The understanding was that
my leg was always on the table for anyone to seize me
by that thought he could swing me as an instrument
to teach himself with. So we had an amusing year.

Frost, of course, was ready to make game of just about any pedagogical
assumptions except his own—certainly he had been less than rever-
ent about the vaunted New Curriculum. By the time that was displaced, in 1966, he was no longer living; yet it is fair to say that the
invoking of Problems of Inquiry courses as a way to signal Learning
(rather than old-fashioned Teaching) would have elicited his contempt, not because they embodied "radical" instead of "conservative"
assumptions, but simply because of their solemnity.

These courses, in fact, were better and less pretentious than the
words used to sell them; but they would have had to have been of
amazing quality indeed to survive the shocks of the next few years, as
"revolution" came to university and college campuses. Until 1970
there was no strong radical presence at the college; it took the killings
at Kent State to effect what radicalizing there eventually was. Students for a Democratic Society (SDS) had made little or no impact at
Amherst and when in 1967 Mario Savio, fresh from his triumphs in
the Berkeley Free Speech movement, appeared on campus, he was surprised to find out how far behind the changing times were its inhabi-
tants. A modest crowd turned out to listen to Savio, who at one point,
obviously frustrated or bored by what he perceived as the relatively
unstirred-up state of the undergraduates, bluntly asked, "Well, what
are you upset about? What do you want to see changed?" One student
responded with "parietal rules," then in the process of being dispensed
with. Savio laughed and shrugged his shoulders as if to say, "What do *I*

care about such chicken-feed changes—I'm interested in restructuring the university, if not the universe."

But the atmosphere of dissatisfaction grew perceptibly in the late sixties. In my own classroom, at the end of a Friday morning hour spent on some poems by William Carlos Williams, a student confronted me and asked why I had said nothing about the assassination of Martin Luther King, which had occurred the previous day. Awkwardly I replied that, indeed, King's assassination was on my mind. Also on my mind was a piano recital I was to give that evening. In class (I told the student) I had mentioned neither my private worry about the concert, nor my distress at the public horror of King's murder. Our subject was, rather, the poetry of William Carlos Williams, and that was what we had spent our fifty minutes on. The student, though clearly unconvinced, did not pursue the matter. But in thinking about it later, I was myself less than convinced that I was in the clear. What right did I have to equate the assassination of an American hero—as an event that had no place in an English class—with my piano recital? Previous to the student's question it hadn't even occurred to me to address the murder in class, and bracketing it with the piano event was something done only under pressure of criticism, on the spur of the moment. In a way the class was a replay of the Cuban missile crisis afternoon when we had occupied ourselves with Alexander Pope. This time I found it more difficult to assure myself that in the classroom nothing ever took precedence over the study of literature.

In the spring of 1969, with the escalation of the war in Vietnam and with serious student disruptions over the past twelve months in Paris, and at Columbia and Harvard, Amherst College declared a moratorium. Classes were canceled; an all-campus meeting was called in which votes were taken on various issues, resolutions passed, and committees to study this and that set up. The moratorium featured the usual paraphernalia of such occasions when, as the loaded phrase went, "business as usual" was suspended in the interest of something presumably more pressing and vital. I heard of these events—and of the subsequent moratorium in which black students had their own "day of concern," with speakers brought in to address the college—at second hand, since I was living in London, on sabbatical. The essential action of the first moratorium was initiated by a body of students and sympathetic faculty members and consisted in the writing of a letter to President Nixon declaring that the college found it impossible to perform its educational function adequately because of the war in Vietnam. The letter, written by Leo Marx—most prominent of the faculty Left—and the dean of faculty, was signed by a reluctant president, the same Calvin Plimpton who three years before had offered a rebuffed Robert McNamara a standing ovation. The letter was prominently featured in the *New York Times* as an example of the principled protest a thoughtful college had been provoked into. Here surely was an example of how far things had come in the course of a few years: the student committee's complaint, from 1966, of faculty indifference to "relevance" and to the lives of its students beyond the classroom, was now, one might say, answered by the insistence that this faculty cared so much about the world outside the classroom that business as usual could no longer be conducted without significant interruption.

Although I had become convinced by Walter Lippmann as early as 1965 that the war was a bad mistake (I even signed a petition—my one and only such act—against it), it was not until Vietnam impinged on Amherst College that its effect was fully brought home to me. I thought of myself as neither a hawk nor a dove; I deplored the war but didn't know what to do about it. And I felt more than uneasy in the presence of those faculty colleagues who presumably did know what should be done; namely, that we were to suspend our bookish concerns so as to address important issues, not just Vietnam, but racism, urban blight, even (in some minds) the coeducation that had not yet come to the college. My first, and indeed last, response to the characterization was that I did not practice business as usual in my classes, since, at least in a good class, the business conducted was unusual. Of course I knew that users of the contemptuous phrase could back off by saying it was simply a metaphor for the continuity of academic routine and that nothing derogatory was meant by it. At such a point I became stubborn, insisting that metaphors really mattered, and that the business-as-usual metaphor invited teachers to adopt a dismissive and patronizing attitude toward the activity they had presumably devoted their lives to practicing.

The notion also began to grow on me, as I sat in London reading accounts of the moratorium and the faculty–presidential letter to President Nixon, that such activities could be viewed as something less than heroic. Theodore Baird's letters to me, describing the events, were full of shocked contempt at the new kind of "community" he witnessed: "people sprawling in front of Frost Library while [the word] 'bullshit' goes reverberating from building to building, a mob in the gym voting, one man, one woman, one Smith girl, etc., one vote." The department meeting with students, to discuss curricular dissatisfactions, brought about the following:

> Then someone said he wanted to be treated as a Human Bean, and he wanted his professor to be a Human Bean. This was too much for me again and I vehemently denied that I was a Human Bean, that he had any claim to this, hastily sketching the application process at Amherst College. Are you or are you not a Human Bean? etc., all with as much bitterness as I could control and I claimed to be a Professor, yes, even a Doctor of Philosophy in English, and I told him he was a Student or nothing. . . . I must say I found a new note here, the Pure Whine.

I suspected that faculty self-importance could be observed as well. In ten or so years of teaching at Amherst, I had come to feel that the job's only unwelcome burden was compulsory attendance at the five or six or more faculty meetings spaced over the academic year. Here, in increasingly longer sessions as the years went on, my colleagues got a chance to sound off on various issues. The "talkers" amongst us could be excruciatingly painful to listen to. Some thought they were in the next best thing to the House of Commons, and embraced the opportunity to set straight the president of the college — or the president of the United States — as the spirit moved them. Unlike Parliament, no one had to suffer the consequences of anything said — it was theater merely. Such meetings, I had begun to say without knowing exactly what I meant, reminded me of death; they certainly had nothing to do with the satisfactions of teaching bright students or the chance to argue about D. H. Lawrence with department colleagues. For my own part I would have been happy to let the administration — mainly benevolent, so it seemed to me — administer the college, leaving me the freedom (again as I felt it) to do my work in the classroom. But many faculty didn't feel that way and wanted instead to be recognized as the body that *really* ran the college. More and more I found myself writhing during these meetings, speaking out only in deflation of some colleague-orator moved by the sound of his own voice. I grew bad mannered enough to blurt out bits of sarcasm or fancied humorous retorts directed at someone even as he was still speaking. These minor outbursts pleased some and annoyed others but did not enhance my reputation as a trusted faculty spokesman.

When I returned from England in July of 1969 the campus had changed, even more so than it had on that awful morning in June of the previous year when, having awakened to the news of Robert Kennedy's assassination, I sat on the quad with George Kateb and Leo Marx in perfect spring weather, trying to figure out what could possibly happen next. (Classes were over, so there had been no question of addressing students on what had happened.) Now, more than a year later, signs of purpose were perceived on the campus: a faculty committee would meet all summer long to see how the proposals for change emanating from the spring's moratorium could be implemented; two white professors, both Jewish, were preparing to give an introductory course in the newly formed Black Studies department, which as yet had no black professors. Three members of my own department were engaged in a summer program to teach teachers of black students in the Springfield public schools. To some extent the ivory tower had become conscious of, perhaps embarrassed at itself, and steps were being taken, no matter how small, to reach out to a wider public and social world.

As the new semester began, things were coming apart at the seams. Our introductory English course, now rudderless after the retirement of Theodore Baird the previous June, was headed by a colleague who agreed to run it only after insisting that his authority would be nominal. It had also been agreed, I was informed, that plays of Shakespeare were to constitute our semester's subject, though no clear idea seemed to have emerged about just what "Shakespeare" meant in the course's pedagogy, if it had one. We were no longer teaching composition, nor were we introducing literature, and aside from the fact that it was required for majors in the department, there seemed no other particular reason for giving or taking this course called, vaguely, Introduction to English. The sense of confusion and drifting was only heightened when directions were handed out for the first unit, presumably to deal with *Hamlet*. Instead of the old-fashioned, carefully worked out sequence of classes and assignments, we were presented with a single page titled *Not About Hamlet* and an opening sentence, "This is a sort of excuse for not writing about *Hamlet,* and a vague statement about what I want to do in my section of English 11." The writer, William Heath, had become interested in new ways of looking at the classroom relation between teacher and student:

> I see my first job to be defining a class—its limits, expectations—and working out the place of a teacher in it. I have gimmicks in mind for this, but no real notion of how long it will take or how successful I'll be in working out ground rules for a situation of trust (real or feigned) where we are willing to tolerate one another's boringness but interested enough to demand the most of ourselves and others.

He said that his class would begin with "role-playing and improvisation, using simple social and family situations at first." There would be "daily reporters" for each class hour, students who would comment on what had gone on, but there would be no formal papers. In fact, he said, having not yet met the eighteen or so people who made up his class, he couldn't be specific about anything.

Here was an extreme instance of disenchantment with the orderly, hierarchical relation between teacher and student on which our course assignments and procedures had always depended. We were being invited instead to consider the possibility that that relationship was an oppressive one and whether a more equal relationship could somehow be substituted in its place. With this question, the notion of learning from the students, much talked about in connection with the courses in Inquiry, was carried to its logical culmination. In an important way it anticipated, perhaps inaugurated, the emphasis on literary theory that would follow in the decades to come, insofar as "theory" flourishes when a consensus has broken down. If the value of studying literature under the guiding hand of a teacher who proposed terms, asked questions, and rewarded or punished answers to them, could no longer be taken for granted, then an inquiry into the whole pedagogical subject—what is a "teacher" or a "student" anyway?—might be substituted for it. After all, in the words of an essay by the poet Allen Grossman that appeared at this time, were we not teaching "literature in a discredited civilization"?

How deep in my unconscious the resistance to theory ran, I cannot confidently say; as far as literature went, I resisted theoretical inquiry only when that inquiry bid to usurp the place of literature itself as the central object of study. But I instinctively and profoundly resented the notion that to conduct a good classroom one had to begin by talking about how to conduct the classroom. That autumn in my section of English 11 (which had "replaced" English 1) there was no role playing and no attempt to create an atmosphere of "trust" prior to dealing with Shakespeare. For better or worse—and it was a more chaotic term than some—we began and ended with literature, something that proved more difficult to accomplish in the spring semester to come.

It did seem, in those years, that springtime especially was the time of troubles. Spring 1968 was grimly marked by the assassinations of Martin Luther King and Robert Kennedy, along with student uprisings in Paris and at Columbia; 1969 featured the "bust" at Harvard, where the police were called in to club protestors occupying University Hall. In a more decorous (some said Amherstian) way, spring 1969 brought the moratorium and days of concern at our college. Then, as if attempting to up the ante, late April and early May of 1970 featured the U.S. "incursion" into Cambodia and the Kent State disaster. In response to these events came the National Strike movement in colleges and universities. To the sounds of the Jefferson Airplane booming over the campus and the audible tearing of orange strips of cloth to be worn as strike armbands, Amherst entered its most active effort to influence the nation's foreign and domestic policy. Different rationalizations were offered for the move: that the incursion had precipitated a "constitutional crisis" in which the government was acting illegally; that the killings of students morally demanded extreme suspension of daily activities; that these activities should be replaced by a countercurriculum, as it were, of lectures and teach-ins about the war and about the racial situation in America. (About collegiate "governance" as well, from the existence of an ROTC program at neighboring University of Massachusetts to whatever iniquity could be perceived in Amherst College's financial, social, or academic policy. Everything was fair game.)

Faculty support for the strike was strong and although—as usual on such occasions—I felt confused and uncertain, I supported it as well, especially since it did not mandate that classes be called off. Instead, and because the semester was winding down, students who chose to suspend any further academic work might receive a "Pass" for the course, while the professor could use the remaining class meetings as occasion for inquiry into the Nixon administration's conduct of the war or whatever contemporary issue seemed of most import. Another possibility, the one I acted on, was to show up for class and continue with our current subject, the poetry of T. S. Eliot. So the strike didn't seem coercive on the face of it, although the pressure not to hold regular classes would be stronger than I anticipated. The schedule of strike-related meetings and lectures included topics (in addition to Vietnam–Cambodia) such as "Panthers," "Political Repression," "Selective Service," and "Defense Establishment," as well as draft counseling, canvassing techniques (the students were going out among the people to bring them a message), and instructions in first aid. This last was preparatory to marching on the University of Massachusetts to demonstrate against the ROTC, a march that some feared would lead to violence. (It never materialized).

In his incisive, splendidly particularized account of the Amherst events, "Journal of a Campus Strike," Benjamin DeMott has vividly brought to life those two weeks in May. A member of the faculty-student strike committee, DeMott canceled his classes but was sympathetic to the situation of those who chose to continue meeting them. He attempted to imagine how such faculty members might have felt as they headed off to teach:

> Despite obstacles, despite majority dementia, say the hardrocks *and* the honest conservatives, *we* persevere. Humor or playfulness, imaginative ease — can they survive that sense of intransigent dutifulness? the feeling of embattled beleaguered virtue? the feeling that the man on strike across the hall — once a colleague — is now a kind of Enemy? I think there's no such thing, when most of us quit, as an uncoercive atmosphere.

This observation is confirmed when I remember the uneasiness I felt when I showed up for the modern poetry course. The room, which held fifty-six students if everyone attended, was now seven-eighths empty, with those in attendance still sitting in their assigned (alphabetical) places so that there were lonely gaping holes. The best student in the class, a young man named Herbert "Chip" Tucker who would go on to an impressive career as a teacher and scholar-critic of Victorian poetry, was there with his usual calm and cheerful demeanor. I had noticed him sponsoring one of the first aid sessions; evidently he could balance such practical advice on how to conduct oneself on a march, with the intricacies of Eliot's *Quartets,* our subject for that class.

I taught it with a mixture of feelings more significant than whatever I had to "say about" *East Coker* or *The Dry Salvages* — with an intense and almost embarrassing gratitude toward the students who had showed up. Any comment any one of them made about *anything* in Eliot's poems, I found myself welcoming out of all proportion to its acuteness. Outside, in the lovely spring weather and in the air of embattled seriousness that characterized the strike, one could hear the rhetorical designs of different voices as they expatiated on grave national matters that had displaced our little collegiate concerns. Yet here, inside, some of us were still listening to the words of a rueful, disenchanted master of the melodious morose:

> Time and the bell have buried the day,
> The black cloud carries the sun away.
> Will the sunflower turn to us, will the clematis
> Stray down, bend to us; tendril and spray
> Clutch and cling?
> Chill
> Fingers of yew be curled
> Down on us?

Was this the right thing to be doing at ten o'clock on a Tuesday morning in what everyone agreed was a very bad time in America's history — reading aloud and talking about a poem by an American expatriate whose brand of Anglican religion and whose cultural philosophy had little or nothing in common with what my students or what I "believed"? And yet there we were, doing it, reading and criticizing poetry again.

During the strike various members of the faculty addressed the undergraduates on topics of current concern: a professor of religion spoke about the practice of religion in Cambodia; a sociologist analyzed the makeup of Northampton's population and presented problems that might be met by community canvassers; an American historian once more detailed the rise of our involvement in Southeast

Asia. By 1970, with compulsory chapel a thing of the recent past, a much weakened form of it was still carried on in something called College Meeting, where faculty members might address the community at greater length than the old morning format of ten minutes. I had been asked by the colleague in charge of scheduling talks for the meeting if I would give one, and had accepted before the strike began. I had planned to say something about my own student days at Amherst and might have thought better of it since its "relevance" to the current crisis appeared to be minimal if not nonexistent. But with the air full of words, I couldn't resist adding to them by seeing how much — in such a charged atmosphere — I could get away with by way of reimagining "relevance."

My strategy was fairly unsubtle, although not everyone caught on. I looked at various aspects and slogans of college life in the early 1950s: the notion of the Well-Rounded Man; the provinciality of a small institution without even a psychiatric consultant; the absolute lack of interest in what was going on in Korea; the wastefulness of life in the fraternities; the absence not only of black and minority students but of any awareness of an absence. I quoted one priceless bit of condescension from the college newspaper's account of how a daring experiment of lodging one foreign exchange student in each of seven fraternities had worked out:

> Comments ran to superlatives at every house interviewed, although one person thought the student at his particular house "took too much for granted." All thought their student was mixing very well. Several remarked to the effect that "we couldn't have found a better fellow," and "this fraternity is very pleased with the whole situation." And one avowed that "If all these foreign students are as fine as the one we have, we hope we can have one every year."

Having satirized aspects of Amherst back then (though my affection for those aspects must also have shown through), I tried in conclusion to compare them with the college's present state. I noted that attempts to think of Amherst in the early 1950s as a place concerned with the cultivation of thinking people (and other words to that effect) needed to be set against the large amount of nonthinking, beer-drinking, bridge-playing reality that concurrently went on. Nor, back then, did a lack of concern for the larger society mean that steady attention was directed rather at contemplative, intellectual pursuits. "The golden haze of college days," as the words of a college song had it, was more likely to have been a blur. Now, in 1970 with the larger society in terrible trouble, there was a group within this academy who were enthusiastic in adapting the sloganeering of others, with invocations of "Solidarity" and "Power to the People." Maybe, I concluded, these words fitted us no better now than "Cultivation of Thinking People" did back then. What had impressed me in talking to individuals during the recent days of the strike was

> that for all the raised fists, all the talk of Solidarity, not everybody is too solid. That for all one's feelings of being swept up, of exhilaration at this *moment of crisis*, there are attendant feelings of depression, uncertainty, dismay at saying, after all, there are things more important than reading books.

I ended with a charge to my audience:

> Perhaps if just for a moment you can imagine under-graduate life at Amherst twenty years back with something besides contempt and amused superiority, you will be well on your way, even in the midst of confusion, of this present nongolden nonhaze of non-college days, to making up the beginnings of a story about your own life here. There will be at least two ways to look at it.

It may have been a slippery way out of things to have taken since I did not in so many words oppose the strike, although I expressed a temperamental disinclination toward rallying round the cause in the language of nonthink (Power to the People!). As usual I came out for ambiguity, for "complexity" — that well-worn New Critical term — and for making sure you had two ways to look at anything. I have no idea what my audience, a mixed one composed of students, faculty, and friends, made of it. It was, at any rate, quite off the main line of the week's events and might have been taken as a sort of entertainment — a jester's performance in the midst of serious business.

Yet within the academy, in those days and perhaps at any time, it was hard to know how "serious" anything truly could be, the line between serious and frivolous having become exceptionally thin. Earlier in that academic year of moratoria and suspensions of business as usual, the English department, one day in winter, declared itself temporarily out of business. It had become increasingly difficult to settle on a mutually convenient time for us to meet and discuss curricular problems, and it was decided that the department needed to engage in a day of self-examination. Accordingly, on a Tuesday or Wednesday of whatever week it was in February, we canceled our classes and adjourned to a hotel, the Northampton Hilton, for a day of brainstorming and self-definition. (Why the Northampton Hilton I can't quite say, except perhaps that it took us out of our routine and out of Amherst into a new situation.) We sat around a table (lunch and drinks laid on, courtesy of the college's budget) and argued to not very much avail. I was coming down with the flu, which served only to heighten the weirdness of this strange holiday happening. It might be seen as some sort of low point in the way a department conducted its affairs; or if you believed that crisis was everywhere, demanding suspension of teaching for reasons as unglobal as a group's inability to schedule a meeting during nonclass hours, you might think of it as groundbreaking. It was never, however, repeated.

Marx's often-quoted remark from *The Eighteenth Brumaire* about how history ironically repeats itself, with tragedy replayed as farce, applies to the pattern of disruption experienced at Amherst College in the early seventies. In 1972, just about two years after the Kent State Cambodia strike, Nixon and Kissinger ordered the mining of Haiphong Harbor, precipitating another campus upheaval that involved a concerted faculty and student act of civil disobedience. About fifteen miles from campus, near Chicopee, Massachusetts, stood Westover Air Force Base, a significant military installation. Pressed by students and some faculty members, the new president of the college, John William Ward, in his first year on the job, offered to lead a "march" on the base—protesters would sit down and block the road leading to it. The point was to get arrested and receive publicity in the papers; this is what happened, as faculty members (and indeed the president's spouse) who had never before practiced such "activism" had their first nonviolent taste of protest. After the arrests the protesters were booked, then immediately released.

The sequence of events leading up to this act of civil disobedience is worth remark. President Ward first addressed a mass meeting of students in the chapel and made his offer to lead a march on Westover. Immediately afterward the faculty held a meeting where Ward's proposal to the students was passed on to us for a vote of support. If the atmosphere of the strike two years previously could have been called coercive, this vote, taken at a moment when groups of excited students were milling about outside the doors of the faculty room, was even more so. Again, as in 1970, I voted affirmatively; in the grip of excitement I hadn't figured out what to do. After the vote a faculty member who strongly supported the action of civil disobedience admonished us not to second-guess our decision publicly. We had voted overwhelmingly in favor of action and that should be that.

Next morning, the protesters having set off early for Westover, I stayed behind without a scheduled class to teach and therefore with no moral prop. As I walked about the visibly less populated campus turning things over in my mind, I felt dissatisfied and embarrassed — for what, it wasn't exactly clear. In my fortieth year, it seemed evidently too late to assume the activist role many faculty had embraced; but I was less than sure, on the other hand, that they weren't in the right. Nixon really *had* gone too far, hadn't he? Looking for company — the English department building was notably vacant, since my colleagues, now fifteen miles away, were being arrested — I walked over to visit a professor of philosophy as disinclined toward protest as I. We sat around and talked about this and that, then were joined by a mutual friend from economics, also a nonactivist. One of us said to him, in that academic kidding vein, "Well, Arnold, why didn't *you* go to Westover?" He looked at us intently and, affecting suddenly to recall that this was the day of the sitdown, snapped his fingers and pronounced, "I forgot!" We all laughed and I felt better for taking refuge in a moment of comic irresponsibility, the last refuge of scoundrels.

Soon reports filtered in that the march had been a success, with a jovial even carnival-like atmosphere prevailing, the police unfailingly polite as they dealt with these obstreperous gentlemen and (a few) ladies from the college community. A subsequent letter to the alumni on Ward's part attempted to define his act as that of a private citizen and his wife (referred to in the letter, reassuringly, as Barbara), rather than a president who represented a prestigious small college. In doing what he did, Ward's credit with the undergraduates and the faculty — though not, let it be said, with the alumni — was measurably strengthened, in marked contrast to the situation of his predecessor, Plimpton, two years previously.

As the semester ended and just before exams were scheduled to begin, I headed to New York for the purposes mainly of taking in some performances of Balanchine's City Ballet. Coincident with the ballet were the NBA playoffs, that year a memorable one between the Knicks and the Lakers. The two activities dovetailed in my mind to make the point that despite Haiphong Harbor and talk of possible nuclear war (would the Russians or Chinese step in to help out North Vietnam?), professional dancers and musicians and athletes showed up for their jobs, put on their acts, did not suspend business as usual in the light of something more important. And not only were these highly paid stars showing up, but all over New York City people kept right on doing what they were doing: garbage got collected, subways ran, and restaurants served food. Riding back to Amherst on the bus, always a good place for meditation, I tried to decide whether the academic community had some sort of special responsibility — to the young in our charges, to American society, to the moral law — to instruct the civil order. It didn't seem to me that the answer was obviously yes. Suddenly it felt as if going to New York, escaping momentarily from our tight little academic community, had cleared my head and made it necessary that I say something to the faculty in defense of my principles.

The short remarks I delivered at our next and final yearly meeting consisted of nothing more than a question whether it was appropriate for us as a group to take "stands" on matters of national and international policy or whether, like the Knicks and the City Ballet, we should continue to perform business as usual in as effective a manner as we knew how. It was a speech in favor of not smoothing out our individual differences, doubts, and reservations about things in order to write a letter to the president or to the world, so as to provide a unified front. A college faculty should be a place, I said, where distinctions and disagreements are always being registered; where we would never be heard to speak in a monolithic voice of rectitude. In a way, I was repeating the sentiment of two springs previously about how, with all the talk of Solidarity, things weren't all that solid for the individual student. Appropriately, a few sympathetic individuals on the faculty spoke to me afterward about my remarks (the unsympathetic remaining silent). Collectively, no account was taken of them, neither agreement nor disagreement expressed.

The six years that had elapsed since the demise of the New Curriculum were in retrospect the most eventful years in Amherst College's history—certainly they remain the most unsettling and troubled ones in my memory. Their motto might have been Doing Without: as if we said, see how an educational institution with a complicated history could function if it did without . . . a structured curriculum . . . compulsory chapel . . . Saturday classes . . . parietal rules . . . a marching band at football games. Earlier in the decade the moribund public speaking requirement (one hour per week for every sophomore) was unanimously dispensed with, and our collective sense was good riddance. Now, with requirements falling thick and fast, there was little exultation in their jettisoning—it felt more like participation in the inevitable. The requirement that every student should be able to demonstrate a proficiency in one foreign language was about to go, its abolition strongly prompted by members of the language departments who, like teachers of Saturday classes, did not want to teach students who were not there voluntarily. By 1975 the physical education requirement for freshmen and sophomores would also disappear, prompted especially by the tragic drowning of a black student trying to pass his swimming test. Nor did the much heralded Problems of Inquiry courses escape decapitation. By the fall of 1971 they were so unpopular that, as an experiment, they were made voluntary rather than required in the next term, just to see what would happen to enrollments. From the three hundred or so freshmen compelled to elect each course, there was left an embarrassing remnant: sixteen students signed up for the social science course (too much reading); twenty-five for the natural science one; a more respectable but drastically diminished eighty-five for the humanities, whose subject, Eros, continued to exert a certain appeal. Abruptly those courses were scrapped; in their stead came something called Freshman Seminars where any professor offered a course in any subject his or her heart desired. Students would elect such a course. The name of the place was indeed Liberty Hall.

What one had witnessed, over the years 1966 to 1972, might be described as the dismantling of a college in preparation for reconstituting itself in another style. That style would first of all be coeducational: after an initial setback, in which the trustees were divided on the issue, the move to two-sex education became official in 1974, the first class of men and women entering in the fall of 1976. Second came the opening up of the college to minority groups, with active recruitment of black students, Latinos, and an ever-expanding group of Asian Americans. On a less noticeable but still significant front, there was the attempt—a highly successful one, since it brought some remarkable students to Amherst—to recruit promising undergraduates who had attended community college for a year or so. These students, usually older than the typical undergraduate, were inevitably equipped with a sense of purpose and seriousness that made them more than a pleasure to teach. In other words, giving up a central intellectual core of requirements and splitting apart consensus on what should be taught and how, brought positive as well as negative results, depending on how you looked at them. For example, without the hurdle of a first-year math–physics course to overcome, students could be admitted with weak backgrounds in science but with impressive talents in music, theater, or the fine arts. The result was that the college's artistic groups became much more numerous, varied, and in most instances more sophisticated than their predecessors. But the professor of physics, teaching many fewer students and wondering what he was doing at this small college where he had expected to teach an audience larger than a few confirmed physics majors, might well have had second thoughts about all those heavy enrollments in serigraphy, music of the Third World, or dance.

Some of these changes registered only superficially on me: could I care, really, that there was no longer a compulsory swimming test, since as an undergraduate I barely managed to scrape by it myself? Certainly the loss of a marching band at football games could be absorbed. But collectively the change, or drift, was near glacial. Frost has some lines at the end of his poem "Carpe Diem," about how impossible it is really to seize the day, to take hold and heed of what's going on about you when you are in the middle of it:

But bid life seize the present?
It lives less in the present
Than in the future always,
And less in both together
Than in the past. The present
Is too much for the senses,
Too crowding, too confusing—
Too present to imagine.

After this country had undergone the humiliation and disaster of Vietnam, swiftly followed by the shambles of Watergate, it became fashionable to declare that we had lost our innocence; that never again would there prevail the unthinking assumption of American privilege, superiority, and moral rightness. Without drawing an extended parallel between the national and the local college scene, what happened at Amherst in the late sixties and early seventies, too present for me to imagine it at the time, now seems as momentous as anything academic can be.

A historical moment in American education at a small college had come to its end. For twenty years there had existed a virtually unanimous consensus about the best way to educate young people; about what they needed to know and the order in which they needed to know it. I doubt that the moment could have existed or been as prolonged as it was if it had not followed directly upon World War II, with its legacy of returning veterans intent upon making up what they had lost in the previous four years. Nor could it have existed without a homogeneous climate of white male idealism and privilege. To adapt Matthew Arnold's phrase, the power of the man (the men, actually) and the moment had come together to produce not a "great creative epoch of literature" (Arnold's phrase) but something as close to a "great college" as there was likely to be. It was an education that the undergraduates of those years—most of them, anyway—never got over, as testified to their returning to the campus at their various reunions, still ready to hold discussions and symposia about their most influential courses; still assuming that something unique, or at least memorably distinctive, had been theirs. Were they mainly deluded, the victims of sentimental memories of male bonding in the classrooms and on the playing fields? Should an Amherst education be compared to a long-term disease from which the infected never quite recovered? For better or for worse the college in its twenty years of the New Curriculum was felt to be unlike other places of higher education; from the early 1970s on that distinctness was felt less and less, as what was now done at Amherst began to look more like what, with minor differences, all comparable institutions, large and small, were doing.

VIII
Reviewing Books, Reviewing the Profession

Back in 1958, as I was preparing to begin my teaching career at Amherst, Reuben Brower (who had left the college four years previously) advised me to find something else to occupy myself there in the hours not spent teaching and reading papers. Brower may not have used the word "hobby," but he was suggesting something like it. He himself was a devoted gardener, but that line of recreation held no attraction for me. I had my musical interests — playing the piano, listening to classical and jazz records, reading music criticism — but they were less an alternative to the academic life than an expression of my deepest self. I had begun to publish in the early 1960s, and the 1963–64 year abroad in Italy and England yielded a manuscript on the writer and painter Wyndham Lewis that, after some delay, would see print. But the process of writing essays and sending them out in hopes of acceptance by periodicals was a frustrating one. One might, as I did, spend a summer writing a longish piece on Eliot's *Waste Land* or on the novels of Anthony Burgess or the criticism of R. P. Blackmur, then have a periodical keep the essay for months, eventually deciding it was not for them. By contrast I was pleased that the few reviews I had written had a shorter circuit between submission and publication.

It was thus with some elation that, in the spring of 1967, I received a letter from Frederick Morgan, editor of the *Hudson Review*, inviting me to review a number of volumes of recently published poetry for his magazine. At that time *Hudson* was close to completing two decades of publication and seemed to me the best of the quarterlies, acting as both a medium for creative and critical work. It had published poems by Eliot, Ezra Pound, Wallace Stevens, and William Carlos Williams; fiction by Wyndham Lewis; and essays and reviews by some of the livelier critics, such as Hugh Kenner, Northrop Frye, and Robert M. Adams. And its quarterly roundups or "omnibus" reviews of new fiction and poetry had for years been useful to me in the attempt to keep up with what might currently be of worth. The notion that I would now appear in its pages was, to say the least, gratifying.

Accordingly, over the course of a couple of weeks forty or so slim volumes, products from the past three months of the poetry world, appeared at my house. From these I was to select those that appealed to me—or that I found unappealing, but wanted to write about nonetheless—and weave together, perhaps with some thematic continuity, an essay of five thousand or so words. I ended up reviewing about fifteen volumes, which was doubtless too many, but Morgan was pleased and accepted the piece for publication. I wrote it while the semester's teaching was going on, feeling quite important that I now had a task *beyond* the classroom whose results would secure me at least a few readers in addition to my Amherst colleagues to whom I sent course handouts and exercises.

My way of grouping the poets in that chronicle was one that I had seen practiced in *Hudson,* a progress from approbation or disapprobation for a younger poet, with passages quoted to suggest the flavor of his or her work (a first book by Yale Younger Poet James Tate, say), to slightly fuller commentary on more established figures (Robert Creeley and Denise Levertov), to a conclusion in which older poets such as John Hall Wheelock and Kenneth Rexroth, or posthumous collections by Ford Madox Ford and Louis MacNeice, were evaluated, in the main, positively. But *Hudson* was hospitable to sharp-tongued critics (James Wolcott once referred to them as "hard throwing"), and I came out aggressively, even pugilistically, toward slim volumes I disliked, as in the following sentences about May Swenson's *Half Sun Half Sleep:*

> May Swenson begins and ends in mannerism. She is
> forever tinkering, taking apart a cat, a watch, a poem.
> Without evident embarrassment she can tell us (in
> "The Watch") that the watchmaker
>
>> leaned like an ogre over my
>> naked watch. With critical pincers he
>> poked and stirred. He

lifted out little private things with a magnet
    too tiny for me
to watch almost. 'Watch out!' I
    almost said.

> I'm not just sure what kind of good fun this is. . . . For
> May Swenson things exist so that poems can be writ-
> ten about them, and if most things have been discov-
> ered there's always "A Basin of Eggs"; "Their cheeks
> touching, / their cheeks being / their bellies, their /
> bellies being undimpled, / dimples of dark being." I
> suppose so, but why couldn't they have been left
> alone just to lie there as boring old eggs, instead of
> taking their place in a hyped-up poetic universe? May
> Swenson has nothing to say, and her many ways of
> saying it drove me to exasperation.

In this manner I skewered a number of what I thought were pretenders
to poetic talent; whether I was right or wrong, or whatever might be
said in judgment of the reviewer's tone, passages like this were the
liveliest part of the chronicle. By contrast, and by the time I reached
Louis MacNeice, whose *Collected Poems* I wanted to praise, my inven-
tiveness seemed to have given out and my phrasing become threadbare,
as in this sentence: "And there are moments in the poems when the
personality revealed seems incomparable, like to nothing but itself."
What, for heaven's sake, was the use of saying *that* — "like to nothing
but itself"? At that point, or soon thereafter, a fundamental truth about
reviewing dawned on me, namely, that it is easier to find fault than to
praise convincingly. A writer's pretentiousness or fashionableness —
qualities I thought May Swenson's poems revealed — were easy targets
for ironic and satiric dismissal; but the subtlety and refinement of a
poem or poet were not so easy to articulate.

Back in those salad days I thought that it was the critic's task to
stand vigilant against inferior work, since I had no idea how quickly
that work, whether inferior or even superior, would surely fade away
on its own. I was also, of course, a young man on the make in search of
a career parallel to my teaching one, and was not above a bit of showing off, especially since *Hudson* in this and subsequent efforts allowed
me to do it and even praised me for it. But my senior colleague and
severest critic, Theodore Baird, to whom I showed the review, took a

rather different view. In a letter he professed to fear for my physical safety, conjuring up a vision of outraged poets descending upon my office, intent on paying me back for what I had doled out. "I cannot see why you do this," he went on:

> Are you going to pursue this course and sacrifice every poet's (except for a dead Limey) goodwill for a witticism? There you are, I say, dancing around the flames occasionally throwing in another slim volume. Well, I read and laughed and then as always felt guilty. . . . But I am finally on the side of the bad novelists, the bad poets, when they are made fun of. Perhaps I have no idea of good clean fun — certainly your imbecile examples are imbecile. But, you will say patiently, holding your head in your hands, Somebody has to do this. And I reply like lightning, Why? And more personally, why you? I do not believe that this single omnibus performance will ruin life for you. But I cannot see any future in it. The attention finally turns from the poets to the personalities of the Reviewers. It is much better than here expressed, I think.

Did somebody have to do what I had done? The letter floored me; but after getting up and brushing myself off, I decided that I was more interested in more reviewing than in seriously entertaining Baird's questions — especially since Morgan immediately held out another title (the first volume of Bertrand Russell's *Autobiography*) as something to write about for the next issue of *Hudson*. It felt as if I were launched. In due course invitations to review elsewhere began to show up and four years or so later I was asked to do something for the *New York Times Book Review*, an event that at the time seemed nothing less than momentous.

Soon after my first appearance in *Hudson*, while spending a sabbatical year in London I occupied myself with trying to lead what I called, with only half-meant irony, the literary life. During that year, and on another London sabbatical four years later, I worked at getting published in weeklies like the *Listener*, the *New Statesman*, and the *Times Literary Supplement*, as well as in monthlies and quarterlies like the *London Magazine* and *Essays in Criticism*. Those years in England and the modest success I had in breaking into print now and then probably

did more to confirm and satisfy my identity as a reviewer than did anything else. Here the example of one man was crucial—Julian Symons,
whose name had been given me as someone interested in Wyndham
Lewis. My book on Lewis had just appeared, although not in England,
but I had brought along some copies of it in my trunk and sent them
out to a few known Lewisites. The first to acknowledge receipt was
Martin Seymour-Smith, whose postcard from Bexhill-on-Sea claimed
that he greatly looked forward to reading my book. When his review
appeared a few months later in the *Spectator*—the first review I had
had anywhere of anything—it was a pan, a put-down designed especially for that awful species, the American academic. My critiques of
Lewis's novels were "inept, sixth-form condensations, shyly tinctured
with tiny Aristotelian 'objections','' and my manner in general toward
Lewis was "timid, donnish, obtuse." The review went on in that manner. By contrast, Symons's review in the *TLS* was incisive, civilized,
and sensible: that is, he liked my book, and I determined to make
myself acquainted with the work of this critic.

Like his English contemporaries V. S. Pritchett and Geoffrey
Grigson, two other formidable reviewers, Julian Symons was unacademic, never having attended a university. He was also, like them, a
reviewer for all seasons, able to deliver the requisite number of words
on varied subjects, not at all confined to poetry and fiction. He, Pritchett, and Grigson shared a common respect for criticism written in a
language their readers could speak, and they believed further that a
reviewer needed to be skilled at quoting appositely from, and making
judgments about, the work at hand. Symons was less fierce in his judgments than Grigson, though more so than Pritchett (who tended to be,
whenever possible, kind to the books he reviewed). But of the three it
was Symons who provided me with a prime example of the ideal
reviewer: flexible and diverse in his approach; in bondage to no particular critical system; possessor of a strongly vivid irony; not above
occasional self-depreciation, but stubborn in his judgments. Like
Orwell, with whom he was friends in the 1940s, Symons seemed to
me (in Orwell's own words) one of "the minority of gifted, wilful people who are determined to live their own lives to the end."

Of course Symons was more than a reviewer. He turned out with
regularity a series of expert crime novels and was also a biographer and
a cultural critic of distinction. His example made me feel not only that
reviewing books was a respectable thing to do, but also that it could be

a significant part of one's life. Part of this significance was practical, since reviewing provided short-term dates and goals by which life could be organized: twenty-five hundred words by November 15, with the knowledge that the written review would appear in print by, say, December, rather than the endless wait between the submission, acceptance, and appearance of an article. More important, reviewing turned out to be a way of keeping fit, as it were. Confronted by new subjects and writers one might be acquainted with only slightly, reviewing, when practiced properly, required familiarizing oneself with the subject's earlier work and previous volumes. One would then, given the time, be in a position not only to describe and evaluate the new novel or book of verse to hand, but to place it in relation to what had come before it. Practically speaking, it was often impossible to do this, especially if it were an "omnibus" review of fiction; and there was, on occasion, the impossible reviewing assignment to be undertaken in the spirit of adventure—such as Byron's correspondence in twelve volumes, or the massive three-volume edition of Tennyson's poems edited by Christopher Ricks. That the reviewer didn't always feel as authoritative as he managed to sound began to strike me as inevitable, rather than irresponsible. In reviewing, as in life, you never knew enough.

Needless to say, this wisdom was unavailable to me at the beginning of my reviewing career. But I soon knew enough to distrust the kinds of things I had heard some academics say in disparagement of the activity—for example, a colleague who had been asked to review a biography of Dreiser for the *Nation* but declined because he saw no point in wasting time on someone else's book when he could be getting on with his own. On the contrary, I found that the habit of writing and the seizing of any occasion, however humble, to practice that habit, was an incitement rather than a deterrent to my own critical-scholarly production. I also found that reviewing fed into my teaching, and vice versa. For example, when teaching William Carlos Williams's poetry I noted a statement in one of Wallace Stevens's letters to the effect that Williams cared more about form than content. By way of critique Stevens wrote: "The fact remains that we are always fundamentally interested in what a writer has to say. When we are sure of that, we pay attention to the way in which he says it, not often before." It just so happens that I was using that pronouncement in my poetry course when I wrote my first poetry chronicle for the *Hudson*

Review. What better way than to begin my review with Stevens's pronouncement and test its truth or falsity by reference to the books of verse that presented themselves? And just as often I used a formulation, discovered in some book I was reviewing, to organize a class around or make the subject of an assigned paper.

The effect of habitual reviewing on my teaching style was to make it even less academic. Perhaps the influence went as much the other way; at any rate, both in the classroom and in reviews I cultivated an informal style of address, emphasized the first person, used plenty of contractions, and tried to make a joke where it was conceivably relevant. And I encouraged my students, many of whom had been taught in secondary school never to use "I" in their papers, to write out of their own sense of things, rather than deferring to "objective" authorities by way of telling me what was really "in" this or that poem. The emphasis on informality of course had its perils: I was more than once accused of being "chatty," and as for the students, too devoted an emphasis on what they personally thought or felt could lead to no more than airy self-indulgence. Still, the risk seemed worth taking. The style I cultivated in reviewing and encouraged in my students put a high premium on literary performance as something to admire both in works of art and in the critic's sentences about those works. Some remarks from Frost's *Paris Review* interview were never far from my mind, and I probably quoted them too often: "The whole thing," he said to Richard Poirier (who would himself write a book titled *The Performing Self*), "is performance and prowess and feats of association. Why don't critics talk about those things? — what a feat it was to turn that that way, and what a feat it was to remember that, to be reminded of that by this? Why don't they talk about that?" "That" was what I tried — and helped others try — to talk about.

Elsewhere I have described some of the interesting by-products of reviewing: of wide differences in editorial behavior, or of the violent temper a review may provoke in certain readers or in the author of the book. B. H. Haggin insisted, on principle, that his reviews appear exactly as he had written them and considered any editorial tampering with the finished product as grounds for severing his connection with the offending magazine. With a less towering ego than Haggin's, I was never able to uphold his standard, partly since my writing was sometimes improved by such tampering; more often because it hardly seemed worth losing a desirable place to publish. But a reviewer's relationship is not likely to thrive with any editor who engages in wholesale rewriting. Just once in my career did I encounter an editor who declined to print something (part of a longer review) because he disliked my judgment of the poet in question. He said he was tired of printing things he disagreed with, and I found his frankness so surprising that I couldn't feel offended (also, I recycled the piece someplace else).

Reviewing had the further consequence of separating me from my departmental colleagues in a way I had not foreseen. The first glimmer that everyone around me was not absolutely delighted to see my name frequently appearing in print came when, after generously passing out offprints of my latest piece, I found the responses to it fell short of the acclaim I must have assumed was my due. Indeed, silence was the response of more than one recipient. It is a truth universally acknowledged — although not known to me then — that recognizing someone else's effort is not easy. And after all, as Theodore Baird said about the initial poetry chronicle, why should anyone do this? Yet once I had started — and continued — to write reviews, the activity served as a substitute for more conventionally professional ways of self-definition. Early in my teaching career I decided, dutifully, that I had better join the MLA and duly sent a letter requesting a membership form, which for some reason never arrived. I was content to take this silence as a sign that my presence in "our" professional organization was not essential. (Decades later, I finally joined, for more or less anthropological reasons.) The reviewing game, then, furnished an area in which to extend myself beyond Amherst. With plenty of reviews to do, I didn't look for academic conferences or symposia at this or that university on such and such a topic, nor did I attempt to latch on to some organization (the Friends of Wyndham Lewis would be an imaginary one) in which I could play a leading role. As long as I continued to extend my reviewing venues, with *Hudson* always there as a solid base, I could feel more or less fulfilled as a writer and contributor to the world of critical discussion. As Henry James put it in his seminal essay "The Art of Fiction": "Art lives upon discussion, upon experiment, upon curiosity, upon variety of attempt, upon the exchange of views and the comparison of standpoints." Criticism, most especially reviewing, it seemed to me, could facilitate the discussion and help keep current the life of art.

In the early and mid-seventies, as I became more certain about the sort of reviewer-critic I wanted to be, life in the Amherst English department became by degrees, not always perceptible, more destabilized and uncertain of purpose. The uncertainty could be observed most noticeably in our introductory staff course, still called Reading but ever shakier in the degree to which assumptions about reading, teaching, and criticism were shared. In 1972, with the college on the verge of becoming coeducational (it did not, in fact, become so until 1976, the trustees first rejecting the proposal), the dean made it known that we would do well to hire a woman, thus desegregating our all-male department. By the time I returned from sabbatical in 1974, there were three tenure-track women in the department, a fact whose consequences, on my assuming the chairman's role in the Reading course, I had not guessed. From England I had sent back a suggested reading list for the course that coming fall, consisting of books by Salinger, Turgenev, Shakespeare, Beckett, H. G. Wells, Stevenson, Henry James, John Updike, plus a contemporary poetry anthology. I said that I wasn't inextricably committed to any of these titles; what I didn't realize—or at least not to the point where it caused me to revise my syllabus—was that it consisted wholly of works by dead white males and a few living ones. By the time a group of us met that summer to plan things further, most of these writers had been axed, although oddly enough no woman was brought in as a replacement. But the first staff meeting that fall made it clear that new factors had come into play as far as pedagogy was concerned.

I suggested an introductory exercise on a recently published poem of Richard Wilbur's titled "Playboy," which I thought was witty, not too difficult, and a good vehicle for introducing old reliable terms—tone, voice, dramatic situation, and the like. "Playboy" is about a young man working in a store who in an idle moment is perusing the current issue of *Playboy* ("High on his stockroom ladder like a dunce / The stockboy sits, and studies like a sage / The subject matter of one glossy page, / As lost in curves as Archimedes once"). As the poem continues it speculates on why this boy seems so preoccupied, lost in his fantasy:

> What so engrosses him? The wild decor
> Of this pink-papered alcove into which
> A naked girl has stumbled, with its rich
> Welter of pelts and pillows on the floor,

Amidst which, kneeling in a supple pose,
She lifts a goblet in her farther hand,
As if about to toast a flower-stand
Above which hovers an exploding rose

Fired from a long-necked crystal vase that rests
Upon a tasseled and vermillion cloth
One taste of which would shrivel up a moth?
Or is he pondering her perfect breasts?

Eventually we get inside the boy's head as, in the consummatory last line of the poem, the *Playboy* girl "consents to his inexorable will." It was by no means a major poem (that was part of the point), and I had selected it as something I thought we could have fun with: no more Sir Philip Sidney and "Leave me, O love," as in that first class at Harvard.

But "fun" it turned out was the very thing that some members of the staff—notably the female ones (two of whom were beginning their first year of teaching) but also supported by some sympathetic males— were convinced they would not have with "Playboy." Pain was more like it. "I should feel extremely embarrassed," said one of the young women, "standing up there and 'teaching' this poem to a class composed entirely of males." Another woman agreed, and a male colleague said that he understood their embarrassment in such a situation, especially as first-year teachers in newly defined circumstances. The outcome of our extended discussion of the merits and demerits of Wilbur's poem was that some of us used it while others substituted something else. It seems to me now that the lame and embarrassing start to which we were off was absolutely symptomatic of the divisions, increasing by the year, that were to characterize Reading (or Reading and Writing, or Writing about Reading as we changed the title) until its eventual demise in the late 1980s. The wonder is, I suppose, that the course limped along for as long as it did.

This controversy over the Wilbur poem was perhaps the first of a number of "extra-literary" arguments that, for a staff to hang together through a course, had somehow to be dealt with. One was reminded that not only were these young women untenured and new to the classroom, but they were being asked to deal with an almost all-male student population (there were a few women exchange students) and with a staff composed entirely of white males, almost all tenured, and significantly older than they. Put yourself in their place, think how they must feel — thus the claims for sympathy presented themselves. It was no longer simply a matter of arguing whether D. H. Lawrence or Henry James or Henry Miller would better serve to ensure a successful unit of the Reading course, but rather whether we should be reading Richard Wilbur at all, especially this poem of his. Over the course of that term I became sufficiently sensitive to the new spirit — every man and woman regardless of his or her (mainly her) rank deserved equal participation and an equal voice in the running of things. This democratic new world extended beyond the internal workings of the staff course into matters one hadn't thought about making an issue of before, such as the scheduling of classes. In the past, older members of the department chose their preferred time slots, less desirable ones being filled in by the younger people. (I once taught courses at 9, 10, 11, Tuesday, Thursday, and Saturday.) Now each person signed up for class meeting times as convenience and preference dictated. Convenience and preference usually dictated that teaching three classes a week, one of them on Friday, should be avoided; thus the eighty-minute slots on Tuesday and Thursday, or Monday and Wednesday afternoons, became the popular spots — to the inconvenience, often, of students who found too many courses scheduled in the same hour. Younger departmental members were also invited to participate in the hiring process, even though their own futures were in doubt — this, again, in the name of democracy.

When it came time to prepare the next fall's reading list, I cautiously exercised my chairmanly powers and, instead of assembling on my own a suggested syllabus, invited staff members to send me their suggestions. One of the young women shot back a list that included titles by, among others, Italo Calvino, Oriana Fallaci, Gabriel García Márquez, Camara Laye, Carlos Casteneda, and Anaïs Nin. Was this deliberate provocation or simply a sincere effort at charting a new direction for the course ("contemporary things with an international emphasis," as she put it)? Whatever it was, I didn't know how to deal with the list, so subversive of the assumption that book titles would be chosen largely from the Anglo-American canon (a word that had not yet come into general play) and would not in the main be works in translation. But had these assumptions been spelled out? Certainly not, since, like the college itself, the course was moving from a time in which things were not spelled out ("Conduct befitting a gentleman is expected from Amherst students at all times") to a time when everything needed to be codified, then argued over, if not litigated. Should not a secretary be delegated to take notes on our meetings, so there would be fewer misunderstandings? (Smith College's English department at the time was embroiled in a lawsuit brought against it by two female members.) In the past decisions were usually not put to a vote, as it was assumed that eventually a consensus had been worked out. Should we not, as a rule, vote and tabulate the votes about any issue of significance, of which there seemed to be many? Increasingly, nothing could be taken for granted.

A certain level of writing literacy also could no longer be taken for granted. The college's laudable aim to attract a mixed group of undergraduates—a significant minority population, an increased number of community college and transfer students—was an attempt to shake up the old monolithic male Amherst population composed almost wholly of WASPs and Jews (the number of Roman Catholics had always been relatively low). In many ways the new mixture of students was more interesting than the old, but one could make fewer assumptions about their command of English prose. For years we had excepted ourselves from the need to deal, at any intensive level, with matters of sentence structure—the "mechanics" of writing students had supposedly mastered in high school—so that we could talk instead about "higher" things. It was also assumed that the main baggage with which students entered the college was an unexamined mind-set that could be referred to, shorthand, as Cleveland Heights or Upper Montclair—educated (often expensively so) but still provincial. As clever resourceful teachers, we would show them their unexamined assumptions and initiate the process whereby they began to argue with themselves. Now it was questionable just how truly that model fitted the new makeup of an entering class. It might be that the furniture of their minds was not at all of such uniformly high style (for all its dubiousness) as we were pretending. Perhaps our questions to them were too indirect, oblique, vague ("Tell me what's interesting about this poem"), and they needed more straightforward directions. Expressing dismay by picking out bonehead student sentences has always been fair game for professors, but more of these sentences seemed to be showing up in their papers: "I enjoy the piece because it made for very pleasurable reading. By pleasurable I mean it did not pose big problems in language as did Wordsworth"; "My visual and audible senses flowed in a clear and comprehensible manner"; "I responded to him with all the animus of an emetic" (this student had used both a dictionary and a thesaurus); "Emily Dickinson did have character though. She knew her works were unacceptable but she kept on writing. This shows courage."

These sentences occurred early in the English 11 term, but a boy from my section late in the semester produced a final report on Martin Scorsese's *Mean Streets* (we were now attempting, from time to time, to teach film) that began like this:

> This movie had a lot of effect on me. I did not feel like a critic. I actually felt as though I was in the movie myself. The actors did not seem as strange to me as they did to other people. My roommate, who lives in Miami had trouble understanding what was being said. He said the actors talked too fast, cursed too much and had heavy New York accents. I live just 2 miles outside of Queens, N.Y. in a town with a very large Italian population. I have seen real men like the ones in the movie. The movie itself was very real to me.

These sentences punctured any illusion that I had usefully commented on this student's writing over the previous ten weeks. In fact, although throughout the seventies and well into the eighties we engaged in argument within the staff meetings (sometimes fierce and sometimes with good results) that argument had little effect on most students in the course. Perhaps it was ever thus, yet the often abstruse nature of materials now chosen as texts made connection with the freshman mind unlikely. I think, for example, of our attempts to deal with Claude Lévi-Strauss's *Tristes Tropiques;* or Walter Benjamin's collection of essays, *Illuminations;* or Marx's *Eighteenth Brumaire of Louis Napoleon.* The effort spurred in each case by someone's passionate advocacy was to expand the repertoire of "teachable" books by selecting challenging, difficult kinds of theoretical writing without the familiar patterns of literary organization we were used to exploring in a novel by Jane Austen or a poem by Keats. But as I struggled in front of a group of eighteen-year-olds with Benjamin's dense, obscure essay "On Translation," I had an inkling that this was not the best position for a teacher—at least for me—to occupy. In fact, the semester when we read, briefly, Benjamin's essays was the same one that concluded with the film unit on *Mean Streets,* though doubtless, to the fellow from Queens, the prose of Walter Benjamin was less real than Scorsese's movie.

Not until the late seventies did I even begin to realize that we were living in an age of Theory, so what was happening to the Reading course I understood only imperfectly at the time. Instead of the shared assumption that animated Brower's Hum. 6 and that for decades had stood behind our Amherst introductory course—namely, that students could be taught to perceive intelligible imaginative structures in works of literature and to articulate their perceptions—there was now a heavy emphasis on the problematics of reading. Indeed, "problematics" was a word I began encountering more and more frequently, along with related friends such as "valorize" (one was not supposed to do this to works of literature), "slippage," "recuperate," and others of that ilk. The idea now seemed to be, at least on the part of some hands in the department, that the business of reading was extremely difficult to negotiate and, in fact, probably could never be done successfully. We were no longer dealing with books—novels, plays, poems—but with "texts," each of which presented conflicting evidence as to how it should be "read." Indeed one didn't merely read literature; one "read" film and fashion, cartoons and dance, the aim being to make that reading a complicated and unresolved activity. I remember my puzzlement in those lists of suggested readings I solicited, by the omnipresence of an essay by the anthropologist Clifford Geertz about a Balinese cockfight. For heaven's sake, I asked myself in my ignorance, not having read the essay, what is this doing in an introductory course in Reading? Although we never actually assigned Geertz, his presence in the list of suggestions was symptomatic of a movement away from "primary" literary work to secondary-theoretical elaboration and instruction in how difficult it was to read a work, a cultural artifact, a phenomenon.

There was also a good deal of contention about the canon (the term came into its own in the early 1980s) and our proper relation to it as teachers. On one occasion when Philip Larkin's poetry had been proposed for inclusion, some colleagues felt uneasy about "privileging" this highly successful "traditional" white male Englishman by making him, as it were, the representative contemporary poet. It was suggested that we include another poet, someone as different from Larkin as possible, so as to bring a proper balance into the poetry unit. Accordingly,

Imamu Amiri Baraka (Leroi Jones) was read in tandem with Larkin. Anticipating the political correctness wars of the nineties, it remains in my mind as one of the most curious solutions to what was perceived as a problem, especially since almost no one on the staff, including myself, thought much of Baraka's poetry. What were the undergraduates supposed to make of our whimsical decision? The question was not satisfactorily answered, at least in my section. In fact, and as might perhaps be expected, students—at least the ones I dealt with—were not in the least troubled by reading lists consisting entirely of canonical works, and I can count on fewer than the fingers of one hand the times when someone questioned the exclusion of a book or writer from a classroom syllabus. On the contrary, the students showed an eagerness to grapple with "high" culture materials, and when once in English 11 as a prelude to Roman Polanski's film *Chinatown*, we assigned Raymond Chandler's novel *The Big Sleep* with its tough-guy first-person narrator, my class was confused and somewhat disapproving. Had they come to Amherst to read *this* sort of product?

Once when I deliberately introduced the notion of a canon—an established, anthologized (at the moment) body of writings and writers called English literature—the result was revealing. A group of students in a course in criticism for honors candidates had read an essay advocating an enlarging of the canon to embrace X, Y, or Z's writing. What did they think of this notion? I asked them. They responded affirmatively, nodding their heads—yes, this seemed like a good idea, open and expansive and forward-looking. I then provided them with some names from the, as it were, unopened unexpanded canon, such as Bernard Shaw, John Henry Newman, Andrew Marvell, Anthony Trollope—admittedly all white male Anglo products. To a person, man and woman, the class could barely confess the slightest acquaintance with any of the names I had trotted out. I was hardly shocked at their ignorance, since I was exactly in that position myself as a college sophomore. But it was proof, if proof were needed, that far from oppressing students with the accepted names and works from the canonical list, we were doing nothing of the sort; the unopened canon was there, ready to be explored, should anyone feel adventurous enough to undertake the journey. I said that I found such exploratory activity just about enough to keep me going.

The fragmenting of our English department reflected something happening in the academic professional world of literary criticism, as

[handwritten marginal note:] GOD KNOWS THEN (I CERTAINLY DON'T) WHAT MY STUDENTS IN 1977 THOUGHT OF THE ASSIGNMENT TO READ ANY 200 PAGES OF SADE'S JULIETTE, IN CONJUNCTION WITH THE DIALECTIC OF ENLIGHTENMENT. DID I NOTICE? DID I CARE? DID I SHITE!

New Criticism was replaced by alternate modes of commentary —
feminist, materialist-Marxist, deconstructive — or by one or another
species of theory. Often the theory tended to avoid dealing directly
with specific literary works. In defense or rationalization of the
change, it was often said that, after all, decades of New Critical "close
readings" of various poems and plays and novels had exhausted themselves: in other words, there was simply no more to say "internally"
about *Hamlet* or Marvell's "Horatian Ode" or Austen's *Emma*. The
profession had to keep its wheels greased; thus it was inevitable that
other forms of *nouvelle critique* should take up the slack. Surely there
is some truth in this, especially the part about the profession's need to
invent new movements and schools in which a young person could
enlist and contribute to so as to achieve professional status. Yet there
is also something abject about the argument. To say, for example, that
nothing more could be said, after forty years of commentary, about
T. S. Eliot's *Waste Land* seemed to me ignoble as well as false. As both
reviewer and teacher I welcomed the opportunity to deal not just with
new work but with work around which a body of critical commentary
had accumulated. It was and still is inconceivable to me that anyone
who pretended to some originality and liveliness of mind could admit
that, really, there was nothing new to say about Pope or Yeats. If I had
been magically presented, in 1975 or 1985 with *The Dunciad* or
"Among School Children" along with its inherited commentary, I
would have jumped at the chance to "review" it. This was my way of
further exploring and acquainting myself with the canon, and to
enable me to do this I needed the activity of teaching in a classroom as
much as private reflection in the study.

Something analogous to expanding the canon was to be seen in our
English department as, in the seventies and eighties, it grew more
diverse, pluralistic, incoherent — and, of course, larger. As it became
easier to satisfy the requirements for a major in English, student
enrollments increased. And as "English" became an umbrella under
which all sorts of quite different majors were pursued, any sense of
common purpose could be perceived only at a fairly high level
of abstraction. The most convenient place to watch this splintering of
effort was in the Reading course, which for some time had been taught
by a staff (eight to thirteen department members) with a common
reading list, common assignments and writing exercises, and a weekly
meeting where things were planned out and argued about. Gradually

this format was chipped away to the point where it was judged no longer viable. Instrumental in this judgment were younger members who had been hired, to use the rhetoric that accompanied their hiring process, because they were "different" from us — "us" being the older white-male tenured members. The phenomenon deserves some attention in its assumption that because we were white and male and more or less of a certain age, "we" were deeply alike in our convictions and predilections about the teaching of English. To an extent this was true, inasmuch as we had succeeded in keeping going a cooperative staff course. But, as I came to feel about it, the assumption of "sameness" devalued individuality by pretending such individuality was less crucial than class or sex or age. So to hire someone "different from us" was already to set fairly crude standards of discrimination to the process. I had thought that *I* was different from "us"!

Naturally it turned out that "we" lacked the various specialties and fields that a university English department would offer but that a small college might not necessarily want or be able to. In the early seventies, with coeducation on the near horizon, what we did not have that was most different from "us" was a woman. If the woman were au courant with literary theory and knew something about linguistics, so much the better for filling in curricular absences. Accordingly such a person was hired. Then with the emerging awareness of black writers, an African American woman joined the department. What about the Caribbean and its literary contribution? Did we not need someone who could present these writers and engage in the important task of informing and educating students in a burgeoning new field? And what about movies? The move toward studying film was effected without new hirings, since a couple of our members began to devote half their teaching schedules to film criticism and theory. Then sexuality reared its head, especially gay and lesbian sexuality, and some members began to devote half their time to teaching cross-listed courses in the new Department of Women and Gender Studies; accordingly, a woman was hired to teach lesbian literature and engage with issues of gender. With the recent canonization of the word "queer," courses in "queer" reading of literature and film presented themselves. Meanwhile the teachers of American literature, in accord with the new emphasis on hitherto marginal writers and races, began to replace the outdated surveys of writers in the North American canon with interdisciplinary and cultural studies.

*Liberal Solution- Blacks teach about blacks-

The extent of this evolution or development or redirection of interest may be seen in the following list of titles selected from the offerings in English from a recent course catalogue and arranged for
convenience under certain rubrics:

> *Film Studies:* Film and Writing; Studies in Classic
> American Film; Film Noir; Contemporary American
> Film; The Nonfiction Film; Topics in Film Study.

> *Sexuality:* Lesbian Literature; Reading Gender, Read-
> ing Race; Issues of Gender in African Literature; Stud-
> ies in the Literature of Sexuality.

> *Theme Courses:* Literature of the Civil Rights Move-
> ment; American Men's Lives; Democracy, Culture,
> and the Media; The Literature of Madness; The Mode
> of Romance.

> *Comparative and "Third World" Courses:* Per-
> ceptions of Childhood in African and Caribbean
> Literature; Oral Traditions, Literature, and Culture;
> Contemporary Literature by Asian-Americans and
> Latinos; Performance of African-American Litera-
> ture; Authenticity and Audience: The "Third World"
> in the Literary Marketplace.

These courses are not explicitly theoretical; certainly they do not
highlight a deconstructive approach to materials. Yet most of them are
fairly strongly ballasted by theoretical material even though the only
"straight" course in theory currently being taught is one titled "The
Linguistic Turn."

The college's current enrollment stands at 1,600, a substantial
increase from the school of around 1,000 I attended, but still a small
college. In its admission process, Amherst is more "elite" than ever,
the ratio of applications to acceptances being about eighteen to one.
Most of the elite come here with only the slightest acquaintance with
literature. To be sure, many of the courses listed above employ the
word "literature"; the people who teach them require frequent papers
from their students and take seriously the task of reading and commenting on them. And the catalogue still contains courses, taught by
me and a few others, in some of the traditional "period" classifica-

tions: seventeenth-century English literature; Romantic poets; and so on. No one has set out purposely, it seems, to do in the canon; it is not a matter of "tenured radicals" (in the words of Roger Kimball's book against what he sees as the theory-oriented academic Left) conspiring to ensure that the fate of literature is a dark one.

Yet despite such assurances, and despite the fact that my individual colleagues are bright, hardworking, and serious about their teaching and their principles, I am filled with a sense of absence. For I am inclined to suspect that the people around me care more about modes of signification, gender talk, issues of sexuality and race, screwball comedies and the films of Douglas Sirk, than they do about poetry (by "poetry" I mean to refer to what we used confidently to identify as "literature" — and without the nervous quotation marks). The absence is most specifically identifiable in the demise of the Reading course, whose fortunes I have been tracing in these pages. Some time in the mid-1980s, after a semester of especially intense and prolonged argument about the wording of our common assignments, we decided to compromise. The assignment maker would submit his or her exercises, and people at the meeting would make suggestions for changes, but finally anyone was at liberty to make up one of her own; this would save time and perhaps spare wounded feelings of those whose words got changed in the process of arguing. What it did in fact was to reduce the course's collective impact: in section A you were asked to write about this aspect of *Lear* whereas in Section B a rather different emphasis was pursued. It was no surprise when a few years later our inability to agree on a common reading list with books read in a certain order over the term led to some colleagues declining to teach Y and substituting Z instead. This meant of course that the weekly meeting lost much of its significance, since really there was no reason for someone to attend the meeting on Thomas Middleton's *The Changeling* if he were teaching Thomas Pynchon's *The Crying of Lot 49*. The following year things became even more chaotic when the staff divided itself into groups that taught only a couple of books in common, therefore meeting among themselves for most of the term. From here it was the shortest of steps to declaring the course at an end and replacing it with a number of courses taught by groups of two or three (or one) that were connected only insofar as they involved a fair amount of writing. In most of them the absence of literature as a central subject of concern could be noted. One of the new courses involved students doing tutorial work with minorities at a neighboring high school; another was about "how we create ourselves textually" and featured autobiographical writing plus films; another, "Representing Sexualities in Word and Image," paid particular attention to same-sex sexualities; yet another featured the work of Jean Genet and offered reading in comic book literature and documentary films. Although three or four of us persisted in teaching a course with traditional literary materials, the "traditionalists" (a term now used to pigeonhole anyone whose primary interest is in "literature") included no one under the age of fifty-five.

To what extent is the devaluation of traditional literature symptomatic of far-reaching changes in the academic world of English today? At least one commentator, Frank Kermode, blames what he calls a hostility toward literature on the great efflorescence of literary theory in recent decades, especially theory's dismissal of "quality" as irrelevant to the study of writing. Such a dismissal, Kermode argues, entails a denial of literature; indeed, he goes so far as to suggest that the change in the character and purpose of literary criticism—its depressingly arcane lack of reference to anything that an intelligent layperson might be interested in—may have as a consequence the destruction of reading. These days, Kermode writes, people essentially get taught to read at universities and colleges. At the same time, and after the impact of theorists like Derrida, de Man, and their followers, "the whole business of reading is . . . acknowledged to be very difficult, so difficult that until recently nobody ever really managed to accomplish it."

Surely the university must be the proper place in which to teach reading:

> But how? To a few, in very rigorous classrooms, on a narrow range of Mallarmean texts? Or to the many who could not hope to get around such an assault course. Or perhaps one should instead take the opportunity to explain to students what they are doing when they watch Western movies? Should one try to impart to people who have only the slightest acquaintance with literature an expert knowledge of the modes of its production?

He concludes that many people—though not he himself—would give positive answers to these questions. From the evidence of English at Amherst in the early nineties, I conclude that a number of my colleagues would most surely give such positive answers, as testified to by the courses they want to teach.

Kermode's complaint has the more authority for coming from someone who has put in his time studying and writing about literary theory and theorists. His concern that the activity of valuing, of making judgments about literary quality, has been excluded or attacked or finessed by these theorists and their disciples now teaching in the academy, surely has something to do with the fact that, throughout his literary career, he has continued to make such judgments in the large amount of reviewing he has undertaken. Many of Kermode's complaints about the aridity of current literary discourse and its remoteness from the conceivable interest of intelligent lay readers, had been anticipated forty years previously in Randall Jarrell's famous essay "The Age of Criticism." This of course raises the question whether these complaints—about the pedantry and obfuscation of others—have not always been and will not always be with us. I defer that question, remarking here only the paradox—or perhaps merely the moral—of this chapter: as I became clearer and more committed to the essential practice as a critic, in the classroom and in the pages of the reviews, I found myself more out of touch with, less in accord with, the academic practices going on about me, and not just at Amherst College. Could I, after all this purposeful work, have become an anachronism? A dinosaur? Replaceable?

IX
Autumn of a Teacher

Yeats's brief essay of 1898, "The Autumn of the Body," celebrates in its hushed and evocative cadences the new art he saw emerging in fin-de-siècle Europe, an "internal" kind of poetry and painting that featured

> instead of the dramatic stories and picturesque moments of an older school, frail and tremulous bodies unfitted for the labor of life, and landscapes where subtle rhythms of color and of form have overcome the clear outline of things as we see them in the labour of life.

I turned sixty in the fall of 1992, thus was provoked to look back on my life's labor and muse on whatever dramatic stories and picturesque moments it contained. To a degree, I even played the sixty-year-old smiling man of Yeats's "Among School Children," graciously rehearsing his past, sometimes to the amusement of others. But the autumnal note was prospective as well, having to do with anticipations of winter, a time when one decides (or it is decided for one) that the body is too frail to engage further in the labor of life that is a teacher's daily occupation. Not so many years ago, at Amherst and other academic institutions, age sixty-five, seventy at the latest, was the cutoff age for retirement. Now, with no such enforced termination, continuing to inhabit the classroom depends on individual decision, made with who knows how much wisdom. Still, whenever the time comes to call it quits in the academy (and surely in other professions and trades) there

179

is an overhanging mood of what Samuel Johnson once referred to as "the secret horror of the last." Johnson believed, rightly, that such a horror was inseparable from all thinking beings, and the autumnal landscape over which this mood hangs may induce a special kind of brooding, since the century is also winding down. For years when I taught Hardy's "The Darkling Thrush," I would ask students — back there in 1967 or whenever — what will happen when December 31, 2000, comes round and "the land's dark features" may be compared again to another "century's corpse outleant"? We look to the poets for support and anticipation, and suddenly we are living what they told us would happen. When Frost was not yet forty, he composed a series of one-line glosses to the poems for his first book, *A Boy's Will*, the final four of which read as follows in sequence: "It is time to make an end to speaking"; "It is the autumnal mood with a difference"; "He sees days slipping from him that were the best for what they were"; "There are things that can never be the same." And though the final poem in *A Boy's Will*, "Reluctance," has no gloss, its last stanza concentrates the essential message:

> Ah, when to the heart of man
>   Was it ever less than a treason
> To go with the drift of things,
>   To yield with a grace to reason;
> And bow and accept the end
>   Of a love or a season?

In May of 1994 when my sabbatical year drew to its close, I received a dreaded communication in the form of a note from the current head of our department telling me that (unhappily for me, he knows) I have been designated as his successor for the next two years. It is my turn. We pass the office along on a rotating basis; twenty years ago it fell to me and now, despite strenuous efforts to remove myself from the rotation, it has come round again. So my attempt to set myself apart from colleagues has ironically been brushed aside by the demands of corporate responsibility. It is as if a minor league Coriolanus, intent on showing citizens of the community that there is a world elsewhere, were suddenly interrupted in his private dream and called back to the world of institutions and administrative routine. In my previous years as chairman (it was still called that, rather than the current "chair"), I did my best to avoid holding department meetings, discouraged the taking of notes at such meetings when they occurred, and never got around to advising the committee of students that was supposed to have "input" in departmental decisions. It was a relatively easy term (there were no tenure cases and almost no hiring), and things are not likely to be as relaxed in the coming two years. Still, there is something to be said for designing the job so that no one can aspire to or electioneer in behalf of it. A professor so odd as to covet this position of responsibility will just have to wait his or her turn, and must surrender it, in two years, to the next in line.

As for the profession at large, one combats isolation by looking out for and occasionally finding evidence, in the writing of another scholar, that one's own convictions about literary study are something more than the crotchets of a curmudgeon or a "traditionalist" (as the abusive word has it for someone with his head presumably in the sand). I have no credentials as a critic of Shakespearean drama, but I read and teach the plays and try to keep up, in a modest way, with criticism of them. Recently there has appeared an enormous book by an authoritative Shakespearean, Brian Vickers: titled *Appropriating Shakespeare: Contemporary Critical Quarrels*, it concerns itself with recent ways of approaching the plays, "schools" of criticism Vickers thinks are deleterious in the main. He takes them up one by one — deconstruction; New Historicism; feminism; psychoanalysis; cultural materialism — and attempts to demonstrate the insufficiently "literary" quality of their dealings with Shakespeare's art.

I ordered the book for our library, read a hundred pages or so, mostly liked what I read, and decided to review it, since it confirmed dissatisfactions I had been feeling about new trends in Shakespearean criticism. By reviewing it I can publicize a little more widely opinions I'm sympathetic to, as well as say something on my own about other recent critics who are still doing what strikes me as valuable writing about the poet. Brian Vickers is primarily against what he calls the "abstractionism" of recent schools, the way in which they are willing to sacrifice concreteness — details of plot, character, and dramatic sequences — in favor of what they think are larger significances. Since I don't think there's any significance in Shakespeare larger than the art of his poetry, I want to add my voice on the side of the good. The only possible place for me to write about Vickers is the *Hudson Review*, a venue that will also give me enough words — thirty-five hundred or so—to make it worth doing. I manage to get the review commissioned, thanks to Frederick Morgan's confidence in me, and I write it with some enthusiasm—though as always with doubts that I have read enough and with the uncertainty that I've been "fair" to what others see as innovative approaches to Shakespeare. As often, the question occurs to me at some point: Am I just digging in my heels, automatically resisting current fashions in criticism? Do I have anything better to put in their place? I try, in the review, to build in at least some sense that things aren't wholly cut-and-dried—that it is possible to argue about these matters. In due course the review appears, eliciting total silence.

Evidently a number of my professional colleagues share my unhappiness with the current state of English studies. The mail brings a letter inviting me to join a new association of literary critics and scholars open to anyone with "a serious scholarly and critical interest in literature, without regard to political persuasion." The final words are welcome since I have been tempted to join neither the National Association of Scholars, a group of academics more or less on the Right, nor the Teachers for a Democratic Society, an organization formed in opposition to the NAS. (But everything is political, a colleague informs me.) The new organization, named the Association of Literary Scholars and Critics, speaks of "current deficiencies" in contemporary literary studies and assumes I know about them (I do). The ALSC will reassert "our general faith in the validity of the literary imagination and in the value of literary studies." It sounds a bit like signing on for God, freedom, and country, but I like the idea of opposing, however vaguely, organizations that are indifferent or hostile to such a belief in literary studies. So I sign on and enclose a note telling the president that I hope to be told more specifically what is going on.

Soon afterward, another professional communication arrives, forcefully reinforcing my conviction that things have taken a very strange turn in the field of what I used to think of as English studies. This is a pamphlet announcing the program for the annual meeting, in Cambridge over Labor Day weekend of 1994, of the English Institute. The English Institute was founded in 1942 by American professors of literature who had grown dissatisfied with the annual MLA convention in its gigantism and its frantic concentration on the interviewing and hiring of candidates. The MLA had become more of a job market than an occasion for literary discussion and debate, and the new organization pledged to devote itself wholly to intellectual matters. Each yearly session featured four topics; for each, three or four papers were read, papers of the leisurely fifty minutes to an hour variety instead of the MLA's fifteen to twenty minutes. The English Institute was a successful idea, and though one could (and did) complain about this or that individual paper, the overall quality of the sessions was impressive. A typical four-day meeting might include — as did the thirtieth anniversary one in 1972 — "Pastoral Modes in Modern Literature"; "The Poetry of Samuel Taylor Coleridge"; "Recent Linguistics and Literary Study"; and "The Literature of Fantasy: Children's Literature." If a session yielded a number of what were judged good papers, a volume of them would be published, and among the many institute volumes are *Literature and Belief, Style in Prose Fiction, Sound and Poetry,* and *Edwardians and Late Victorians.* The assumption, which nobody ever thought to question, was that English teachers would gather to talk about literature.

This has all changed, as was confirmed by the program of the 1994 session. Titled "Human, All Too Human," it consisted of four sessions under the following rubrics: "Humane Societies"; "Things"; "Conceiving the Child"; and "Science Fictions." Titles of individual talks ran as follows: "Heavy Petting"; "Barring the Cross: Hybridization and Purity in Eighteenth- and Nineteenth-Century Britain" (under "Humane Societies"); "Muteness Envy"; "The Dream of a Butterfly" (under "Things"); "Dismembered Selves and Wandering Wombs" (under "Conceiving the Child"); and "Fertile Facts and Fantasies: New Reproductive Practices and the Politics of Life" (under "Science Fictions"). I hadn't a clue, from the titles, what any of these papers could conceivably be about; nor did I satisfy my curiosity by attending the conference. But what I took to be noteworthy was that the English Institute, culminating a trend that developed over the past few years, had almost completely succeeded in excluding literature, as a "traditionalist" conceived it, from consideration. To be sure, many of the talks alluded to literature (if not poetry), but in not a single case was a book or writer or even a literary topic (for example, "Style in Prose Fiction") put in the forefront of things. Was this the deliberate intent of the supervising committee who planned the 1994 program? But why should they so aggressively contend to demote literature from central consideration?

I suppose that the label cultural studies is as accurate as any for what engages these English Institute people, the interdisciplinary

nature of the topics signaling that anything too wholly tied to literature is excluded. In a similar fashion, it is extremely rare for anyone
today to apply, say, for a National Endowment for the Humanities fellowship with the intention of working on "merely" the poetry of
George Herbert or the novels of Dickens. Evidently such a project
would on the face of it be disablingly old-fashioned; whereas a reach
out to other writers and modes of discourse gives the air of validity to
a project—this person is in touch with things in the field. The ascent
of cultural studies has further implication for what used to be called
the study of literature. For example, it is not clear to me how the
model of cooperative disagreement among different approaches to literature, as proposed by Gerald Graff in *Beyond the Culture Wars*,
could be stretched to include teachers whose inclinations are, in
effect, to replace literary with cultural studies. Graff's well-known
position has been that the crisis in English studies, the lack of shared
assumptions by competing interest groups, is best addressed by
acknowledging these conflicts openly—indeed, by "teaching" them.
In other words, a study of the debate about how to teach a text would
be an important part of that text's presentation in class.

Graff's book is an attractively presented defense of an idea that for
a number of reasons doesn't persuade me. (One of them is that by
turning "conflict" into a subject for the classroom, real conflict is
defanged and too easily "understood.") In an imaginary vignette that
opens his book and is designed to show the necessity for staging
debates between different approaches to literature, a senior "traditionalist" male professor, having just taught a class on "Dover
Beach," gets into an argument with a younger, female professor
whose views on the poem greatly differ from his. Graff argues the
value of having these conflicting viewpoints aired in the same classroom, rather than espoused in different rooms by teachers isolated
from one another. But to put in conflict different ways of reading a
short lyric is one thing; in fact, a single teacher, credibly informed
about contemporary styles in literary criticism, could, with sufficient
detachment, construct for the class a debate among various ways of
getting at Arnold's poem. But how can a movement like cultural studies, which refuses to allow the work of literature any kind of privileged or primary status, be "taught" in the classroom without in
effect displacing literature as the object of concern? I don't want to
endorse this displacement.

At the end of his earlier *Professing Literature,* an extremely informative "institutional history" of the English profession in America, Graff calls on a sympathetic fellow professor, James Kincaid, in support of a vision of literary studies in a classroom whose subject is competing versions of the text. Kincaid writes about this ideal course:

> Wouldn't it seek to define the subject matter, literature, and to discuss the various and competing assumptions about texts, language, meaning, culture, readers, and so forth that we make? Wouldn't it show that these assumptions are themselves constructions? Wouldn't it also show that these assumptions were not themselves innocent, that they were value-laden, interested, ideological? You are starting to suspect that this is a course in theory. And so it is. But all courses are courses in theory. One either smuggles it in or goes through customs with it openly. . . . We need to teach not the texts themselves but how we situate ourselves in reference to those texts.

As with Graff's own prose, Kincaid bids to strike the reasonable, fair-minded, "realistic" note. Either you are a smuggler, or you declare the goods openly, concealing nothing about your person. It is a choice unlike the one made in the final stanza of Frost's "I Could Give All to Time":

> But why declare
> The things forbidden that while the Customs slept
> I have crossed to safety with? For I am There,
> And what I would not part with I have kept.

Is Frost's attitude arrogant and outrageous — the sort of thing a poet of distinction can perhaps get away with but that a professor in a democratic classroom must reject? Is it essential to explain to students that the teacher's principles are value-laden and ideological, just like everyone else's?

Perhaps the question is whether not just English studies but all studies and courses should have as their aim to unmask the "interestedness" of all assumptions and bring that aim to the fore. The model is something like that of a sophisticated show-and-tell in which "we," students and teachers of various persuasions, come together and, after admitting divergent, sometimes opposing interests, proceed to talk them out with sincerity and understanding. Leave irony and double-mindedness to the poets: let *them* be mischievous and willful, but let their explicators avoid such devious smuggling in of an unconfessed personal agenda. I look again at Kincaid's final sentence quoted by Graff: "We need to teach not the texts themselves but how we situate ourselves in reference to those texts." The trouble with this sentence is that both the man who wrote it and the man who quoted it evidently thought its meaning perfectly clear. It goes something like this: for years, in a world of literary studies that is less fractured than today's, we could agree that "Dover Beach" was one of the texts to be taught, and then we proceeded to teach "Dover Beach" "itself" without considering or acknowledging our position as readers of it. But as I have tried to make clear in these pages, good teaching of a poem should never be, and has not been for a good many decades, subject-free. Kincaid talks about the newfound importance of how we situate ourselves with reference to a text; I would say rather that it is essential to talk about how we *read* it and that, as with Brower's principle in Hum. 6, the question should be, what does a poem feel like? What it is *like* to read it (rather than what does it mean as a text)? It's perhaps a question of how you define "situate," and I think my definition would vary significantly from Kincaid's and Graff's.

That may be because I am a believer in the romance of texts, or rather books; the belief that they can speak for themselves in such a way as to lift us into a new, absorbing world. And it's that new world that is of supreme importance as a promise of happiness. Perhaps this belief is yet another species of digging one's heels in by someone fortunately situated in an "elite" college where there are still numbers of readers to whom books do, with a little help from the teacher, speak for themselves. Perhaps trying to hold on to a notion of what constitutes the "right" way to go about teaching literature in the classroom (the old Amherst–Hum. 6 staff course way) is really a form of nostalgia, a sense that there was a time when things were done in a way that, alas, they are not done anymore. And perhaps this habit is especially tempting to a male professor moving toward retirement who finds that not enough people are interested in what he, so it feels, is just beginning to learn about the art of poetry. There is a poem of Jarrell's I have quoted more than once whose final quatrain confronts something like this question, in the course of remembering a long-dead love affair:

How poor and miserable we were,
How seldom together!
And yet after so long one thinks:
In those days everything was better.

By emphasizing "one thinks," we can hear the poem as a sadly wry take on a habitual but misconceived human tendency, which teachers are as prey to as lovers insofar as they have a romance with literature.

The sense of a time when it was assumed that we read to extend ourselves, and that imaginative literature provided the most vivid possibilities of extension, is perhaps but another species of longing ("In those days everything was better") that spurs my dissatisfaction with things present, both at the local college level and in the culture at large. If such is the case, so be it; I don't see that we should necessarily welcome change of every sort, nor contemplate, without a seasoning of irony and resentment, huge changes in the realm of what we have cared about most. And who knows how accurate our assessment of current trends and conditions may be? Recently I delivered a talk called "Criticism in an Age of Theory" to a university audience of English faculty and graduate students, where I made the point, again in line with Kermode's preface to *An Appetite for Poetry*, that recent literary studies seemed pretty much to have eliminated the activity of valuing—of making judgments of literary worth—from its business. At dinner after the talk, one of the graduate students, about to begin his first regular teaching job at a small college, hastened to correct me on that point, insisting that in fact he and his friends argued about literary value all the time. I said I was glad to hear it. (On the other hand, how much did the fact that he had graduated from Amherst and written his undergraduate thesis under my direction have to do with it?)

Near the beginning of *After Strange Gods* T. S. Eliot says that while prose may legitimately concern itself with ideals, poetry must deal with actuality. I think the trouble with most books about teaching is that in the end (or the beginning) they put themselves behind some big idea that, if carried into practice, would alleviate or resolve crisis. Harold Bloom's invigorating *The Western Canon* is but the latest of these. I have no such idea, but feel as I used to when students, disappointed in the comments I had written on their papers, asked me if I could not be a little more "positive" in my criticism. Tell me what you *want*, sir, was the implied directive. But I could not tell them, except in abstract terms. These critical comments about English studies may be thought comparably negative, although if only by their distance from the actuality of things, certain ideals about teaching and writing have been implied.

Rather than ending, then, with advice freely rendered, a recipe for new and improved English teaching, or final guesses about the future, I choose to do so more poetically by suggesting what goes on in an actual classroom—my own—as observed over a few weeks during a recent fall term. This seems fitting inasmuch as, increasingly, I depend on my students—the more interesting of them—to engage with me in the conversation about literature I want to see continue. It is they who refute the current wisdom (not very wise at all) of pundits who would tell us, say, that the poetry of T. S. Eliot is no longer of concern to younger readers. They refute it, in my classes, by reading and writing about "Prufrock," *The Waste Land,* and *Four Quartets,* as if these poems still constituted a formidable and dazzling exercise in the use of words. On more than one occasion, they show the teacher how a poem he has forgotten about or has always avoided facing up to, such as Browning's long one, *The Ring and the Book,* can be addressed with freshness, seen and heard with new ears and eyes by an individual reader. The more adventuresome of them become free spirits by being granted the privilege of acting as if, just for a few years, there were nothing more important and fulfilling than reading works of imaginative literature. The following concluding pages are essentially entries from a diary I kept during a term in which I taught a course—Reading and Writing—for twenty or so freshmen, and a somewhat larger course in seventeenth- and eighteenth-century major British writers, beginning with Ben Jonson and John Milton. Each course involved a fair amount of writing, especially the freshman one.

★   ★   ★

Labor Day: the course catalogue arrived and I am held up by an offering titled "What is the Self?" It will deal with questions like: "Is it a concept or is it really 'there'? . . . Is it something that we are taught in order to be members of a particular society and culture, and if so, does that mean that it is culture-specific or is it something that is universal to all humans? . . . What do we think of as 'ourselves'? Does our idea of what the self is have to do with what our idea of what 'others' are or what others think of us? . . . Can we act as a self without being a self?

Is it impossible to do that, and would it be liberating or would it lead to a kind of nihilism? Or both, or neither?" None of the above, I snarled to myself, and thought about the impertinence of much bright-eyed academic pursuit with its oh-so-challenging questions designed to "shake up" the young person. I had been reading Arnold Bennett's *The Old Wives' Tale*, the passage where Constance learns that her mother is dying but also hears her newborn baby cry upstairs:

> She picked up the night-light and stole round the bed. Yes, he had decided to fall asleep. The hazard of death afar off had just defeated his devilish obstinacy. Fate had bested him. How marvelously soft and delicate that tear-stained cheek! How frail that tiny clenched hand! In Constance grief and joy were mystically united.

That's what the self is, I thought, and no amount of chatter about nihilism and culture-specific will get you within a mile of it.

* ⋆ ⋆ ⋆

Students arriving back, calling up to make appointments. How was your summer? Great! They run and frisk about the quad, tossing the Frisbee, and one feels a long way away. A friend and colleague of many years is about to have an operation on a cancerous esophagus. Another has a leaky heart valve to be replaced. What is this perpetual summer camp we live in, presided over by kindly deans and a benign administration making sure everybody's needs get fulfilled? Learning has a place here, but is kept in its place. HOW WAS YOUR SUMMER?

⋆ ⋆ ⋆

Classes begin in the usual oppressive weather, the summer we missed earlier on; both rooms overfilled, the usual chaos. I talked about why the Major English Writers, Ben Jonson to Samuel Johnson, should be read, but I also quoted an admonition from the novelist Anthony Powell: "Literature illuminates life only for those to whom books are a necessity." There were many students at Amherst College, I told them, to whom books, at least these books, were not a necessity, rather something to be read, if at all, in order to get degrees and good jobs. Nobody is required to be interested in Milton, except in this course. Quoted Eliot from "Tradition and the Individual Talent":

"Someone said 'The dead writers are remote from us because we *know* so much more than they did.' Precisely, and they are that which we know." We spent some time on Ben Jonson's poem to his dead daughter, with its wonderful closing line about her mortal remains in the grave: "Which cover lightly, gentle earth." One student put his finger on that moment as the really surprising, touching thing about the poem. I then read aloud Anthony Hecht's poem in memory of a one-time friend of his and mine, now dead of AIDS:

> "Men die from time to time," said Rosalind,
> "But not," she said, "for love." A lot she knew!
>
> From the green world of Africa the plague
> Wiped out the Forest of Arden, the whole crew
> Of innocents, of which, poor generous ghost
> You were among the liveliest.

Then a sudden line about the dead man's scattered ashes descending "Even to the bottom of the monstrous world" and how this took us back to Milton's "Lycidas" and why we need to know "Lycidas" to read Anthony Hecht. You read one poem the better to read another one. They seemed interested and agreeable, attentive even. Well, it's the first day and spirits are up.

In the freshman class that same day we talked about an idiotic article in a recent *New York Times* about how college students send their parents oblique messages of loneliness and confusion, spelled out to Mom and Dad: "Their phone calls home may contain complaints about the workload ('I have to read four books and write two papers this week!') or; fanciful descriptions of the school's food ('We call it mystery meat, Mom. Someone said it was owl')." The article was suggesting that we disregard the ostensible subjects of the phone call in favor of their real concerns, but I said that in this course we were going to try to keep literature, poetry, in all its odd particularity, in *front* of us, rather than trying to see through it to what it "really" means. So we would treasure the lively language about owl-as-mystery-meat, and take pleasure in it, rather than saying it meant frustration or loneliness. Frost's "Stopping by Woods" is really "about" a man and his horse and a woods-filling-up-with-snow, rather than "about" suicide. Poetry is excess, excessive, like the owl, and we turned to Sir Walter Raleigh's little poem to his son, urging him to avoid being hanged:

Three things there be that prosper all apace
And flourish, while they are asunder far;
But on a day they meet all in a place,
And when they meet, they one another mar,
And they be these: the wood, the weed, the wag.
The wood is that that makes the gallows tree;
The weed is that that strings the hangmans bag;
The wag, my pretty knave, betokens thee.
Now mark, dear boy, while these assemble not,
Green springs the tree, hemp grows, the wag is wild;
But when they meet, it makes the timber rot,
It frets the halter and it chokes the child.
Then bless thee, and beware, and let us pray
We part not with thee at this meeting day.

How can we understand this, I asked, and someone said, well it's like warning a child about AIDS. Yes . . . but no, what about this voice, what's its tone? A number of possibilities, not so easy to tell. I can hear, but they can't, Frost taking great delight in reading the poem aloud, especially "The wag, my pretty knave, betokens thee." What did *he* get out of it? A student said she liked the way "the wood, the weed, the wag" went together. Good enough, me too—so let's keep the owl in front of us. They went home to write about their first poem, Coleridge's "Frost at Midnight."

In that same class, for ten or so minutes, I asked them to write down a few sentences about reading poetry, their thoughts on it, their experience of it. The previous year when I'd tried it, the responses showed a high degree of poetry-anxiety ("frankly, I loathe it," said one truthteller) but this year almost everybody was positive, to the point—in one case—of really turning my stomach:

Poetry is a written representation of all that is beautiful in the world. Reading its verses one becomes a part of that beauty and is allowed to explore the realms of his own self-conscience. I read poetry, not to critique, but to absorb. Analyzation, though helpful in comprehending the author's "true" meaning, seems to tear at what cobweb-thin threads are desperately trying to hold together.

Dreadful writing, with its beauty, its self-conscience, its critiques and analyzation: yet nobody wholly insensitive to language (I told myself) speaks of cobweb-thin threads as what makes a poem cohere. I said that this was a course called Reading and Writing, and that they would write frequently (six times in the first five weeks) but I was more concerned with working on how they read than how they wrote. Your parents are concerned about how you write, I know (said I), but do they worry about how you read? How and what and how much do *they* read? For most of you, your writing will take care of itself more or less, through practice, repetition, just getting older and having some experience. But if the reading bug doesn't bite you now, it may never.

★   ★   ★

Loud and lively classes yesterday, probably because I felt hyped-up, a little manic. I scoffed at the notion, in reading Ben Jonson's *Volpone* that you could condemn these rascals in any way, since Jonson's language at the beginning of the play elevated them into another realm, beyond condemnation and eliciting admiration. Asked them what other writers reading Jonson reminded them of: one said Shaw (good), another said Dickens (excellent), and one said Trollope. I said this was the first time a student had ever mentioned Trollope in my classroom, and I was touched, since I'd been reading him all summer. (The Trollopian was from Bombay and had been subjected to a rather elitist education.) A girl said Tennyson, and that took some wiggling around, since I didn't see how it could possibly be a sensible answer. But she was pretty, and I managed to dismiss her suggestion without a touch of sexual harassment. Later an earnest economics major came to my office, a very nice boy, and said he felt a bit lost when people began mentioning other writers, comparing them to Jonson. How would I feel in an economics course, I thought? English studies is in fact a discipline—it helps to have read more than one writer.

★   ★   ★

Deep in the midst of my regular-as-clockwork end-of-second-week-of-classes cold, I had conveniently asked the freshmen to be prepared to say something about a poem that interested them from the day's batch. Somebody asked about Sylvia Plath's fierce "Daddy," which places the blame for her suicidal disposition on her father, whom she caricatures as a Nazi ("And your Aryan eye, bright blue. / Panzer man,

Panzer man, O You— "). Various people said what a fine poem it was, terrific rhythm, an arresting voice; then a girl admitted that one line "Your Luftwaffe, your gobbledygoo" made her almost sick. I asked, shouldn't these feelings of repulsion, of being assaulted by an unpleasant voice, count in our response, maybe more importantly than whatever it is Plath is "saying" about suicide? This is a loud performance. Was it "fair" to poor old Otto Plath, a mild-mannered professor of biology? Or does it matter? Then after class a student came up and asked me something about "gobbledygoo" and I noticed that she was holding a volume titled *Critical Essays on Sylvia Plath* where she had come across one William H. Pritchard's review of the *Collected Poems*. Suddenly we were into something besides objective judgment and commentary: poor kid, she'd just been led to the Plath shelf and innocently picked up this volume and there was her teacher, an authority evidently. We had a good time about this and I professed not to remember what I'd said about "gobbledygoo." When I looked at it, it was the same thing I'd just said in class. This was somehow just slightly embarrassing, though not to her.

⋆   ⋆   ⋆

Hardest part of Milton is getting started and trying to figure out what satisfactions or pleasures the reader of 1992 can take in "On the Morning of Christ's Nativity," "L'Allegro" and "Il Penseroso." And what about *Comus*, a masque? I recommended they adopt the light touch in dealing with it, remembering that Frost used to have his students put it on as a play. On the other hand, I read them some sentences from a recently published essay on sexuality in *Comus*:

> This paper moves from a psychoanalytic reading, which operates in the essentially biographical context of what is sometimes called the young Milton's chastity cult; to a politico-cultural reading, set in the context of what Foucault calls the history of sexuality, in which the chastity cult appears no longer as a biographical phenomenon but as a political statement and instrument of control as generalized sexuality; to a socio-economic reading in which the chastity cult and generalized sexuality appear under the aspect of the reification imposed by emergent capitalism and

the conditions of possibility of the confluence of sexual and political messages are clarified.

This I said is a way of taking *Comus* seriously, if not solemnly. No
need to fuss about the poetry, the verse; just transform it into interpre-
tations, into large cultural meanings. I said this is what graduate students in literature did these days, were encouraged to do, and was why
I like teaching at Amherst College instead. All we were going to do
with *Comus* was read aloud some passages, some exchanges, and see
what could be said in praise of it as a work of the imagination.

Next hour something of the same message seemed to surface. The
freshmen had rebelled a bit at end of last hour, saying we're tired of all
this talk about voice in the poem, why can't we talk about themes,
man vs. nature (as they learned to do in high school). After spending
half an hour on a selection of moldy, incompetent sentences they had
written in response to an assignment — it turns out we needed to pay
some attention to their writing after all ("The contrast between the
two stanzas enable me to understand the feeling's Larkin relates to us
at the end of his poem")—we turned to Frost's poem "The Most of It."
I read it aloud ("He thought he kept the universe alone; / For all the
voice in answer he could wake / Was but the mocking echo of his
own / From some tree-hidden cliff across the lake.") up through the
coming of the great buck that "powerfully appeared, / Pushing the
crumpled water up ahead, / And landed pouring like a waterfall, / And
stumbled through the rocks with horny tread, / And forced the under-
brush, and that was all." We talked about how the voice was odd, hard
to locate, strange yet fascinating, gripping, how it was difficult to say
who the "he" was in the poem or where Frost-the-poet was in writing
it. They said some lively things. But, I pointed out, there *was* a way of
"understanding" this poem, the *way* their anthology editors suggested
in the headnote to Frost when they wrote

> He was a poet in the Romantic tradition who sought
> to criticize and correct Romantic emotions from a
> standpoint that seemed to him more realistic. Frost's
> "The Most of It," for example, interplays with the
> Wordsworthian theme of a consciousness in nature
> answering to human consciousness (etc.).

Here was the language of literary history, old-fashioned official Harvard grad-school English, academic classification, man-nature "theme" talk, used in the service of smoothing out the rough uncertainties of "The Most of It." I told them I could talk this way myself ("Wordsworthian theme of a consciousness in nature answering to human consciousness") and they could take notes and then write papers giving me back this language. Wasn't it more interesting, more risky, more manly and womanly, to eschew such "understanding," bought much too cheaply, and try instead to live in, live with, the voice of the poem? I'm not sure how much of this got across, probably not much. For after all this was Old Amherst English Talk and I had become, have become Old Amherst. What can be done about that?

Classes yesterday a bit on the droopy side, people seem weighed down as the semester complicates itself. We paused a long time over the "Whilst thee the shores and sounding seas" passage near the end of "Lycidas." One slightly adenoidal fellow confessed he "didn't get much out of 'Lycidas'" and I wanted to yell at him, "of course you didn't if you sound that way," and I began to say aloud "Yet once more O, ye laurels, / And once more ye myrtles brown, with ivy never sere". But how much is this a mere attempt to effect continuity between my present self, among schoolchildren, and my twenty-year-old self, which sat on a sunny winter morning in 1953 in Appleton 14 and listened to Armour Craig read out boldly those lines? How much is my belief in, my commitment to "Lycidas," a commitment to the rightness and value of my own past? Off for a walk in the crisp-late-afternoon air as breathed in around the college observatory and the Amherst Golf Club, I tried to see how much of "Lycidas" I could say aloud. A fair portion— I surprised myself. But you can't "teach" that.

★   ★   ★

Suddenly, something works, you're on a roll, and it's the best of all ways to spend an hour. A very satisfying class on Milton, just beginning *Paradise Lost*. We started with Matthew Arnold's fine praise of Miltonic "movement," what Arnold calls Milton's "laborious and condensed fullness." I illustrated by a comparison of Satan—chained on the burning lake of hell in Book I, and talking with his mate Beelzebub—to a Leviathan:

With Head uplift above the wave, and Eyes
That sparkling blaz'd, his other Parts besides
Prone on the flood, extended long and large
Lay floating many a rood, in bulk as huge
As whom the Fable name of monstrous size,
Titanian or Earth-born, that warr'd on Jove,
Briareos or Typhon, whom the Den
By ancient Tarsus held, or that Sea-beast
Leviathan, which God of all his works
Created hugest that swim th'Ocean stream;
Him haply slumb'ring on the Norway foam
The Pilot of some night-foundered Skiff,
Deeming some Island, oft, as Sea-men tell,
With fixed Anchor in his scaly rind
Moors by his side under the Lee, while Night
Invests the Sea, and wished Morn delays:
So stretcht out huge in length the Arch-fiend lay
Chain'd on the burning lake . . .

And it goes on, Satan getting "fuller" as a character by means of
Miltonic labor in the long comparison. A good feeling in the class, as if
people were finding it possible to read *Paradise Lost* and even — by
God, or by Satan — enjoy it. Milton can be fun.

And so can teaching, as long as you forsake certainties and wait for
the unexpected, even as your routine solidifies and your values grow
rigid. Emerson, who didn't know everything — as some of his present
admirers presume — nevertheless had this one right in his wonderful
essay "Circles":

> Whilst we converse with what is above us, we do not
> grow old, but grow young. Infancy, youth, receptive,
> aspiring, with religious eye looking upward, counts
> itself nothing and abandons itself to the instruction
> flowing from all sides. But the man and woman of
> seventy assume to know all, they have outlived their
> hope, they renounce aspiration, accept the actual for
> the necessary and talk down to the young. Let them
> then become organs of the Holy Ghost; let them be
> lovers; let them behold truth; and their eyes are
> uplifted, their wrinkles smoothed, they are perfumed

again with hope and power. This old age ought not to creep on a human mind. In nature every moment is new; the past is always swallowed and forgotten; the coming only is sacred. Nothing is secure but life, transition, the energizing spirit. No love can be bound by oath or covenant to secure it against a higher love. No truth so sublime but it may be trivial tomorrow in the light of new thoughts. People wish to be settled; only as far as they are unsettled is there any hope for them.

Life is a series of surprises.

The optative mode is the proper one for such poetry, which as Auden said makes nothing happen but is a way of happening. So it may happen in the autumn of a teacher.

WILLIAM H. PRITCHARD is the Henry Clay Folger Professor of English at Amherst College. He is the author of two important biographies, *Frost: A Literary Life Reconsidered* and *Randall Jarrell: A Literary Life*. He reviews regularly for the *New York Times Book Review*, and his literary criticism is published in the *New Republic, Hudson Review, American Scholar,* and *Boston Sunday Globe*. His latest book, *Playing It by Ear: Literary Essays and Reviews,* was published in 1994 by the University of Massachusetts Press.

This book was designed by Will Powers.
It is set in Trump Medieval type
by Stanton Publication Services, Inc.
and manufactured by
Edwards Brothers, Ann Arbor, Michigan,
on acid-free paper.